Modern Science Fiction:
A Critical Analysis

Modern Science Fiction: A Critical Analysis

The Seminal 1951 Thesis with a New Introduction and Commentary

JAMES GUNN

EDITED BY MICHAEL R. PAGE

Foreword by Gary K. Wolfe

McFarland & Company, Inc., Publishers
Jefferson, North Carolina

ALSO OF INTEREST
Star-Begotten: A Life Lived in Science Fiction,
   James Gunn (McFarland, 2017)
*Saving the World Through Science Fiction:
   James Gunn, Writer, Teacher and Scholar*,
   Michael R. Page (McFarland, 2017)

LIBRARY OF CONGRESS CATALOGUING-IN-PUBLICATION DATA

Names: Gunn, James E., 1923– author. | Page, Michael R., 1967– editor. | Wolfe, Gary K., 1946– writer of foreword.
Title: Modern science fiction, a critical analysis : the seminal 1951 thesis with a new introduction and commentary / James Gunn ; edited by Michael R. Page ; foreword by Gary K. Wolfe.
Description: Jefferson, North Carolina : McFarland & Company, Inc., Publishers, 2018. | Includes bibliographical references and index.
Identifiers: LCCN 2018022637 | ISBN 9781476673196 (softcover : acid free paper) ∞
Subjects: LCSH: Science fiction—History and criticism. | Science fiction—Authorship.
Classification: LCC PN3433.5 .G86 2018 | DDC 809.3/8762—dc23
LC record available at https://lccn.loc.gov/2018022637

BRITISH LIBRARY CATALOGUING DATA ARE AVAILABLE

ISBN (print) 978-1-4766-7319-6
ISBN (ebook) 978-1-4766-3237-7

© 2018 James Gunn. All rights reserved

No part of this book may be reproduced or transmitted in any form or by any means, electronic or mechanical, including photocopying or recording, or by any information storage and retrieval system, without permission in writing from the publisher.

Front cover illustration © 2018 iStock

Printed in the United States of America

*McFarland & Company, Inc., Publishers
   Box 611, Jefferson, North Carolina 28640
   www.mcfarlandpub.com*

To the late Professor John M. Hankins, who had
the open-mindedness to allow a graduate student
to venture into a strange land,
and to Michael Page, who retrieved the unlikely result.

Table of Contents

FOREWORD *Gary K. Wolfe*   1

PREFACE: "WHEN MODERN SCIENCE FICTION WAS MODERN"
James Gunn   5

EDITOR'S INTRODUCTION *Michael R. Page*   9

Modern Science Fiction: A Critical Analysis
by James Gunn

Introduction   34

Part One—"Some of Us Are Looking at the Stars":
The Philosophy of Science Fiction   37

Part Two: "Through Caverns Measureless to Man":
The Plot Forms of Science Fiction   60
   Section One: Plots of Circumstance   65
      Chapter One: A Being in an Alien Environment   66
      Chapter Two: Modern Man in the Modern World   91
      Chapter Three: A Past Being in the Past   111
      Chapter Four: A Future Being in a Future World 114
      Chapter Five: Mutations   121
      Conclusion to Plots of Circumstance   133
   Section Two: Plots of Creation   134
      Chapter One: The Creation of New Life or New Forms Thereof 137
      Chapter Two: Experimentation in Other Fields   157

CONCLUSION   163

APPENDIX: DISTRIBUTION CHART   167

CHAPTER NOTES *Michael R. Page*		169
BIBLIOGRAPHY		183
Fiction Works Cited *James Gunn*		183
Critical Works Cited *James Gunn*		188
Works Cited in Editor's Introduction *Michael R. Page*		188
INDEX		197

Foreword

Gary K. Wolfe

Any sort of fiction worth writing is also worth writing *about*. That insight may sound obvious, or even a bit of a bromide, to literary scholars, but it's an argument I've found myself making in many ways over many years—not only to fellow scholars who might question my interest in science fiction, but to professional science fiction writers who might question the value of any sort of criticism at all. Although the situation is largely improved today, for a long time being a science fiction critic was an excellent way to invite suspicion from both writers and academics. But it's an insight I've held onto doggedly, because I can remember exactly when I learned it, and whose fault it was.

By the time I was ten or twelve, I'd been a fan of whatever science fiction I could find in the not-quite-small town of Sedalia, Missouri, and it wasn't much. Eventually, my brother and I persuaded our dad to drive us to Kansas City, where there were *real* bookstores, and somehow we discovered a used bookshop on 12th Street with what seemed a huge collection of science fiction paperbacks and even pulp magazines, most of which were being sold for something like a quarter apiece. The bookstore is of course long gone, and a couple of years ago, when Kansas City hosted the World Science Fiction Convention, I tried to figure out where it might have been (I concluded its site was probably somewhere beneath the concrete apocalypse that surrounded the convention center that was the Worldcon site).

But if the bookstore is gone, I still have most of what I bought there, and two of those 25-cent pulps were issues of *Dynamic Science Fiction* containing portions of James Gunn's master's thesis, under the titles of "The Philosophy of Science Fiction" and "The Plot-Forms of Science Fiction." I was fascinated not only by how Gunn seemed to give order to what I'd been reading all along, but also by the litany of stories I knew

I needed to track down. It was the first time I'd even conceived such a thing as science fiction criticism, and for that matter the first time I'd read any literary criticism at all (it was inexplicably absent from the fifth-grade curriculum back in Sedalia). About a decade later, I found myself knocking on Jim's office door at the University of Kansas, hoping to persuade him to supervise my honors thesis on Ray Bradbury—although technically he was still in administration and public relations at the time, rather than in the English department. Both he and the department graciously agreed—Jim even gave me Bradbury's address, so I could interview him by mail—and I ended up writing my own first piece of science fiction criticism.

Looking back at Jim's original thesis after a half-century, I was surprised at how useful and insightful it remains, not only as clearly written practical criticism and not only for students of James Gunn, but also for anyone interested in the development of (mostly) American science fiction during what is arguably its most formative period. Gunn's thesis came at a crucial juncture: science fiction as a self-conscious genre (if we date that from the launch of Hugo Gernback's *Amazing Stories* in 1926) was scarcely a quarter-century old in 1951, and the market for science fiction books from major publishers was just emerging (Gunn mentions new science fiction lines from Doubleday, Crown, Simon & Schuster, Dutton, and Little, Brown). Within a couple of years, the pulp market would begin to collapse under the competition from paperbacks (and perhaps television), while the paperback and hardcover publishers would present opportunities for new SF novels conceived as novels, and not as magazine serials. The classic novels of the 1950s—by Asimov, Heinlein, Clarke, Sturgeon, Bester, Pohl & Kornbluth, Brackett—were only a couple of years off.

So Gunn was compelled, except for a few glimpses back to Verne, Wells, Burroughs, Bellamy, and others, to draw the bulk of his observations from the magazine stories he obviously knew very well. None of these stories had achieved the canonization that comes from repeated appearances in anthologies (the SF anthology itself was only a few years old in 1951), from SFWA "Hall of Fame" votes, or from retro-Hugo Awards, so Gunn was largely on his own in determining which stories might last. And his batting average here is pretty impressive; he clearly describes the virtues of stories by Kuttner and Moore ("Vintage Season," "The Twonky," "Mimsy Were the Borogoves"), Moore alone ("No Woman Born"), Campbell ("Who Goes There?"), Williamson ("With Folded Hands"), Bester ("Adam and No Eve"), Clarke ("Rescue Party"), Heinlein (several titles), Leiber ("Coming Attraction"), Leinster ("First Contact"), Sturgeon ("Killdozer!"), and others.

Remember that no one *told* Gunn these stories were going to become classics; the only previous criticism he had at hand were J. O. Bailey's *Pilgrims Through Space and Time*, which barely touched upon contemporary SF, and the various editorial comments from magazine editors or anthologists like Groff Conklin and August Derleth.

As gratifying as it is to see Gunn identifying stories that would still be read and discussed more than 60 years later, what I found most fascinating in revisiting this thesis were those writers—like Nelson Bond, Arthur Leo Zagat, Maurice Hugi, Noel Loomis, Thomas Calvert McClary, Nat Schachner, Peter Phillips—and stories that didn't quite make it, and are virtually forgotten today. Since Gunn's thesis is largely concerned with matters of plot, their mostly forgettable stories (though some sound fascinating) can provide examples just as illustrative of "plot-forms" as the more famous stories, and together they provide a kind of anatomy of what the world of magazine SF was like in the 1930s and 1940s—not simply a few canonical tales from writers later celebrated, but the more workmanlike contributions that really kept the magazines going from month to month, and that occasionally produced tales that (from Gunn's descriptions) ranged from forgotten but worthwhile curiosities to absolute howlers.

Gunn's overriding concern with plot and theme—which would not necessarily become the focus of later more academic studies of science fiction—is entirely understandable given that his critical approach is that of a working writer seeking both to move the genre forward and to realistically address the markets available to him. It's interesting how often he comments that a particular plot-form "does not have the inherent possibilities of some of the others" or "will never achieve anything important in the field," while others pose challenges: "if someone were to overcome the difficulties and write such a story," he says of one plot-type, "it might be a tremendous influence on the development of science fiction." These are not the concerns of a theorist, but of a writer who has to face the problem of what to write next, and this practical approach characterizes the whole thesis. Not only are there some forgotten but intriguing writers discussed here, there are also themes that loomed much larger in 1951 than in more recent science fiction; mutants, for example, have waned as concerns over atomic radiation have waned (although arguably they just moved over to the comic books and superhero movies), while the notion of "dimensions" has either disappeared or been replaced by alternate histories and parallel worlds. The vocabulary of science fiction may have moved on since Gunn's thesis was written, and so has the vocabulary of science fiction criticism, but that feeling of raw discovery that I felt way back when first reading it as a kid—the realization that *you can actually write about this stuff*—was its own form of the sense of wonder that science fiction so often boasts about.

So no: this thesis and James Gunn did not make me a science fiction critic. Circumstance, and perhaps sheer perversity, did that. But they did first open up the possibility, and inasmuch as there is blame to be apportioned, I am happy to find Gunn guilty.

Gary K. Wolfe is an emeritus professor of humanities at Roosevelt University. One of the leading scholars in science fiction studies, he is a senior reviewer for Locus *magazine and science fiction reviewer for the* Chicago Tribune.

Preface
When Modern Science Fiction Was Modern

James Gunn

I entered the graduate program at the University of Kansas with a small cadre of fellow students, maybe half-a-dozen of us, few enough that Professor Bill Paden could take us all to lunch at a steak house about ten miles south of Lawrence. I was a little older than some of the other students, since I had served three years in the U.S. Navy during World War II, and I had spent a year as a freelance writer and was the only one of my group who had actually been published. My first two stories came out in September and October, and three others would be published before I got my degree in 1951.

The GI Bill (and assistance from my wife's parents) allowed me the freedom to focus on school without having to work to support my family—now consisting of a wife and a newborn son—and I could take three or four classes a semester and another couple in the summer. Still, though, it took me two years because I had earned my bachelor's degree in journalism and had a number of undergraduate English classes to make up. Even with all that, I continued to write science fiction, including a script for a Dick Tracy comic book and a memorable three-act play for Professor Carroll Edwards, which I adapted as a science-fiction novella and sent off to the new magazine *Galaxy Science Fiction*. I got a telephone call from Horace Gold, an editor, telling me that he liked "Breaking Point" but thought it needed cutting. Why it didn't get published in *Galaxy* and wound up in *Space Science Fiction* is another story. At that time I was also doing some editorial work for E. Haldeman-Julius of Little Blue Books, reading and sending reports about current science-fiction novels to the firm that would employ me after graduation. The point of all this is that I was involved in an ongoing engagement with a category of fiction that I had become fascinated with at an early age. This was before my transformative experience of attending my first science-fiction convention, the World convention of 1952 in Chicago, where I met many of the authors I had read and admired, a couple of famous editors, and the agent I ended up acquiring (probably through the recommendation of Gold), Frederik Pohl.

So, when my faculty adviser, Professor John Hankins, asked me what I wanted to write my thesis about, I told him "science fiction." It is a tribute to Hankins's open-mindedness and avuncular good will—that he didn't look horrified or disdainful (unlike Professor Paden, who when I told him my plans replied, "I view science fiction as, at best, sub-literary"). These were the early days of science fiction in higher education. There were no classes in science fiction—the first of these wouldn't be taught until 1966— and science-fiction books, of which there were beginning to be a few published after a long, dry period between 1926 (when the first American science-fiction magazine, *Amazing Stories*, began publication) and the end of World War II, would never be noted in the book-review pages of the general media. There were no academic studies, either. J. O. Bailey, professor at the University of North Carolina at Chapel Hill, had been allowed in 1933 to write his doctoral dissertation on a survey of science fiction, but it would not be published until fourteen years later as *Pilgrims Through Space and Time*. Bailey was a Victorian scholar and the additions he made to his discussion of nineteenth century works for the later publication had little on contemporary fiction, including the magazines. A year later, Columbia University's Marjorie Hope Nicolson published her *Voyages to the Moon*, but this reached even further into the past.

By 1950, science fiction was still considered pulp fiction, and, indeed, the science-fiction magazines were proliferating on the newsstands, some fifty of them during the late 1940s and early 1950s before the publishing boom (influenced by the fact that World War II had been largely won in the laboratory and its validity confirmed by the use of rockets and atomic bombs, among other technological innovations). Fan publishers were turning their favorite magazine serials into books, and a few were even wandering into mainstream publication. A series of important anthologies had come out—some of them covering a large swathe of literary history, some of them focused more narrowly on what came to be known as "the Golden Age"—the period between 1938 and 1950, when John W. Campbell, Jr., edited *Astounding Science Fiction* and transformed the field. *Adventures in Time and Space* by Raymond J. Healy and J. Francis McComas and *The Best of Science Fiction* by Groff Conklin were published in 1946, and a series of annual anthologies—beginning with *Strange Ports of Call*—were produced by August Derleth in 1948. The magazine-publishing field was just being revolutionized by two new magazines: *The Magazine of Fantasy* (which became *The Magazine of Fantasy and Science Fiction* with its second issue) in 1949 and *Galaxy Science Fiction* in 1950. Articles about the surprising rise and unusual message of science fiction were beginning to appear in the mainstream media. Included in that was an article I wrote for the *Kansas City Star* that got me a letter from Hugo Gernsback and a note from the editor saying I was "over-enthusiastic."

So it was a time of change and a time of promise, although no one could have predicted the way it would turn out, with the implosion of the magazine field in the mid–1950s, the proliferation of book publication from some 70 books in 1952 to a thousand a decade later and then two thousand and on upward, the ascendance of fantasy over the long dominance of science-fiction, the big-moneymaking films, the TV series, the comic books and the comic-related giant conventions—all that was in the unanticipated future.

But in the innocence and energy of youth, I tackled the task of pouring what I knew and loved about science fiction into a text that must have surprised Hankins by its scope and size. He invited me to his yellow-stucco home in downtown Lawrence and had me read from my tome to a living room of his faculty colleagues and a few of my fellow students. Buoyed by all this, I sent the manuscript off to Fred Pohl, who submitted it to several publishers, none of whom were ready to venture into the relatively untouched field of academic consideration—at least not by a recent and untried graduate. So Fred sent it over to his Futurian buddy, Robert A. W. Lowndes, who had been editing a variety of magazines for Columbia Publications for some years. Lowndes, in his willingness to try something different, began to serialize my thesis in *Dynamic Science Fiction*—first as "The Philosophy of Science Fiction" in two parts and then as "The Plot-Forms of Science Fiction" in two sections—before the magazine folded.

I like to think that I didn't kill it (I've killed a few in my time), but I also like to think that its publication was an appropriate response to Professor Paden. I may have had the only master's thesis published in a pulp magazine.

Editor's Introduction

Michael R. Page

I was delighted when James Gunn responded enthusiastically to my idea of editing an edition of his historic 1951 master's thesis, *Modern Science Fiction: A Critical Analysis*, and I was especially delighted that the folks at McFarland immediately accepted the proposal and were excited to have another James Gunn book in their catalog. Gunn's thesis is one of the great "lost" manuscripts (although never really lost, just unavailable without diligent search) of science fiction scholarship, and it is an important one. I need not make a case for James Gunn's importance and centrality to science fiction and science fiction studies here. His career speaks for itself. Thus, this edition is, I hope, a valuable addition to the library of scholarly books about science fiction and fills a gap in James Gunn's bibliography that scholars and general readers of science fiction will find useful.

The scholarship, criticism, theory and teaching of science fiction is a lively and significant—although, perhaps, still small—part of academic literary studies. Similarly, these activities no longer sit on the fringes of the overall spectrum of the science fiction community and its activities, but are an important segment of it—as witnessed at the 2016 World Science Fiction Convention in Kansas City where the Academic Track programming held over forty panels, most of which had larger audiences than one would anticipate at a typical academic literary conference. Most colleges and universities offer courses in science fiction, dozens of academic monographs and anthologies appear each year from academic presses, and at least four academic journals—*Extrapolation, Science Fiction Studies, Foundation, Journal of the Fantastic in the Arts* (there are probably others)—are devoted to science fiction and the other genres of the fantastic. Increasingly, undergraduate honor's theses, master's theses, and Ph.D. dissertations focus on science fiction or include the analysis of texts that are decidedly science fiction side-by-side with mainstream literary texts.

This was not always the case. Not surprising, really, everything must start somewhere. The story of how science fiction became legitimized in academia, in many ways, begins with James Gunn and this thesis, which he submitted for his master's degree in the English department at the University of Kansas in May 1951. Arguably, Gunn's story is the story of how science fiction came to college. And James Gunn was instrumental in making that happen.

Of course there was one academic pioneer (or pilgrim, if you will) who predated Gunn's historic thesis: J. O. Bailey. Bailey is rightfully recognized as the founding father of academic science fiction criticism for his 1947 monograph *Pilgrims Through Space and Time*. The book began as a dissertation submitted in 1934 at the University of North Carolina. As Gunn points out in the thesis, Bailey's book was the only academic attempt at grappling with science fiction up to that point. (Two other studies from the decade, Philip Gove's *The Imaginary Voyage in Prose Fiction* (1941) and Marjorie Nicolson's *Voyages to the Moon* (1948) are significant for exploring what later was termed proto-SF, but their subject matter was even further removed from contemporary science fiction than was Bailey's). Like Gunn would later experience when his thesis was sent to publishers, Bailey had a hard time getting *Pilgrims* published, and it was only after World War II that Ben Abramson, a bookseller and science fiction fan, published it under the imprint Argus Books. Nonetheless, the book made its way into most major university libraries and became a starting point for scholars interested in science fiction. But Bailey's book is primarily centered on eighteenth and nineteenth century writers, such as Mary Shelley, Poe, and Bellamy, and Edwardians and Modernists, such as Wells, Huxley and Stapledon. Modern science fiction, as Gunn defines it—that which emerged in the American genre magazines starting in 1926 with the publication of *Amazing Stories*— gets some slight attention in Bailey's book. What attention Bailey does give it was added in later for book publication and his knowledge of the scene current with his introduction, which frames his study with some degree of inspiration in terms of the emergent "Atomic Age," is spotty at best. Nonetheless, Bailey does take a look at a handful of stories from the emerging genre and a list of the titles he covers is revealing: Wylie and Balmer's *When Worlds Collide* and Wylie's *Gladiator*, the Binder's "Adam Link's Vengeance," Burroughs's *Tarzan at the Earth's Core* (but no other Burroughs titles), Clyde Crane Campbell's "The Avatar" (but no John W. Campbell, Jr.), Ray Cummings's *The Girl in the Golden Atom* and *The Man who Mastered Time*, Stanton Coblentz's *After 12,000 Years*, John Russell Fearn's "The Blue Infinity," Edmond Hamilton's "The Metal Giants," L. Taylor Hansen's "The Prince of Liars," Otis Adelbert Kline's *The Planet of Peril*, Leinster's "The Man who

Put Out the Sun" and "The Storm that Had to Be Stopped" (two works by a master that have never been collected or anthologized), Lovecraft's "At the Mountains of Madness" and "The Shadow Out of Time," George McLociard's "Television Hill," Simak's "The Creator," "Doc" Smith's *The Skylark of Space*, George O. Smith's "Identity" (the most recent story—published in *Astounding* in November 1945—Bailey considers), John Taine's *Before the Dawn* and *The Iron Star*, A. Hyatt Verrill's "Beyond the Pole," and Donald Wandrei's "The Red Brain." This list hardly represents the classics of the genre, let alone the best work coming out of the early magazines, although a number of the novels Bailey considers are of significance. The short stories, and many of their authors, in particular, are all long forgotten, with the exceptions of Leinster, Lovecraft, Simak, and possibly Wandrei. Readers will notice that most of the novels in the list were from the general interest pulps of the teens, twenties, and thirties.

We see no engagement with Campbell's *Astounding*; let alone Tremaine's and the compelling string of "thought-variant" stories he published—by Williamson, Campbell writing as Don A. Stuart, Schachner, Gallun, and others. There is no sign of Asimov, Heinlein, Sturgeon, or Van Vogt. This is not to dismiss Bailey's achievement, but to show that he left a significant gap in his analysis, which left room for another scholar to intervene. Gunn was the first to make that intervention. Indeed, Gunn addresses Bailey's shortcomings in the early chapters of *Modern Science Fiction*, recognizing the significance of Bailey's contribution, while hoping that his work will fill the gap left by *Pilgrims* and open the discourse for later scholars to examine modern science fiction.

Bailey's achievement, in its way, ranks with Hugo Gernsback's launching of *Amazing Stories* in April 1926, and like Gernsback, whose name graces the annual Hugo Awards, Bailey has been acknowledged through the annual Pilgrim Award given by the Science Fiction Research Association (SFRA) for lifetime achievement in science fiction scholarship. Bailey was the initial recipient in 1970, the year the SFRA was founded; Gunn was the seventh recipient in 1976.

Although Bailey's *Pilgrims* represents the first formal academic study of science fiction, this is not to say that there was no other science fiction scholarship and criticism out there. Since the launching of *Amazing* in 1926 and Hugo Gernsback's inclusion of letters from readers beginning in 1927, science fiction scholarship and criticism—mostly amateurish likes and dislikes, but sometimes sophisticated in its analysis—was active. In the fan letters, the study of science fiction was in its infancy. Another important critical intervention was the editorial column, instituted by Gernsback with the editorial "A New Sort of Magazine" in the first issue of *Amazing*, an important feature in most science fiction magazines, which included occasional guest editorials by writers that made steps toward genre definition, theory, and praxis.[1] Important early guest editorials include Jack Williamson's "Scientifiction, Searchlight of Science," which appeared in the Fall 1928 *Amazing Stories Quarterly* slightly before Williamson's first story, "The Metal Man," which appeared in the December 1928 issue. Williamson enthusiastically proclaimed, "The chief function of scientifiction is the creation of real pictures of new things, new ideas, and new machines. Scientifiction is the product of the human imagination, guided by the suggestion of science. It takes the basis of science, considers all the clues that science has to offer, and then adds a thing that is alien to science—imagination. It goes ahead and lights the way" (1). Following Williamson's essay, Dr. Miles J. Breuer, one of the leading pioneers of magazine science fiction, contributed "The Future of Scientifiction" to the Summer 1929 issue of *Amazing Stories Quarterly*, where he more measuredly considered the budding field: "*Amazing Stories* is a pioneer. Our Magazine is ineradicably down in history as the leader with the far-flung vision. A hundred or a thousand years in the future, men will point back to it as the originator of a new type of literary art. In the meanwhile, the art is spreading.... Some day the public will wake up to an intense, conscious interest in Scientifiction" (417).[2]

When Gernsback lost *Amazing* through a shady takeover by a rival publisher, he immediately began publishing a competitor, *Wonder Stories* (initially *Air Wonder* and *Science Wonder*) and there he created a space for the coalescence of science fiction fandom by forming the Science Fiction League through which fans from across the country (and overseas) could correspond with one another. The enthusiastic young fans, faced with having to write multiple letters to several correspondents, began sharing their thoughts about stories and ideas about science fiction in mimeographed booklets that they could share with multiple correspondents. Thus the first fanzines were born, another avenue through which science fiction scholarship and criticism developed. As the 30s moved forward and the fans themselves grew from pre-teens to teens to adults, the fanzines got more sophisticated and the critical discourse in turn became more sophisticated—and sometimes contentious. Without question, there was a strong base of amateur criticism (both from fans and the writers themselves) prior to the academic intervention by Bailey, and then a few years later, by Gunn. Although, it should be noted that Gunn, a Midwesterner away from the science fiction scene in New York, Philadelphia, Chicago, Los Angeles, and elsewhere, was largely unaware of the fan discourse, except for what he might have picked up in the pages of the magazines.

The major editorial voice by the 1940s was John W. Campbell, who used the editorial column in *Astounding* to engage readers, inspire writers, and argue for science fiction as the searchlight Williamson proclaimed and the literary art Breuer hoped for. Gunn later wrote of Campbell in his essay "The Gatekeepers": "He proselytized for new kinds of writers; he encouraged and redirected more established ones. In editorial and letter and personal conversation, he inserted irritating ideas in the oyster shells of author's minds, and he repeated the requirements for good SF so often it was like chiseling them into stone" (60). Through *Astounding*, Campbell shaped science fiction into a coherent mode of imaginative inquiry and not only laid the foundation for modern science fiction, but for science fiction scholarship, criticism, and theory. As Gunn puts it, "In *Astounding*, between 1937 and 1950, SF was shaped and reshaped by the writers attracted to the vision Campbell held up for them and by Campbell himself, and out of this intense experience of creating and shaping and debating came the conventions and methods that mark SF to this day and which later generations of writers would use, often unconscious of their origins, or react against" ("Gatekeepers" 60). In *Modern Science Fiction* Gunn draws on a number of Campbell's editorials and articles in defining the philosophy of science fiction, and Campbell was, certainly at the time, the central voice in Gunn's own thinking about the genre and its significance. Arguably, Campbell's editorials were the central body of science fiction criticism in the 1940s.

Those who have traced the history of science fiction criticism, such as Gary K. Wolfe in his excellent essay "Pilgrims of the Fall,"[3] point to only one other book from the 1940s that directly engaged with contemporary science fiction: *Of Worlds Beyond*, a symposium of essays on the writing of science fiction put together by Lloyd Arthur Eschbach and published in 1947. The slim volume includes essays by many of the leading writers of the 30s and 40s: Heinlein, John Taine, Williamson, Van Vogt, De Camp, "Doc" Smith, and Campbell. Gunn draws upon the Williamson and Campbell contributions in the thesis. But none of the essays can really be called criticism; the volume is more about the techniques of writing. Its value lies mainly in these insights for writers and for the historical and biographical interest the volume represents. As Wolfe points out, perhaps only Jack Williamson's contribution, "The Logic of Fantasy," makes overtures to a critical approach by outlining "a number of principles that he saw governing internal consistency in a fantastic story and anticipated more formal attempts to describe the genre by later critics" (191). Between the publications of *Pilgrims Through Space and Time* and *Of Worlds Beyond* in 1947 and the completion of Gunn's thesis in 1951, no other work of science fiction criticism or scholarship appeared in book form.

A case can be made, then, that had Gunn's thesis been published as a book in the early 1950s—Gunn's agent at the time, Frederik Pohl, had taken it to a number of publishers without success—it would hold an equal, if not greater, place in the history of science fiction scholarship than Bailey's *Pilgrims*. Book publication, however, did not happen—until now. Nonetheless, Gunn's thesis did circulate in a way appropriate for a genre that received little attention from academia at the time, but that had an enthusiastic and intellectually engaged readership hungry for a critical discourse for the genre. Although Pohl wasn't able to secure a book publisher, he did sell the thesis to his comrade from the Futurian days, Robert Lowndes, who published portions of Gunn's thesis in one of his pulp magazines called *Dynamic Science Fiction*. Anyone who knows much about science fiction magazines knows that they were (and still are) sought out, treasured, and read by writers, fans, and budding scholars alike, unlike other magazines and journals which, once having been read (if at all), were often tossed in the trash and forgotten. Many budding scholars (Gary K. Wolfe, for one) found Gunn's articles in *Dynamic* or sought them out when they began their graduate work. Others may have found the thesis through interlibrary loan or on microfiche as they pursued their studies, graduate and undergraduate. In spite of this, Gunn's audience was, admittedly, limited—much more limited than Bailey's, especially when *Pilgrims* appeared in a second edition in the 1960s from Advent.

Portions of the thesis appeared in *Dynamic* in four parts. The first section, "The Philosophy of Science Fiction," appeared in the March 1953 and June 1953 issues. Parts of the second section, "The Plot-Forms of Science Fiction" appeared in the October 1953 and January 1954 issues (the magazine's last). Lowndes would have published the rest of the thesis, but the magazine folded before completion of the serialization.[4] The serialization ends with Gunn's discussion of Arthur C. Clarke's "Rescue Party" with the promise that "Mr. Gunn continues his survey in our next issue" (48). In the first installment, Lowndes presents Gunn's work with no fanfare; there is no mention of it in his editorial column, "The Lobby," and the table of contents and the title page provide no blurb, both only referring to Gunn's piece as a "special article." There is no mention of the article in the advertisement for the March 1953 issue in the inaugural December 1952 issue, although it is possible that Lowndes announced the piece in earlier issues of *Future* and *Science Fiction Quarterly*, as all three magazines under his editorship appear somewhat interdependent.

The second part of "The Philosophy of Science Fiction" is blurbed in the table of contents of the June 1953 issue as "Final sections of Mr. Gunn's introduction to contemporary science fiction" and in "The Lobby" editorial Lowndes wrote, "This article is the first part of a book-length essay on science fiction, written as a Master's Thesis. We'd like your votes on whether you'd care to see the rest of the essay: it is titled, 'The Plot-Forms of Science Fiction,' and we would have to spread it out over a number of issues" (11). A similar note asking for readers' opinions on whether to publish "The Plot-Forms" appears at the end of Gunn's article. A letter by one Dave Hammond praised Gunn's article: "I hope you continue the series until you publish Gunn's entire book. It is really great to see an article on science fiction by someone who reads and knows science fiction; this is almost a novelty. For that reason, and because it struck such a responsive chord in me, I want to rate that article in top place for this issue!" (114). Another reader, Joe Keogh, wrote, "If 'The Philosophy of Science Fiction' is the kind of articles you're going to be handing out... you can be sure this reader will keep liking them. I don't know if Gunn said all there can be said about stf, but if he hasn't, bring it on" (118). Another, perhaps younger reader, Irvin Norfleet, Jr., remarked, "I liked Mr. Gunn's article. I think that you should continue these articles, but don't get so darn technical about it" (121).

The August issue, which is almost entirely taken up by the novel *The Duplicated Man* by James Blish and Lowndes (under the pseudonym Michael Sherman), announces the first installment of "The Plot-Forms" in the next issue: "And finally, better watch out for our forthcoming issue; we're starting that James Gunn essay you all approved our using" (118). Lowndes didn't have room for the letters column in that issue, but teases us with a note indicating that a letter by one Bob Silverberg "found favor this time" (104). One wonders what Silverberg might have had to say about Gunn's articles.

It's worth noting that in the gap between the publication of "The Philosophy of Science Fiction" and "The Plot-Forms of Science Fiction," Lowndes published the first article by Thomas Clareson, "The Evolution of Science Fiction," in the August issue of one of *Dynamic*'s companion magazines, *Science Fiction Quarterly*. Clareson, who was then working toward his Ph.D. at the University of Pennsylvania, went on to become, along with Gunn, one of the important foundational academic scholars in the science fiction field, founding the journal *Extrapolation* in 1959. In his essay, Clareson traces the history of science fiction (much in the manner of Bailey) and cites Gunn's "Philosophy of Science Fiction" essay as a point of argument, putting it into play with Dorothy Scarborough's 1917 study *The Supernatural in Modern English Fiction*, thereby bringing the practice of academic criticism (engaging in conversation with the recent critical literature) to science fiction. Clareson contends that Gunn's remark that "the 'Gothic' romance of the eighteenth century had even less to contribute to the movement which culminated in modern science-fiction" does not accurately reflect the impact of the novels of Charles Brockden Brown and, most importantly, Mary Shelley's *Frankenstein*. Clareson says that "[t]o dismiss it as the first of a series dealing with a mad scientist is to base one's interpretation upon the movie, *not* upon the novel" (89), anticipating Brian Aldiss's famous argument in *Billion Year Spree* that *Frankenstein* is the ür-text of science fiction (7–39). At the end of Clareson's article, Lowndes includes an advertisement for the next installment of Gunn's thesis in the upcoming issue of *Dynamic*: "A significant article for all science-fictionists, 'The Plot-Forms of Science Fiction,' by James Gunn, starts in the October issue of *Dynamic Science Fiction*. Watch for it; this is the essay that you, our readers, stated, by overwhelming majority vote, that you wanted to see!" (98). Lowndes reciprocates by plugging Clareson's article in an advertisement in the October *Dynamic*: "Ordinarily, you'd think we'd plug one of the stories and you'd be right, nine times out of ten—but this is the tenth time, the time when an article has already brought such glowing praise, that we want to draw your attention to 'The Evolution of Science Fiction' by Tom Clareson. It's but one of the many topflight features in *Science Fiction Quarterly*" (53).

The table of contents of the October *Dynamic* states, "Beginning the thorough survey you wanted to see" and the blurb on the article's title page reads: "Here is the first of a series of articles, which add up to one of the most significant essays written about science fiction—published by your request" (44). Lowndes's continued appeal that his readers have "requested" Gunn's thesis comes across as at once true, given the response in the letters column, but also somewhat hesitant—as if Lowndes still feels the need to justify publication in the eyes of new readers, unsure how readers will respond to sophisticated critical analysis. In the letters, a reader from Toronto named R. R. Anger commented "James Gunn's 'The Philosophy of Science Fiction' is a masterly handling of this subject and is absolutely fascinating reading. I would say that his viewpoint is too much influenced by recent science fiction, and that part of the older material which has been reprinted recently; but the conclusions he draws are not harmed by this. By all means continue the series. It is something that marks *Dynamic* out from its competitors as showing great originality in articles" (69).[5] Joe Keogh returned with another enthusiastic endorsement: "*Dynamic* No. 3 exemplifies a growing trend (all to the good) in this magazine of catering to the scientifan by means of fact articles, but even more important, articles that have to do with present day science fiction" (87).[6] A letter from Wilkie Connor with the heading "Give Us Gunn!" closes out the column. Connor requests "Definitely *do* run the second section of Gunn's essay! The work would be of great value to anyone who aspires to writing stf. And who can read science fiction without feeling the urge to write it?" (94).

The table of contents and title-page blurbs in the January 1954 issue,

Dynamic's last, repeat the previous issue's blurbs. The letter column is mostly taken up with letters disputing L. Sprague de Camp's skeptical article, "A Modern Merlin" about Charles Leadbetter and Theosophy, from the June issue and de Camp's response, and a lengthy letter by Al Lewis taking to task a piece on E. E. "Doc" Smith "Skylark Smith: An Appreciation" by Anthony K. Van Riper that appeared in October. Although Lewis mostly concerns himself with defending Smith against Van Riper's "damning with faint praise," he does make one remark suggestive that he was also thinking of Gunn's assessments when he says, "His plot-form is quite admittedly the adventure plot. But he handles it better than anyone else. He writes it with a verve and an optimism and an irrepressible enjoyment that other would be practitioners of the type—Simak, for instance—can't approach" (92). Unfortunately, *Dynamic* folded before Lowndes could publish further reader reaction to Gunn's thesis.

Gunn was not a mere beginner when he started composing the thesis in 1950, and certainly by the time it appeared in *Dynamic*, his name was known across the magazines. By the time Gunn had entered graduate school at the University of Kansas in the fall 1949 semester, he'd already written about a dozen science fiction stories and an article on the history of science fiction for the *Kansas City Star*, which garnered a note of thanks from Hugo Gernsback.[7] Indeed, that fall his first two stories would be published almost simultaneously in the sister magazines *Thrilling Wonder* and *Startling*. The stories "Paradox" (*Thrilling Wonder*, October 1949) and "Communications" (*Startling*, September 1949) appeared under the byline Edwin James; at this point, Gunn was reserving the use of his own name for "serious literary scholarship."[8] He stopped this practice while working on the thesis and the first story to appear under his own name was "The Misogynist" in the November 1952 *Galaxy*. Gunn sent the first chapter of the thesis to John W. Campbell as early as May 23, 1950, claiming that "It represents, I believe, a beginning of what science fiction very badly needs at this time—a summation of what it has been trying to say during the last ten to twenty years and an indication of the possibilities ahead."[9] Although Campbell didn't want to publish it in *Astounding*, his response was positive and Gunn was encouraged to complete the project. In addition to starting the thesis during his first year in graduate school, Gunn also wrote a science fiction play as an independent study project, which he converted into his breakthrough novella "Breaking Point" that summer. The story of the publication process of that novella can be found in my *Saving the World Through Science Fiction*.[10] Gunn received approval for his thesis project from Professor John Hankins that fall. When he told another faculty member, William Paden, Paden scoffed and said "Science fiction is at best sub-literary."[11] Nonetheless,

Gunn proceeded to work diligently, while continuing to write science fiction stories. At this time, Gunn was also doing piecework for Lloyd Smith at Western Printing of Racine, Wisconsin, the publishers of Dell Books. Gunn's task was to write publication reviews for science fiction books that were brought to the firm's attention and to keep Smith informed about what was happening in the science fiction field. One of the books he reviewed was Isaac Asimov's *Pebble in the Sky* (strangely absent from discussion in the thesis); another was Van Vogt's *The Voyage of the Space Beagle*, which includes Van Vogt's classic "Black Destroyer," discussed here in *Modern Science Fiction*.

Gunn completed the thesis in May 1951, graduated, and within days, he and his family, wife Jane and baby Christopher, packed up and moved to Racine where Gunn took a post as junior editor at Western Printing. A little over a year later, Gunn convinced Smith to pay for him to attend the World Science Fiction Convention, held in Chicago that year. That experience proved a revelation and when Pohl told him he'd sold several of his stories, including one each to the top markets *Astounding* and *Galaxy*, Gunn decided to leave Western, move back to Kansas City, and write full time. This led to Gunn's most productive period and established him as one of the top writers in the science fiction field. But by the time the 1950s concluded, Gunn had transitioned into an administrative position at the University of Kansas, which would take up most of his time for the next decade. Had Gunn, perhaps, been more active in science fiction when Advent expanded their publishing of science fiction criticism in the mid-1960s, the thesis would have most likely found book publication then.

A very slow drip of science fiction criticism appeared in the 1950s in book form. In 1953 Reginald Bretnor put together a volume of essays by major writers and editors in the field—including Campbell, Boucher, Fletcher Pratt, de Camp, Asimov, Clarke, and Wylie—not unlike Eschbach's *Of Worlds Beyond*, but much larger and focused on the social function of science fiction and its place in intellectual discourse and literary culture; it was called *Modern Science Fiction: Its Meaning and Its Future*. Important essays in the volume include Asimov's "Social Science Fiction," Campbell's "The Place of Science Fiction," Clarke's "Science Fiction: Preparation for the Age of Space," and Wylie's "Science Fiction and Sanity in an Age of Crisis." A short but insightful, and somewhat tentative, attempt to define key qualities of the genre in a book largely aimed for the literary audience, titled *Inquiry into Science Fiction* by Basil Davenport, a well-known critic and reviewer for the *New York Times* and elsewhere, appeared in 1955. Advent published the first edition of Damon Knight's *In Search of Wonder* in 1956, although it didn't really become a library standard until the second edition of 1967; the original edition was 180 pages, the expanded second edition 306. The anonymously edited (probably by Davenport who provides the introduction) *The Science Fiction Novel: Imagination and Social Criticism*—a set of essays from Heinlein, Cyril Kornbluth, Alfred Bester, and Robert Bloch from a symposium held at the University of Chicago in 1957—was published in 1959. Kornbluth's essay is of special interest because it appeared only a year after his untimely death.

During the decade of the sixties, interest in science fiction criticism began to grow. Kingsley Amis's *New Maps of Hell* (1960) brought new attention to the genre just as the magazine market was collapsing and as a number of the writers of the fifties went into other fields or lines of work. Advent brought out a series of critical works during the sixties, in addition to a second edition of Knight's *In Search of Wonder*. Of particular importance was James Blish's *The Issue at Hand* (1964) and its sequel *More Issues at Hand* (1970), published under the pseudonym William Atheling, Jr. Both writers had reviewed books and written criticism since the forties in fanzines and magazines. Like Gunn, they were important early critics that straddled the writer-critic divide. As Wolfe puts it in "Pilgrims of the Fall," "The importance of the genre's major internal critics in establishing the context for later science fiction and fantasy criticism cannot be overestimated, although it remains surprising how few academic researchers are familiar with the work of these critics/reviewers" (196). Aside from these works, some books by fan critic Sam Moskowitz are also of note, including *Explorers of the Infinite* (1963) and *Seekers of Tomorrow* (1966), both of which frequently made it into university and municipal library collections. Despite their flaws, Moskowitz's books contributed valuable biographical and bibliographical material, as well as devoted analysis, at a time when little was available outside the magazines.

The aforementioned journal *Extrapolation* was another significant moment in the history of science fiction criticism. It started out as a semi-annual newsletter of less than twenty pages put together by Thomas Clareson as a resource for a small group of scholars who participated in the conference on science fiction at the Modern Languages Association annual convention, the highpoint of academic conferencing. Early contributors were Bailey, Mark Hillegas, Arthur O. Lewis, Lionel Stevenson, and Chad Walsh, among others. But Clareson was the driving force and contributed most of the early material. By the mid-sixties, the newsletter had expanded to around fifty pages and by the end of the decade had the appearance of a large-format journal, finally changing to standard journal format with the December 1970 issue. Important contributors in the late sixties included W. H. G. Armytage, I. F. Clarke, Samuel R. Delany, H. Bruce Franklin, Judith

Merril, and Richard Mullen. Of particular interest is the early contribution by Delany, who was still only twenty-seven when his essay "About Five Thousand One Hundred and Seventy Five Words" appeared. Also of note is the text of an MLA forum (edited by Clareson) on "Science Fiction: The New Mythology," which included Isaac Asimov, Frederik Pohl, critics Darko Suvin and H. Bruce Franklin, and notable audience participation from Philip Klass (William Tenn), Joanna Russ and Robert Silverberg. Clareson gathered a number of these essays, and others, in an important early volume of SF criticism, *SF: The Other Side of Realism*, in 1971.[12] Still, books of academic scholarship about science fiction were relatively rare in the 1960s. Only I. F. Clarke's *Voices Prophesying War* (1966), Hillegas's *The Future as Nightmare: H.G. Wells and the Anti-Utopians* (1967), Armytage's *Yesterday's Tomorrows* (1968), and H. Bruce Franklin's scholarly anthology of nineteenth-century American science fiction, *Future Perfect* (1966),[13] accounted for academic studies of science fiction in the sixties. And none of these important studies spent much time exploring the contemporary science fiction scene.

That changed significantly in the 1970s, just as Gunn was getting back into teaching at the University of Kansas. When Gunn joined the English faculty in the fall of 1970 Robert M. Philmus's history *Into the Unknown: The Evolution of Science Fiction from Francis Godwin to H. G. Wells* had recently been published by the University of California Press. Although focused on science fiction's prehistory, Philmus's study opened the door for later histories of the genre, including Gunn's *Alternate Worlds*, which traced the history of science fiction up to the contemporary. Two new journals, *Foundation*, a British journal, and *Science Fiction Studies* joined *Extrapolation* in 1972 and 1973 respectively. A number of teaching guides appeared, including *Teaching Tomorrow* by Elizabeth Calkins and Barry McGhan, *Grokking the Future* by Bernard Hollister and Deane Thompson, and L. David Allen's *Science Fiction: An Introduction*. The academic interest in SF caught the attention of the writers and fans in the field and some were not happy about it. In a *Galaxy* essay titled, "The Siren Songs of Academe," Lester Del Rey was particularly vehement, barking, "Most of the so-called criticism consists of trying to impose some far-fetched theory onto science fiction, trying to force it into some more familiar mold, or simple attempts at sticking some label or other onto it to replace 'science fiction'" (74). One of the more thoughtful essays, published in *The Magazine of Fantasy and Science Fiction*, came from William Tenn In "Jazz Then, Musicology Now." Tenn compared science fiction to jazz music, at first expressing worry that, like jazz, SF might lose something once it became respectable. But later in the essay, Tenn (who held an academic teaching position at Penn State) conceded that science fiction did belong in the classroom:

> This boom is different: it is significant in terms other than numbers. It's occurring in one place essentially—the university. And the university is where it's always belonged. Science fiction, after all, is nothing but dramatized concept, ideation made into flesh of character and line of narrative. It's come home at last, to its origins, to the one place where the hard sciences become abstract, where the social sciences build reality, where the new frontiers of esthetics and metaphysics are measured off [112–13].[14]

A number of academic books on science fiction appeared in the 1970s following the essays by Tenn and Del Rey. They included historical surveys, such as Robert Scholes and Eric S. Rabkin's *Science Fiction: History, Science, Vision*, published by Oxford University Press, and a thoughtful cultural history of the magazines by Paul A. Carter, who had published a story in *Astounding* as early as 1946 and a handful more in the fifties, titled *The Creation of Tomorrow*. The success of the Scholes and Rabkin volume led to a series of single-author studies (edited by Scholes, a major figure in English studies in general), including Gunn's *Isaac Asimov: The Foundations of Science Fiction*, published by Oxford, in the early 1980s. This association with the globally important university press gave science fiction studies a boost. A number of collections of critical articles in the manner of *SF: The Other Side of Realism* appeared, including many on single authors such as Asimov, Clarke, and Heinlein. An important early critical study that argued that science fiction was part of a larger apocalyptic motif in American literature was David Ketterer's 1974 book *New Worlds for Old*. Samuel R. Delany, like Gunn both a writer and an academic, published his first book of criticism, *The Jewel-Hinged Jaw*, in 1977, followed by his somewhat excessive exercise in structuralist analysis of a single story (Thomas M. Disch's "Angouleme"), *The American Shore*, in 1978. One should also take note of Delany's seminal essay "Science Fiction and 'Literature'—or, the Conscience of the King," which first appeared in, of all places, *Analog*'s May 1979 issue.[15] Indeed, 1979 was a banner year for academic science fiction scholarship and the year marked a critical mass of significant works. The most important academic critical studies of the 1970s all appeared in 1979, and include I. F. Clarke's extremely valuable *The Pattern of Expectation 1644–2001*, Darko Suvin's indispensable *Metamorphoses of Science Fiction* and Gary K. Wolfe's equally indispensable *The Known and the Unknown*. As important as Clarke's, Suvin's, and Wolfe's monographs are, however, the most indispensable accomplishment of SF scholarship in 1979 was the first edition of Peter Nicholls and John Clute's *The Science Fiction Encyclopedia*. My own copy, discovered in a used bookshop in 1983 or '84, is in tatters from my endless fascination with it as a teenage science fiction reader. Another important reference work from the period was Neil Barron's

Anatomy of Wonder (1976) and its subsequent editions. Other early critical works were published in mass market paperback, including Sam Lundwall's *Science Fiction: What It's All About* (1971) and L. David Allen's *Science Fiction Reader's Guide* (1974).[16] But most works of scholarship, criticism, and history in the 1970s still came from the writers within the field: Wollheim's *The Universe Makers*, Aldiss's *Billion Year Spree*, Del Rey's *The World of Science Fiction*, Knight's anthology *Turning Points*, David Kyle's *A Pictorial History of Science Fiction*—and Gunn's *Alternate Worlds*. Aside from Gunn's history, the most important text here is Aldiss's *Billion Year Spree*. In fact, *Billion Year Spree* and *Alternate Worlds* can be thought of as *companion* histories: Aldiss taking the point of view of the British and focusing on the tradition developing from Mary Shelley and the Romantics through the Wellsian scientific romance, and Gunn taking the viewpoint of the long history, dating proto-history extending back to Lucian, but coalescing his argument in the American magazine era where science fiction was defined, codified, and emerged as a genre of contemporary literature. Although Aldiss's history came out a few years before the publication of *Alternate Worlds* (only because *Alternate Worlds* was delayed due to its structure as a large-format book with hundreds of illustrations requiring permissions), we can gather that, in a way, indicated by its subtitle "The True History of Science Fiction," Aldiss is already arguing with the viewpoint taken by Gunn in *Alternate Worlds* (reminding one of Aldiss's classic story "Man in His Time," where the protagonist is slightly ahead of everyone else in time.) Although *Alternate Worlds*, which is certainly one of the most widely read histories of the field (with a new edition forthcoming in China), reflects Gunn's mature understanding of the field, its roots can be traced to the 1951 thesis.

By the 1980s, the trickle of academic books on science fiction became a flood, and now it would take a budding scholar a number of years to read through all of the critical literature in the field (nor would one want to or need to read it all as that would take away from reading the primary texts). Noteworthy works of the first half of the 1980s include: Walter E. Meyers's *Aliens and Linguists* (1980), Patricia Warrick's *The Cybernetic Imagination in Science Fiction* (1980), Mark Rose's *Alien Encounters* (1981), W. Warren Wagar's *Terminal Visions* (1982), and Brian Stableford's *Scientific Romance in Britain 1890–1950* (1985). John Huntington's *Rationalizing Genius* (1989), appearing at the end of the decade, has much in common with Gunn's work in that it centers on a story-by-story analysis of *The Science Fiction Hall of Fame Volume One*, and from this analysis draws conclusions about canon formation that in turn raise questions about the cultural history of the science fiction genre.

I need not give an overview of science fiction criticism and scholarship since the late 1980s, when cyberpunk became the focus of much science fiction scholarship, by scholars whose primary focus was science fiction and by many for whom it was not. However, I will mention some works that, I think, resonate with Gunn's thesis. Thomas Clareson's *Understanding American Science Fiction: The Formative Period 1926–1970* (1990) has a shared sensibility with Gunn's thesis in its discussions of a number of key science fiction texts. Albert I. Berger's *The Magic that Works: John W. Campbell and the American Response to Technology* (1993) gives much additional context to the Campbellian *zeitgeist* at the center of Gunn's study. Certainly J. J. Pierce's ambitious four-volume study, *A Study of Imagination and Evolution*, consisting of *Foundations of Science Fiction* (1987), *Great Themes of Science Fiction* (1987), *When World Views Collide* (1989) and *Odd Genre* (1994), shares similarities with Gunn's approach. Pierce is not an academic, but nevertheless applies a strong argument and academic rigor to the analysis throughout his texts. Equally ambitious is Alexei and Cory Panshin's *The World Beyond the Hill: Science Fiction and the Quest for Transcendence* (1989), a nearly 700-page study of the science fiction of the Gernsbackian era and Campbell's Golden Age, discussing many of the same texts Gunn examines in *Modern Science Fiction*. Gary Westfahl's argumentative *The Mechanics of Wonder* (1998) makes the case for a Gernsbackian and Campbellian nexus at the center of science fiction that concurs with Gunn's 1951 thesis in certain respects. John Cheng's *Astounding Wonder: Imagining Science and Science Fiction in Interwar America* (2012) examines the cultural history out of which science fiction magazines emerged between the two world wars. Although Istvan Csciery-Ronay's *The Seven Beauties of Science Fiction* (2008) is a compelling work of high theory, it also has something of the structure Gunn's thesis modeled. And finally, John Rieder's recent *Science Fiction and the Mass Cultural Genre System* (2017) follows Gunn in setting forth new arguments for science fiction's definition and its place within literary and cultural history.

While science fiction criticism and academic interest in science fiction started to blossom and expand in the late sixties, Gunn himself was about to return to the field, after ten years of administrative work at KU, and so his story parallels the growth of the academic interest in science fiction sketched above. Although a number of Gunn's stories from the 1950s were published in book form in the early 1960s—*The Joy Makers*, *The Immortals*, *Future Imperfect*—Gunn had virtually stopped writing for a period of eight years. That changed in the summer of 1966, following an inspiring conference at the university called *Man and the Future* that Gunn helped organize.[17] Early that summer, Gunn heard from some Hollywood producers who were interested in *The Immortals*, which eventually became an ABC "Movie of the Week" in 1969 and a short-run TV series the following season.[18] For the first time in his tenure as a university administrator Gunn took his summer vacation that year to write the long-delayed sequel to the novella "Witches Must Burn" (about a demagogic and charismatic leader who ushers in an era of ignorance and superstition by orchestrating "burnings" at major universities across the country, leading the "eggheads" to go into hiding), which John Campbell had published in *Astounding* in 1956. Campbell rejected the sequel, "Trial by Fire," after a year of back-and-forth discussions, but Fred Pohl picked it up for *If* and Gunn wrote a final segment, "Witch Hunt," in the summer of 1968, also published by Pohl, which completed the 1972 novel *The Burning*. In the summer of 1967 Gunn wrote his classic first contact story "The Listeners," the beginning of a sequence of stories that make up the novel by the same name, which he continued to add to over the next several years.

By 1969 Gunn found himself back in the classroom when his son Christopher asked him to mentor a student-run class on science fiction, which Gunn ended up teaching, as opposed to merely supervising. One session of the class, featuring Harlan Ellison's lecture at the end of the semester, is captured in "New Directions in Science Fiction," the first film in Gunn's *Literature of Science Fiction* film series. Of special interest for the thesis are some of the later films in the series, especially "The Early Days of the SF Magazines," in which Jack Williamson discusses with Gunn the genesis of *The Humanoids*; Gunn's discussion of the original story, "With Folded Hands..." and the sequel *...And Searching Mind*, as you will see, is one of the most sustained analyses in *Modern Science Fiction*. The discussion of themes in science fiction with Gordon R. Dickson reminds readers of the second half of Gunn's thesis, "The Plot-Forms of Science Fiction," and similar philosophies expressed by Frederik Pohl in his lecture "Ideas in Science Fiction."

Gunn permanently moved from administration to the English department in 1970, where he began to teach science fiction regularly. This was the watershed year in which science fiction came to college across the country and the year that marked the formation of the Science Fiction Research Association, of which Gunn was a founding member. Soon Gunn began to turn his course lectures into a book (although, as mentioned above, publication was delayed for a few years), the essential genre history *Alternate Worlds*, which received a special award at the 1976 World Science Fiction Convention; Gunn would later receive a Hugo Award for his study of Isaac Asimov. A number of the stories featured in Gunn's thesis are also examined in *Alternate Worlds*, and one can see a continuity, but also a *maturing*, of Gunn's ideas about the philosophy of science fiction between the two works.

A few years later, Gunn anthologized a number of these stories in *The Road to Science Fiction* series, which became the cornerstone teaching texts not only for Gunn, but also for many science fiction teachers for several decades. *The Road* is also of monumental importance for the growing science fiction interest in China. Stories and novel excerpts in the first three volumes of *The Road* that Gunn discusses in the thesis include Lucian's "A True Story," Cyrano's *A Voyage to the Moon*, Holberg's *Journey to the World Underground*, Voltaire's "Micromegas" (added for later editions), Shelley's *Frankenstein*, O'Brien's "The Diamond Lens," and Bellamy's *Looking Backward* in volume one; Wells's "The New Accelerator," Merritt's "The Moon Pool," Julian Huxley's "The Tissue-Culture King," Williamson's "With Folded Hands...," Van Vogt's "Black Destroyer," and Asimov's "Nightfall" in volume two; and Kuttner and Moore's "Mimsy Were the Borogoves," Sturgeon's "Thunder and Roses," Merril's "That Only a Mother," Tenn's "Brooklyn Project," and Leiber's "Coming Attraction" in volume three.

Gunn established himself as one of the most important scholars and teachers in the field of science fiction in the 1970s, traveling around the country and the world advocating for science fiction as *the* important literature of the twentieth century, as he famously defined it in volume one of *The Road to Science Fiction*:

> Science fiction is the branch of literature that deals with the effects of change on people in the real world as it can be projected into the past, the future, or to distant places. It often concerns itself with scientific or technological change, and it usually involves matters whose importance is greater than the individual or the community; often civilization or the race itself is in danger (1).

And later in his essay "The Worldview of Science Fiction":

> Science fiction, then, deals with people as if they were creatures as adaptable as the protoplasm from which they emerged. Change the conditions, and humanity will change. The first premise of SF is that humanity is adaptable... although humanity is as much a product of its environment as the other animals, it possesses a quality that the other animals lack—the intellectual ability to recognize its origins and the processes at work upon it, and even, sometimes, to choose a course other than that instilled by its environment (73).

For Gunn, and other science fictionists, SF can, perhaps, save the world, by providing imaginative scenarios, both for the good and the bad, that can help guide us into the future.

To help educate the teachers of science fiction, and, then, in turn, their students, Gunn established the Intensive Summer Institute on the Teaching of Science Fiction held at the University of Kansas in 1974. In the early years of the three-week seminar, participants spent a week each with guest instructors Frederik Pohl, Gordon Dickson, and Theodore Sturgeon, until

Sturgeon's death in 1985 slightly changed the dynamic. Many other writers and scholars participated in the Institute over the years; Tom Clareson helped teach the novels the first year. I found my way to Gunn and the Institute in 2007 where we spent two weeks going through the original four volumes of *The Road to Science Fiction*. By that time Gunn had split the Institute into the short story one year and the novel the next, so I returned in 2008 for the novels. I'd been aware of Gunn's teaching institute as early as my high school days, it just took me around twenty-five years to get there.

A number of Gunn's scholarly essays, many collected in *Inside Science Fiction*, echo the 1951 master's thesis. Students of Gunn will be interested in tracing a number of his ideas from their earliest formulation in the thesis to Gunn's later articulations in his various scholarly articles and activities. The essays in *Inside Science Fiction* that readers may wish to consult are "The Education of a Science Fiction Teacher," "From the Pulps to the Classroom: The Strange Journey of Science Fiction," "The Gatekeepers," "Fifty Amazing, Astounding, Wonderful Years," "The Academic Viewpoint," "Science Fiction as Literature," and "The Protocols of Science Fiction."

Gunn's primary source texts for the thesis were the postwar anthologies that brought magazine science fiction to a broader audience and were largely responsible in making writers such as Robert Heinlein, Isaac Asimov, Theodore Sturgeon, and others, household names. Following the dropping of the atomic bomb and the prospects of future space exploration, the general public got curious about science fiction. Hardcover anthologies by Groff Conklin for Crown (*The Best of Science Fiction* (1946), *A Treasury of Science Fiction* (1948), and *The Big Book of Science Fiction* (1950)), August Derleth for Pellegrini & Cudahy (*Strange Ports of Call* (1948), *The Other Side of the Moon* (1949), and *Beyond Time and Space* (1950)), and perhaps most significantly *Adventures in Time and Space* (1946) published by Random House and edited by R. J. Healy and J. F. McComas, put modern science fiction into public and university libraries across the country and, in effect, created a modern canon of science fiction. Two earlier anthologies were also important: Phil Stong's 1940 *The Other Worlds*, which Gunn draws on, consisting mostly of stories from *Weird Tales*, but containing some science fiction, and Donald Wollheim's *The Pocket Book of Science-Fiction* (1943), an early attempt at paperback publication, and a book which Gunn read several times while traveling across the country during his military service. *The Pocket Book* mostly consisted of earlier stories, but important modern stories—including the two stories that many point to as the beginning of modern magazine science fiction, Weinbaum's "A Martian Odyssey" and John W. Campbell's "Twilight," followed by Sturgeon's "Microcosmic

God" and Heinlein's "—And He Built a Crooked House—" concluded the volume. Surprisingly, Gunn does not discuss any of these stories in *Modern Science Fiction* and it is most likely that he simply didn't have access to his copy of Wollheim's anthology at the time and, given its paperback publication, it was not cataloged in the KU library. Gary K. Wolfe has discussed the significance of these anthologies in *Evaporating Genres*: "These and other anthologies from the postwar period not only vitally preserved stories that had for the most part been consigned to ephemeral publications, but, by finding their way into public libraries, permitted the genre to begin to coalesce as something more than the object of momentary passions of pulp readers. Science fiction now had a more or less permanent set of reference texts from which to derive its characteristic ideologies" (22). Gunn's thesis proves Wolfe's point. Gunn drew upon these anthologies and a few others (Judith Merril's Bantam paperback *A Shot in the Dark* for one) and from the magazines in cases where stories were not yet anthologized. Of particular interest in this regard is Gunn's discussion of a number of stories that appeared in *Galaxy*'s early issues, the most intriguing example being Fritz Leiber's now classic "Coming Attraction."

Gunn's thesis might be best described as an anatomy, in that he sets forth the "philosophy of science fiction," a first attempt at establishing a "theory" of the genre, and then sets out to describe the various types of science fiction, what he calls the "plot-forms," providing a number of story examples that demonstrate each plot-form. Stylistically, it is the manner of the formalistic structure expected of graduate work in literary studies at the time, though the length and scope of Gunn's master's thesis is more like that expected of a Ph.D. dissertation, then and now. Though structured by the stylistic expectations of academia, as in his fiction, Gunn's writing is lively and measured. However, readers of Gunn's later critical works may notice a youthful enthusiasm at times, perhaps fitting for a writer on the cusp of joining writers like Philip K. Dick and Robert Sheckley as a major new voice in the magazines.

The writer most prominently featured in Gunn's thesis is Robert A. Heinlein. Gunn analyzes "Blowups Happen," "By His Bootstraps," "Goldfish Bowl," "The Green Hills of Earth," "Gulf," "Magic, Inc.," "The Roads Must Roll," "Solution Unsatisfactory," and "Universe." The latter is of especial interest; when Gunn went to work for Western Printing, one of his projects was putting together a ten cent paperback of Heinlein's novella for Dell, for which Gunn wrote the anonymous introduction. The slender sixty-four-page book appeared by the end of 1951, not long after Gunn's completion of the thesis.

Another writer that gets a great deal of attention is John W. Campbell,

Jr. At this time, Campbell was still the most significant editor in the science fiction field (although he'd soon be (at least) sharing that appellation with Horace Gold at *Galaxy*) and Gunn certainly aspired to become one of Campbell's regular contributors. One of Gunn's early stories, "Private Enterprise," had already appeared in the July 1950 issue of *Astounding*. As the fifties moved forward, Gold's *Galaxy* and its fantasy companion *Beyond* became Gunn's target market over *Astounding*, although he did continue to occasionally place a story with Campbell. Gunn considers the classic stories "Forgetfulness," "The Machine" and "Who Goes There?" and the late novels *The Incredible Planet* (actually a fix-up of three 1930s stories) and *The Moon Is Hell!* The latter Gunn singles out as an exemplary example of realism in science fiction.

Murray Leinster, the Dean of Science Fiction as he was known,[19] also gets a great deal of attention in *Modern Science Fiction*. Gunn comments on the stories "The Ethical Equations," "The Lost Race," "Nobody Saw the Ship," and "Symbosis," but of most interest is his commentary on Leinster's masterwork "First Contact." Leinster is probably best recognized now for the proto-internet story "A Logic Named Joe" (*Astounding*, March 1946), which Gunn does not discuss here; the story had yet to achieve its iconic status at the time and with the exception of its appearance in a Leinster collection and an obscure British anthology, it was not reprinted again until 1980.

Readers will also be interested in Gunn's discussion of a number of stories by Theodore Sturgeon, including "Killdozer!," "Memorial," "The Sky was Full of Ships," and the classic "Thunder and Roses," given the close relationship the two forged in later years. It's also worth noting that at the time Gunn was writing his thesis, he was corresponding with Sturgeon regarding revisions of Gunn's breakthrough novella "Breaking Point" that Horace Gold asked Sturgeon to "cut." The story about how this all played out can be found in my *Saving the World Through Science Fiction* and Gunn's memoir *Star-Begotten*, both published by McFarland.[20]

I should also mention here Gunn's explorations of the works of A. E. Van Vogt. Here Gunn looks at the stories "Black Destroyer," "Resurrection," "The Weapons Shop" and the novels *Slan*, *The Weapon Makers*, *The World of Null-A* and its sequel *The Players of Null-A*. Gunn might have first read *The World of Null-A* while stationed on Truk Island in the months after the conclusion of the war in the Pacific and the novel became a key text in his later teaching. In the introduction to the novel Gunn wrote for the Easton Press Masterpieces of Science Fiction edition of the novel, he called it "the ultimate science-fiction serial of SF's Golden Age" (*Paratexts* 40).

One thing readers may notice is Gunn's rather limited engagement with the works of Isaac Asimov, especially given Gunn's later book on Asimov for Oxford University Press, *Isaac Asimov: The Foundations of Science Fiction* (1981). For instance, there is no discussion at all of the *Foundation* series. This may simply be that Asimov's *Foundation* stories had not yet been collected in book form: the Gnome Press edition of *Foundation* appeared in August 1951, a few months after Gunn completed the thesis. Nonetheless, Gunn was certainly quite conscious of Asimov and his impact on the field; in fact, he sent Smith a reader's report of *Pebble in the Sky* while the thesis was in draft, where he remarked: "I would say that Asimov is one of the best writers in the science fiction field and in one of the higher (if not, however, the highest) brackets of popularity."[21] Furthermore, Gunn spends little time considering Asimov's robot stories and by this point *I, Robot* was certainly available, although readers might appreciate the attention given to Eando Binder's Adam Link instead. Gunn does, however, quote the version of Asimov's famous Three Laws of Robotics from the original publication in *Astounding* of the final story in *I, Robot*, "The Evitable Conflict," and readers will notice a fascinatingly intriguing change in emphasis, in the Second Law in particular, from the Three Laws as they are generally known. Gunn does give some attention to Asimov's classic story "Nightfall," which he later anthologized in volume two of *The Road*, one of two Asimov stories selected for the series; the other, the robot story "Reason," appears in volume three.

One analysis of special interest here is that of Fritz Leiber's "Coming Attraction," mentioned above, which had just appeared in the fledgling *Galaxy* that fall. Gunn's analysis is cogent and he instantly recognizes the story as something new, something important. He makes this point further when he anthologizes the story in volume three of *The Road to Science Fiction* and it also comes up in his discussion of "Themes in Science Fiction" with Gordon R. Dickson in *The Literature of Science Fiction* film series.

The same can be said for Gunn's astute analysis of C. L. Moore's "No Woman Born," a story which, like Leinster's "A Logic Named Joe," has emerged as one of the most discussed stories from the Golden Age era. As Gunn puts it in his analysis, "'No Woman Born' demonstrates better than anything else the possibilities implicit in the form. At its best, it can epitomize the problems of humanity, of individuality and personality, of the reciprocal emotions of the creator and the created, because, it may be, the mechanical shape startles the imagination into new consideration of old ideas, subtracting all the non-essential qualities and leaving nothing but the eternal core" (149). Indeed, Gunn considers a number of stories by Henry Kuttner and C. L. Moore, both in collaboration and individually, including Kuttner's "The Comedy of Eras" and

"Don't Look Now," Moore's "Black Thirst," and the (assumed) collaborative stories "Call Him Demon," "Mimsy Were the Borogoves," "The Piper's Son," "The Twonky," and "Vintage Season." In addition to the analysis of "No Woman Born," Gunn's analysis of "Vintage Season" and the extraordinary horror story "Call Him Demon" are of particular interest.

Gunn also has high praise for Ray Bradbury's *The Martian Chronicles*, which, incidentally, was just released in its first paperback printing by Bantam, after four hardcover printings, around the time Gunn completed the thesis. Like Moore's "No Woman Born," Gunn sees Bradbury's Martian stories as an important new direction: "Ray Bradbury's Martian stories are an example of something different in the plot form and in science fiction itself, something which, if they are as influential as they deserve to be, presages the start of a new kind of character exposition and development in the genre" (88). Curiously, he is somewhat dismissive of the then newly published "The Fireman," basis for the novel *Fahrenheit 451*, and the other "book burning" stories. Incidentally, Gunn addressed these opinions to Don Ward, an editor at Western Printing with whom Gunn forged a close friendship when he moved to Racine, while he was writing the thesis. In a letter dated March 8, 1951, Gunn wrote: "The burning of the books stories [which includes his novelette in *Galaxy*, 'The Fireman'] go too far in their symbolism and the characters become allegorical figures and the stories allegorical fantasy—it is Bradbury's style carried too far."[22] As these words are almost verbatim to those appearing here in the thesis, one wonders if they were written on the same day.

Gunn also pinpoints a number of the key "atomic" stories of the forties: Heinlein's early "Blowups Happen" and "Solution Unsatisfactory," the emblematic "Deadline" by Cleve Cartmill, the post-Hiroshima stories "The Nightmare" by Chan Davis, "Tomorrow's Children" by Poul Anderson and F. N. Waldrop, Judith Merril's essential "That Only a Mother," and Theodore Sturgeon's poignant classic "Thunder and Roses." Gunn remarks that such atomic war stories are already, at the time of writing, becoming out of favor with editors and readers alike, but as the Cold War continued to escalate during the 1950s and the marketplace for science fiction novels in hardcover and paperback expanded, many such stories and novels written after Gunn's assessment achieved classic status.

I would be remiss if I failed to mention Gunn's brief excursions into the works of H. G. Wells, Edgar Rice Burroughs, and A. Merritt, all three precursors to what Gunn here calls "modern" science fiction, and all three extremely important to Gunn's personal development as a science fiction reader. The list of titles by each author Gunn examines is too long to list here, but I'd highlight his analysis of Merritt's *The Moon Pool* and Wells's

Star-Begotten for the importance each novel held for Gunn's development when he first encountered them in his teenage years.

Finally, Gunn's discussion of Jack Williamson's "With Folded Hands..." and its sequel *...And Searching Mind* is especially interesting, when one considers Williamson was soon to become Gunn's collaborator on the novel *Star Bridge*. Williamson's Humanoids tales get the longest analysis in the thesis. Later, Gunn would write his own robot story in dialogue with both Asimov's robots and Williamson's humanoids, "Little Orphan Android," published in the September 1955 *Galaxy*, which Gunn described as "a sort of satire on all robot stories ever written."[23]

Gunn's thesis is more than an historical curiosity. His insights into the fiction of what we now call science fiction's Golden Age when that fiction was relatively new was (and remains) an important critical intervention, which can contribute to our further understanding of the Golden Age era, its texts, its readers, and the subsequent history of the critical discourse of science fiction.

Furthermore, I hope that some readers will find this edition of *Modern Science Fiction: A Critical Analysis* valuable in understanding the overall contribution of James Gunn to the field of science fiction, not only as a scholar, but also as a writer and teacher. Throughout his career, like no other in the field, Gunn has integrated writing, scholarship, and teaching (of both science fiction as literature and the writing of science fiction) into a cohesive and symbiotic whole. What makes science fiction particularly attractive in this age of academic specialization is the fact that writers, academics, and fans often mingle together in productive ways. I believe that Gunn and his dual-career as writer and scholar has been an inspiring and exemplary model for this interaction between these groups. This 1951 thesis, once partly published in a pulp magazine, illustrates the cross-fertilization that is a paradigmatic characteristic of science fiction.

Some Notes on the Text

For the most part I have preserved Gunn's original words, only intervening where there was a typo, a change in punctuation, compound words, etc. I've also changed Gunn's original mode of citation to current MLA standards so that I could utilize endnotes for my annotations and the notes in this introductory essay. In Gunn's original, he attributed a number of stories to the pseudonyms under which they were originally published—e.g. Heinlein's Anson MacDonald, Kuttner and Moore's Lewis Padgett and Laurence O'Donnell—and for some of Leinster's stories published under his real name Will F. Jenkins. In these cases, I have re-attributed the story with the more familiar appellation.

Readers will also notice on several instances that Gunn refers to a "distribution chart," an analytical chart of the contents of the various anthologies he utilized in the thesis. In the original manuscript, this chart appeared at the beginning of the section on the plot-forms of science fiction. For this edition, I've decided to move the chart to the back of the text as an appendix so the narrative flow of Gunn's overall analysis is not disrupted.

I have preserved Gunn's original citations, except in a few cases where his citation was unclear. Most of these stories have since been reprinted in multiple volumes or, in the case of novels, multiple editions. For readers interested in seeking these stories out, I highly recommend the Internet Science Fiction database (isfdb.org) where you can find information about the anthologies and collections the stories were reprinted in, and the source of original publication.

The text I worked from was the copy held at the Anschutz Library at the University of Kansas, which consisted of 306 manuscript pages. During my work on *Saving the World Through Science Fiction: James Gunn, Writer, Teacher and Scholar* I worked with one of Gunn's personal manuscript copies which had different margins and therefore fewer pages, but the content is the same. I'd like to once again thank KU librarian Elspeth Healey with assistance in retrieving this manuscript through interlibrary loan and for copying a page I discovered missing from my photocopy when I was at work on the transcription. The James Gunn letters quoted in this introduction are housed at the Kenneth Spencer Research Library at KU and I'm grateful for permission to once again use them.

As always, thanks to my wife Susan and my mother Joyce. Thanks to all the folks at the 2017 Campbell Conference celebrating James Gunn's achievements in science fiction, especially my co-organizer Ruth Lichtwardt and Chris McKitterick and Kij Johnson of the Gunn Center for the Study of Science Fiction. Thanks to Gary Wolfe for the Foreword. And thanks to Jim for this foundational work of science fiction scholarship and everything else. Finally, to Mary, for making it through a fourth.

Modern Science Fiction:
A Critical Analysis
by James Gunn

Introduction

It is always interesting to watch the birth of a new literary genre. It is especially interesting when the genre is basically escapist and the two other major escapist genres, the mystery and the western, are—so many critics think—dying a slow death. They have, at least, introduced nothing new in the last decade or so and little beyond what they started with.[1] But, then, they began with nothing but their goal of escapist entertainment. To show that science fiction began with more and has developed into something significant is in part the goal of this work.

There have been predictions that science fiction will supplant in popularity the mystery-detective story or the western or the western movie. One reason for this, noted Fletcher Pratt in the *Saturday Review of Literature*, was the exhaustion of the detective story's somewhat limited possibilities of variation: "There are simply not enough new ways in which people can be murdered or the murder discovered to support a form which depends upon surprise for its major effects" (7). And a well-known critic in other fields, Christopher Isherwood, has this to say about the new genre:

> It is easy to understand why science fiction, and more particularly space-travel fiction, should be enjoying a revival of popularity at the present time. Faced by probable destruction in a third world war, we turn naturally to dreams of escape from this age and this threatened planet. But that is not the whole of the explanation. For, while the "realistic" two-fisted action-story is going through a phase of imaginative bankruptcy, the science-fiction story grows more prodigious, more ideologically daring. Instead of the grunts of cowboys and the fuddled sexual musings of half-plastered private detectives, we are offered adult speculation about the dangers of galactic imperialism and the future of technocratic man. The best of this new generation of science fiction writers are highly sensitive and intelligent. They are under no illusions about the prospective blessings of a machine-age utopia. They do not gape at gadgets with adoring wonder. Their approach to the inhabitants of other worlds is anthropological and non-violent. They owe more to Aldous Huxley than to Jules Verne or H. G. Wells. Insofar as the reading public is turning to them and forsaking the cops and cowboys, the public is growing up [56].

Introduction 35

Whether or not the many predictions of science fiction's coming popularity will come true is a matter that only the future can decide.[2] But several things can contribute to making science fiction's chances better and its content more significant.

Three things a literary genre must have before it can establish itself and begin to realize its potentialities: a knowledge of what it has been, an idea of what it is, and an inkling of what it may become. Science fiction has been too concerned with growing to be analytical: adolescence is too fascinated by new sensations and a changing world to be interested in any sort of organized, objective self-contemplation. But science fiction has reached the stage where it must indulge in this activity if it is to become a sound, firmly based literary type.[3]

The historical review of science fiction has been done, and satisfactorily, by J. O. Bailey in *Pilgrims Through Space and Time*. Whatever else may be said in this work quarreling with Bailey's methods and conclusions, it should not detract from or minimize the trail-blazing importance of his study or its solid, scholarly achievements.[4] That the work does not fulfill all the analytical needs of science fiction is, perhaps, more the fault of science fiction itself and the rapid and radical development it has made in the last decade or so. For the fact is obvious that the science fiction of the 1930s—and the early 1930s at that (beyond which Bailey does not go in any thorough way)—is not the science fiction of today and cast only a faint shadow of what it was to become.[5] It should be realized, however, that beyond this work there is no other critical study of any length or pretensions in the field—and the periodical criticism, if collected, would not fill half an average-sized volume.[6]

This work, then, attempts to fulfill science fiction's other two needs—or, at least, to point in the direction in which this may be done. To determine what modern science fiction is and what it may become are its aims. Along the way some mention will be made of science fiction's history for those who have not read Bailey's work and because, many times, what science fiction is cannot be understood except by understanding what it was.[7]

This work does not pretend to be definitive but to lay a basic groundwork for discussion[8]—something which science fiction has not had and which it needs if it is to analyze itself in any understandable way. Many of the suggestions contained herein are tentative (such as the outline of science fiction by plot type) and will, no doubt, be modified by time and critical comment. But if this work stimulates an ordered and valuable discussion of science fiction, it will have served its purpose.[9]

Because science fiction is primarily a medium of thought, this study has been made on the basis of what science fiction thinks and how it arranges these thoughts—hence the two major sections: the Philosophy of Science Fiction and the Plot Forms of Science Fiction.[10]

Examples of stories have been chosen for their applicability and their availability. Where possible, they have been chosen from the most available source, the anthology, so that the reader may have a ready basis of comparison. The bibliography attempts, without pretensions of being completely exhaustive, to supplement Everett F. Bleiler's *Checklist of Fantastic Literature.*[11]

PART ONE

"Some of Us Are Looking at the Stars": The Philosophy of Science Fiction

> *Inherently, the science-fictioneer believes that any method, any system, which we have today is the rudimentary, crude beginning of the real thing—that any technique known now is a make-shift stop-gap arrangement for the right answer yet to be found. He is deeply, genuinely, and emotionally—not just surface-intellectually—convinced that change is inevitable, necessary, and desirable.*—John W. Campbell, Jr.

Science fiction, once merely a sport of the pulp field, has in the last few years—to somewhat complacent delight of its faithful and vocal adherents—become the fair-haired mutant of the popular entertainment world.

The reverberations from the dropping of the atomic bomb have never ceased echoing through the land where the men are as intelligent as they are strong and capable of facing a three-eyed alien monster and a beautiful blonde with the same unflinching courage; the reverberations have, indeed, been growing ever since, and science fiction has expanded with the mushrooming speed of the atomic cloud.[1]

In the years succeeding that momentous date, more than a hundred science fiction books have been issued in hard covers, eliciting reviews and critical summaries from such magazines as *Time* and the *Saturday Review of Literature*. In 1945 there were seven magazines devoted exclusively to science fiction; five years later there were fourteen; by the beginning of 1951 there were over twenty-one, and there seemed to be no end to the flood, although here and there a magazine was discontinued after a few issues.[2] Science fiction stories have appeared in such "slick" publications as the *Saturday Evening Post, Collier's*, and so forth. Numerous radio and television programs have presented science fiction offerings, and Hollywood has become very much interested in the medium.[3]

Five major publishers at the last counting (Doubleday, Crown, Simon and Schuster, Dutton, and Little, Brown) have started science fiction lines—not to mention a large number of small publishing houses which deal with science fiction almost exclusively.[4] Viking, Pocket Books, Dell, and Random House, among the publishers of pocket reprints, have added their contributions.[5] Several network radio programs, including *Dimension X* and *The Thousand Plus*, have at one time or another aired science fiction from coast to coast.[6] And *Other Worlds* listed almost fifty titles of movies finished, scheduled, or contemplated by motion picture studios, among them *Rocketship X-M, Destination Moon,* and the classic "Who Goes There?" by John W. Campbell, Jr., which Howard Hawks has scheduled for release during 1951 under the title of *The Thing* ("News of the Month" 153–56), while *Publishers' Weekly* predicted that science fiction was due for a wave of movie popularity which might well supplant the westerns (Nathan 2463).

All this is very gratifying to science fiction authors and readers (especially to the authors), but it presents a very real problem to the development of science fiction. To those who know little of the genre or are intent upon exploiting the lowest common denominator of its appeal, science fiction is merely a type of fantasy peculiarly interesting to the modern public. Ignoring or unaware of the development in science fiction's history, tradition, and philosophy, they represent the unfortunate possibility (already evident in many of the new presentations) that science fiction, under the influence of a mass audience, may have to retrace its steps to a much less significant position than it occupies today or might occupy tomorrow. That position is integrally connected with the philosophy science fiction has developed over the years.

I

Two misconceptions are current about modern science fiction: that it is pure escapism and that it differs but little from that written twenty, two hundred, or two thousand years ago. Both of these misconceptions are rooted in a complete or comparative ignorance of the modern field and have as their effect the shunting off of science fiction into the lower regions of the sub-literary or into the limbo of the already explored.[7]

The fact of the matter is that science fiction may be escapism but it is certainly not *pure*.[8] As Leo Margulies and Oscar J. Friend remark in the introduction to their anthology, *My Best Science Fiction Story*, "Science fiction is the only literary escape which the bewildered citizen can seek that offers imaginative relief while keeping him in tune with the apparently insoluble problems confronting him and his fellows" (viii).

The word escapism has, of course, been so overworked that it has lost whatever meaning it ever had. Fundamentally, any and all fiction is escapist literature inasmuch as it is a withdrawal from life—and this would apply to the works of Shakespeare fully as much as to those of Edgar Rice Burroughs. A distinction often made is the possible effect on the reader's life: the greater effect the less the escapist function of the literature. We can readily agree as to Shakespeare's effect, but it might be noted that even Burroughs's Tarzan or John Carter have certain ethical and moral standards which might make a mark on the life of a reader.[9]

The factors that tend to remove literature from the escapist category may be classified as didactic, aesthetic, and philosophic. Almost any work will have one or more of these elements in some degree; it might be postulated, therefore, that there is no such thing as pure escapism.

When one speaks of escapism, then, one is referring not to category but to degree. And the degree is determined by the *usefulness* of the non-escapist elements of the material, although *usefulness* is another term that depends upon the individual critic. He may find a book's didacticism boring, its aestheticism revolting, or its philosophy repugnant; but he must first assess these elements before he comes to a personal judgment.

In modern science fiction all three elements are present. We are not primarily interested in the didactic or aesthetic elements at this time. Didacticism certainly plays a large part, although it has been somewhat overstressed, and, indeed, a reader may find in science fiction much of the theory and technology necessary to orient him in this scientific age. Science fiction is not primarily concerned with aestheticism, although the aesthetic element is often present. It is subordinated, usually, to the reasonable element, which is the foundation stone of science fiction today, as we shall see. Left to consider is one of the most important elements, the philosophic.

Why the philosophic element in science fiction is important is readily apparent on an inspection of a few stories. Science fiction is a medium of ideas; at least nine-tenths, I would estimate, of all science fiction stories came into their authors' minds in the form of an idea rather than with a character or a mood (Ray Bradbury, perhaps, is an exception). The authors, we might speculate, begin a story with such thoughts as: If such-and-such happened or such-and-such was invented, what would be the result?

II

There are two significant but indefinite dates in the history of science fiction as a literary medium, one marking its beginning and the other its development into its present form. The first date might be set around 1830, the second a hundred years later. The period bounded by these dates might be referred to, for purposes of convenience, as the romantic period of science fiction[10]; the present period as the realistic. More will be said of these distinctions later, but first let us examine the patterns of pre-modern science fiction and then see how they differ from those of the present.

Attempts have been made to trace the course of science fiction as far back as *The True History* and *Icaromenippus* of Lucian, a satirist of the second century A.D.[11] These attempts can only be successful under a very loose definition of science fiction. Strictly speaking, the distinguishing mark of science fiction is a rational explanation (present or understood) for every plot development or device included in the story, which is distinguished from ordinary fiction by being about something which might have happened but did not (or not historically recorded) or might happen but has not. In Lucian's work, as in most others of the fantasies written before 1830, the explanation may be present but it is not rational—the means of traveling used by Lucian or his hero were demonstrably impossible, even in Lucian's day (although it should be remembered that pragmatic tests are a relatively new development).

Before going further, it might be well to place science fiction in relation to other allied forms. As Groff Conklin notes in his introduction to *The Best of Science Fiction*, science fiction falls under the general heading of fantasy, which is itself a sub-branch of the species "imaginative writing." Under fantasy there are four primary types: the utopia, the supernatural story, the fairy tale, and science fiction (xix). This division is helpful while it is, at the same time, misleading. A science fiction story can belong as well to any of the three types, depending on whether the story complies with the rational explanation consideration described above. If the story is of a utopia, there must be a rational explanation not only of how the society developed but of how the newcomer, if present, came into contact with that society. If the story is a fairy tale, there must be a rational explanation of the why and how of fairies and of all other non-material elements. If the story deals with supernatural forces, there must be a good explanation of ghosts, demons, werewolves. If not, the stories are fantasy.

Various terms have been in favor for the category of literature I have called science fiction. J. O. Bailey maneuvers the unwieldy phrase "scientific fiction" through his critical work; the editor of one chain of magazines often shortens the Winchellish term "scientifiction" to "stf."[12] The writers' magazines refer to the genre variously: some lump it incorrectly under fantasy or invent an all-inclusive designation, "sci-fantasy." A few incautious or unenlightened commentators fall under the anathema of many science fiction devotees, including the editor of *Astounding Science-Fiction*, by classing the stories as "pseudo-science." As John W. Campbell, Jr., observes:

Science fiction is *not* pseudo-science. Pseudo-science is what the Sunday-Supplement features present. By definition, the term means false, imitation science, attempting to pass itself off as the genuine article. Science fiction is no more pseudo-science than fiction is pseudo-truth. Fiction makes no pretense of being truth; most books and magazines explicitly state, on the flyleaf or in the magazine indicia, than no such characters existed nor did the events actually happen. Science fiction is fiction, purely fiction, and makes no claim to be fact. But it does claim—and with provable truth—that many of its stories are extrapolations of known science into possible future engineering .... The general proposition of uranium fission was described in accurate detail in various stories published before 1941 ended (Preface ix).

For one reason or another (among which are the way the phrase fits to the tongue and its incorporation into the title of *Astounding*), "science fiction" has become the almost universal designation for the genre (a slight debate about hyphenation remains) with only one or two recalcitrant still hanging back.

Before 1830, as Bailey illustrates in his book, the two main themes of the works of fantasy were "the wonderful journey" and "the wonderful machine," categories in which the emphasis, it may be noticed, is on the element of wonder. There is no attempt to achieve probability or even possibility in such examples of "the wonderful journey" as Lucian's works already mentioned, Cyrano de Bergerac's *Voyages to the Moon and the Sun*, and Voltaire's *Micromegas*,[13] and "the wonderful machine" as [in] Bishop John Wilkins' *Mercury; or the Secret and Swift Messenger*.[14] These pre-science fiction tales of wonder derived their chief interest from the wondrous, fantastic qualities of the story or its details; the delight was in the wildness of the imagination. The principal purposes were satire, as in Swift's *Gulliver's Travels*, or wonder, as in Baron Ludvig Holberg's *A Journey to the World Under-Ground*.[15] But most of the novels in the genre, as August Derleth observes in his introduction to *Strange Ports of Call*, were predominantly utopian in character, "and for more than a century the science fiction novel was first and foremost a sociological novel" (1).[16] It might be noted in passing that the Gothic romances of the eighteenth century had even less to contribute to the movement that culminated in modern science fiction; their mysterious events were presented almost always without explanation and were included entirely for their own sake.[17]

III

Science fiction as a distinct literary type probably began, as Groff Conklin suggests, about the time of the industrial revolution, although it would be difficult to pin down any one story as initiating the genre.[18] It is not surprising that science fiction and the industrial revolution should be linked; it was about this time that it was forced on the attention of all thinking men that the world, a comparatively stable thing for many hundreds of years, could be changed radically, for better or worse, by the efforts of their hands and minds. And, if the world could be changed, what could be more interesting or profitable than to speculate on the nature of these changes or what they might reveal about man, the earth, or the universe? Sensitive men (as most writers are) saw in the changes of the industrial age, however, nothing but evil, an attitude that was to influence the thoughts of the people and the philosophy of a literature for a hundred years.[19]

This period is chosen as science fiction's beginnings because, more than anything else, it was about this time that stories began to be written as if they had actually happened or could happen—the identifying consideration of a rational explanation for every plot development. And in the beginning, the first of the three sections into which pre-modern science fiction divides itself, there were isolated men writing isolated stories, inspired individually and more by external circumstances than by any consciousness of writing within a literary movement. The second section began with the growing consciousness among those authors between the turn of the century and the mid-Twenties who have been called the "elder statesmen of science fiction" that they were dealing with a new type of fiction and that they had a new medium, the forerunners of the modern pulps, in which to publish it. This consciousness grew more concentrated and more intense until it moved into the brief third section of science fiction's romantic period: that initiated in 1926 by the founding of the first magazine devoted exclusively to the genre, *Amazing Stories*.

When science, the tool and the prime force of the industrial age, first began to assume a broad, popular interest, the writers of the period were quick enough to capitalize on it. Among them was Richard Adams Locke, a friend of Edgar Allan Poe and a reporter for the *New York Sun*, who, in 1835, concocted one of the most famous of the early science fiction stories. *Concocted* because it was presented by the *Sun* as a factual scientific report reprinted from the Edinburgh *Journal of Science* (defunct a few months before) announcing the discovery through a giant telescope of men and animals living on the Moon's sunward side. This long and detailed forgery which came out under the title *Great Astronomical Discoveries Lately Made by Sir John Herschel, LL.D., F.R.S., etc., at the Cape of Good Hope*, was later to be known as *The Moon Hoax*—but only after fooling, among others, a group of Yale scientists. Just beginning was the willingness—indeed, desire—of the people to believe in the never-ending miracles of science.

Locke's forgery inspired a number of emulators, conscious or otherwise, including Poe and coming down through Orson Welles and his radio version of H. G. Wells's *The War of the Worlds*, but it never succeeded in establishing a particularly significant pattern. A hoax is by its very nature a one-shot affair. A recent and horrible example was a series of stories that ran in *Amazing Stories* until, to judge by comments in that and other magazines, reader protests forced a change of policy and, perhaps, editors. The series, authored by Richard Shaver and presented by the magazine with awe and trembling, swore to the actual presence of hitherto-unsuspected degenerate, malformed "elder races" who controlled human thoughts and events through the misuse of ancient machinery in undiscovered caverns beneath the earth's surface. Becoming known as the "Shaver mystery," it capitalized on more or less mythological sources and suggestive sexual situations in an attempt to overcome hasty and often near-illiterate writing.[20] It is a comment on the sacrosanct position some science fiction magazines feel they must assume that the hoax was never publicly confessed, although it should be mentioned that other hoaxes, such as the Isaac Asimov article, "The Endochronic Properties of Resublimated Thiotimoline," which was published in *Astounding Science-Fiction*, was freely admitted and enjoyed for what it was.[21] The "Shaver Mystery," for what it may be worth, was probably the longest and most extensive example of the type to see print.

The stories of Edgar Allan Poe, running more to dark and mystic fantasy than to science fiction, started, nevertheless, several trends that still persist. Among these are the scientific attack on non-scientific mysteries ("The Gold Bug"), the investigator trapped in his efforts to penetrate earth's secret places ("Descent into the Maelstrom"), the exploration of the hidden powers of the mind ("A Tale of the Ragged Mountains"), as well as the continuation of the adventurous-voyage theme already described ("Hans Pfaall").[22]

One significant pattern, begun perhaps by Mary Wollstonecraft Shelley in *Frankenstein* (1817), began to establish itself as a predominant motif about this time: the theme of the mad, incautious, or unwise scientist who endangers individuals, a society, or a world through his experiments.[23] With slight modifications, this trend produced a science that could contribute nothing in a moment of crisis. For humor it offered the inept, impractical, or absent-minded scientist. Name the authors of stories of this type and you would have (with a few notable exceptions) a roster of the science-fiction writers up to the third decade of this century. Poe has stories in this vein, as does his contemporary Fitz-James O'Brien ("The Diamond Lens").[24] After O'Brien, the numerous well-known writers who flocked to the genre as an outlet for their talents were almost all infected with this philosophy at one time or another; Jules Verne, Conan Doyle, Ambrose Bierce, Jack London,

H. Rider Haggard, Frank Stockton, Mark Twain. The patterns of thought that produced this literature were symptomatic of the attitudes of several generations impressed by the iniquities of early industrialism and sighing for the safe, sane, good-old-days.

The tradition of the villainous or dangerous scientist was not peculiar to the industrial age, of course. In a broader sense, it was an attitude inherited from the Middle Ages, when distrust of science and knowledge (influenced by the dictums of the Church) was even more widespread (for example, the Faust legend and its various interpretations); it was based on the firm conviction that science and knowledge—already threatening the stability of the society—were inevitably evil and encroached upon the exclusive domain of God. It was the modification of this attitude, however, which came so near being the keynote of pre-modern science fiction that the plot and the character of the "mad" scientist became stereotyped.

IV

This type carried over into the second subdivision of science fiction's romantic period, the era in which the "elder statesmen of science fiction" dominated the scene and published their long, serialized novels in the old *Argosy, Black Cat, Cavalier, All Story,* etc. Such authors as H. G. Wells, George Allan England, Charles B. Stilson, Austin Hall, Homer Eon Flint, Garrett P. Serviss, Julian Hawthorne, and a number of others remembered now only by initiates presented as a dominant motif, either on its own merits or allied with that of the mad scientist, the theme of world cataclysm—the threatened or actual destruction of a civilization or a world.[25] The causes were almost always external and unilateral: the machine which gets out of control; the sun which becomes a nova or grows old; the cloud of poisonous gas, sun-obscuring dust motes, or meteorites which invades the solar system; the nomad planet which menaces the earth; the natural law which runs wild. The emphasis was almost always on the worldwide aspect of the cataclysm.

From the time that the theoretical possibilities of nuclear fission became apparent until the dropping of the atomic bomb, there was a sprinkling of stories of the atomic cataclysm type; after Hiroshima the sprinkling became a deluge so great that the theme was soon played out. At least once chain of magazines, The *Thrilling* group, placed an editorial ban on all stories involving the threatened destruction of earth, and another magazine, *Astounding,* decided to stop printing stories about an atomic war. Today the theme is seldom seen except in those pulpier of the pulps which go in for the orthodox adventure story with interplanetary trappings—now happily on the decrease—or else in greatly mutated form. The difference is this: when the cataclysm theme is used, the causes are internal and/or multilateral and the emphasis is upon its individual not universal effects. In general, however, stories today concentrate upon the human effects of a small change in environment or condition. Max Ehrlich's *The Big Eye*, describing the threatened destruction of earth by a wandering planet, despite its other merits, seems thematically naïve from being outside and behind the main stream of modern science fiction.

Three authors, writing three different types of stories, stand out in this pre-modern period of science fiction and are largely responsible for popularizing the science fiction novel: Jules Verne, H. G. Wells, and Edgar Rice Burroughs. The types of stories they introduced or brought into public acclaim have been defined, in that order, by John W. Campbell, Jr.:

1. Prophecy stories, in which the author tries to predict the effects of a new invention.
2. Philosophical stories, in which the author presents, in story form, some philosophical question using the medium of science fiction simply to set the stage for the particular point he wants to discuss.
3. Adventure science fiction, wherein the action and the plot are the main point [Preface vi].

Although the emphasis and the technique may change, these types still sum up the field of science fiction today. It was not, however, to achieve a unity of effect or a distinct philosophy of its own until it won to the dignity of its own magazine. The honor of recognizing science fiction's possibilities and its popular appeal rests with Hugo Gernsback.[26]

Gernsback, publishing a popular science magazine called *Science and Invention* in the mid–1920s, began to insert a few science and fantasy stories. Faced by an enthusiastic response, he launched, in April 1926, the first magazine devoted exclusively to the new medium, *Amazing Stories*. Moved out of control in a few years, Gernsback started two competitors which he later combined into *Wonder Stories* (now *Thrilling Wonder Stories,* although Gernsback left the field for good in 1936).[27]

Of equal or even surpassing importance was the appearance in 1930 of *Astounding Stories* and its falling into the editorial hands of John W. Campbell, Jr., in 1938. *Astounding* under Campbell brought to science fiction a standard of competence and, at times, excellence of writing and the dignity of true scientific knowledge and of appearance (both symbolized by the emphasis of the "Science-Fiction" and the de-emphasis of the "Astounding" on the cover of the magazine). To the other magazines in the field, *Astounding* has shown the way, and they have—willingly or unwillingly—followed or are in the process of following. In *Astounding*, with a few exceptions, have been developed the outstanding authors in the genre; it has set the tone and established much of the philosophy of science fiction.[28]

V

About 1930—a few years either way—I have set the date for the entrance of modern science fiction upon the scene. About this time it slowly became apparent to the authors of science fiction that the industrial, scientific civilization was here to stay and that man must learn to live with it. While leading authors in the main literary stream were—and are still—yearning and sighing for a return to the safety of the ordered, static civilization where values were firm and fixed and there was no necessity for soul-searching or mental struggle (an obvious impossibility), the science fiction authors were searching for new viewpoints, for new values, for new answers to new problems. They found their basis—appropriately enough—in science.

At first their attitude amounted to near-idolatry; their attack was external: science—mystically, superstitiously—would provide the answer to the problems of yesterday, today, and tomorrow; progress was certain if science had its way (or was not thwarted by the non-scientific bias of mankind); the future was a rosy technological miracle. This attitude, evident as early as Edward Bellamy's *Looking Backward*, made its first appearance as a thematic trend almost coincidentally with the founding of science fiction's first magazine in such stories as Austin Hall's "The Man Who Saved the Earth" and reached its peak in the space epics of Campbell and Dr. E. E. Smith.[29] The theme eventually—and fortunately—developed into absurdity, both logically and as fiction. Phil Stong succinctly summed up the objections to these stories in the foreword to his anthology, *The Other Worlds*:

> To me, E. E. Smith's "Skylark" stories ... besides being clumsily written are as dull as ditch water, because there is no possible way for the hero to lose out. When the pilot of Skylark finds himself in a difficulty he quickly works out a ray, formula, or dimensional trick which is more invulnerable—and if you think that "invulnerable" is not subject to modification you should read the stories—than the one that failed him (9).

Gradually the attitude died out—though it died hard and there are still evidences of it in current stories. It isn't hard to understand: pedestalled science provided as firm, as sound, as mystical a repository for faith as Henry James's stratified society, T. S. Eliot's Anglo-Catholic Church, or

William Faulkner's pre-Civil War South. The search for values could be ended, the burden of responsibility could be shifted to other, broader shoulders. Naïve this attitude may have been, but it was one necessary step toward a significant philosophical content. There could be no constructive thought in science fiction while the one progressive element in its subject matter was viewed with alarm. The natural movement was the complete reaction: from the scientist as villain to the scientist as hero. But science fiction could attain no philosophic significance until its attack moved inward and it adopted the doctrine of human and individual responsibility.

After the failure of idolized science as a complete answer—a fact apparent in the physical as well as the literary world—science fiction adopted instead its present philosophical position: the scientific method; science as a means instead of science as a goal. The implications of this shift were far reaching; it opened up entire new worlds. Where science fiction had been a fairly insignificant band in the literary spectrum, a segment entitled "explained fantasy" devoted to the condemnation or glorification of science, it became a literary medium with a mission, a tool in the hands of investigators into the possibilities of the human race. Instead of an attempted justification of science, it became the long needed and still not completely realized conscience of science. Instead of descriptions of wonderful machines, it became a study of the complex relationship between man and the creations of his mind and hands. Instead of stories about the adventures of implausible heroes in strange, new worlds, it became a flexible device for the analysis of the manifold aspects, past, present, and future of the human spirit in contest with something new and vital. All these possibilities, of course, have not been realized; some of them have been attempted, some suggested, some hinted at, but all are potentially present in the medium at its present stage of development.[30]

The scientific method is more than a technical device; it is a way of thought. It has been summed up by Campbell thus:

1. Gather all available data that is, or appears to be relevant.
2. From the data, form a hypothesis.
3. On the basis of the hypothesis, make a prediction.
4. Experiment to check the validity of the prediction.
5. Vary the experiment and collect more data.
6. When the new theory breaks down, take the now collected data and formulate a new hypothesis.
7. Go back to step 3 ["Concerning Dianetics" 4].

The scientific method has no place for absolutes or for authority; a theory must stand on its own merits, but it does not need to be true: "A scientific theory is a useful tool; it need not be true so long as it is useful. Dalton's theory implied atoms were hard little balls; it was incorrect but it advanced chemistry. Therefore it was a good theory" ("Concerning Dianetics" 5).[31] This is, of course, undiluted pragmatism, and pragmatism is the basic philosophy not only of science fiction but of the majority of science in the world today. It can be the only proper philosophy for a free, effective science; when the science is not free, as it is not in Russia, absolutes, other philosophies, and Lysenkoism are possible and the effectiveness of the science diminishes proportionately to the decrease in freedom (as many Americans are counting on in the armament race).

In fictional practice, this irreverent pragmatism results in such a story as Poul Anderson's "The Double-Dyed Villains," which poses the problem of administering and keeping the peace in a diversely populated and civilized galaxy. The sheer complexity of administrative detail would be inconceivable, suggests Anderson, and with only one percent of the total population in the government service it would add up to about ten to the thirteenth power persons. Anderson's solution: a loosely organized Galactic League in which the peace is preserved by a small patrol.[32] Its members may not kill, but they go to all underhanded lengths of thievery, bribery, lying, blackmailing, kidnapping, procuring, sabotaging, encouraging the narcotics traffic, etc. Dishonorable?—true, but it preserves the lives of countless billions of beings. As one of the members of the Patrol answers the objections of a victim that peace can be bought too dearly, that peace is not worthwhile without honor:

> "Honor!" he sneered. "Another catchword. I get so tired of those unctuous phrases—Don't you realize that deliberate scoundrels do little harm, but that the evil wrought by sincere fools is incalculable .... if we can't use force, we have to use any other means that comes in handy. And I, for one, would rather break any number of arbitrary laws and moral rules, and wreck a handful of lives of idiots, who think with a blaster, than see a planet go up in flames or ... or see one baby killed in a war it never even heard about!" (28–29).

The *science* part of science fiction is usually justified on the basis of subject matter. But, to add another facet to the discussion, science is not only the subject matter of science fiction, it—or, to be more precise, the scientific method—is often (and in the best stories almost always) the technique used in story construction. The scientific method has been described above, and the same (if less tedious) pattern is used in fictional form: a new situation or phenomenon is encountered, the protagonist forms a hypothesis, checks it, and when the hypothesis breaks down uses that data to form a new hypothesis. Ideally, this forms a story as suspenseful as Campbell's "Who Goes There?"—in which an isolated group of Antarctic explorers must discover how to detect a non-terrestrial monster able to assimilate any kind of protoplasm and imitate it perfectly.

VI

The utilization of the scientific method both as a technical device and a philosophic basis has resulted in an admirable concentration of fundamentals instead of appearances. Science fiction authors are often trying, manfully and seriously, to probe the depths of our civilization, fishing for the bases of life today and tomorrow, undeterred by traditional concepts of ethics, morality, or philosophy. In the field of science, this has produced an intellectual examination of the technical aspects of new environments.

Hal Clement's "Fireproof" demonstrates that, since convection currents depend on gravity, there can be no danger of fire on such a weightless "space platform" or artificial satellite as the Army suggested a few years ago and rocket enthusiasts have been advocating for more than a decade. In similar stories a number of observations have been made which may well prove useful to future engineers. As Campbell notes in the *Atlantic Monthly*:

> The idea of the rocket spaceship is so completely accepted today that the normally conservative Armed Forces are displaying spaceships on their recruiting posters. Science-fiction authors have discussed spaceships—specifically, rocket spaceships—for twenty years or more. Genuine engineering minds have considered the problems, mulled them over, argued them back and forth in stories, and worked out the basic principles that will most certainly appear in the first ships built—partly because their builders will have read the magazines, seen those stories, and recognized the validity of the science-fiction engineering ["The Science of Science-Fiction" 97].

Among the ideas and devices that have been worked out, Campbell lists: A small hydroponic garden of green plants is the most efficient oxygen convertor (it also absorbs odors). In a weightless ship, books would float aimlessly around unless they were provided with magnetic backstraps, liquids would climb out of wettable cups or glasses and spread themselves in an even layer over the thirsty space-voyager—in a non-wettable container they would float out in a perfect globular form (the answer is flasks with tube necks from which the liquid could be sucked). The prime example, perhaps, is in rocket motors: Major de Seversky (not a science fiction reader) conceived a spaceship with two dozen different rocket motors for propulsion, braking, and directional control; science fiction has evolved the answer that only one rocket motor is necessary if the ship is equipped with three flywheels mounted at right angles to each other. Rotated, they will rotate the ship (much slower, of course) in the opposite direction until the ship's one set of jet tubes is pointed in the desired direction ("The Science of Science-Fiction" 98).

From these technological details science fiction has derived much of its reputation for prophecy. From Jules Verne and his submarine up to the modern writers and their atomic bombs, the history of science fiction is filled with instances of authors who added realistic detail to theoretical possibility and astonished the world when their fiction came true. It is the basis, as well, for science fiction's boast that it teaches while it entertains, giving its readers not only a foretaste of the future but the knowledge necessary to understand it—or be prepared for it.[33] If one would like to know the problems and details of the establishment of a lunar camp (and one which may very well come true), for instance, let him see Mack Reynolds's "The Man in the Moon" or Campbell's recent novel *The Moon is Hell!* So much for the mechanical or technical side.[34]

On philosophic points the fundamental theories advanced by science fiction authors are even more interesting, if their practical value is less certain. To sample a few, there are, in the sociological branch, such stories as Jack Williamson's "The Equalizer"; as the author described his purpose in a critical symposium:

> My premise was the philosophic idea that the prevailing form of government, in any historic period, depends on the current state of military technology—or, more broadly, that social institutions are functions of technical progress. To demonstrate that idea dramatically, I wanted to show how a simple invention causes people to toss aside, overnight, the whole elaborate fabric of what we call civilization ["Logic of Fantasy" 40–41].

The simple invention was a means of wiring an iron bar, elementary enough to be constructed by anyone, which provided unlimited energy for daily existence or for use as a weapon.

Peter Phillips's amusing story, "Dreams are Sacred," is an example of the psychological possibilities implicit in the freedom of science fiction. Phillips postulates that if a means could be found (in this case an accidental improvement of the encephalograph) to project a personality into another's mental world a cure might be found for schizophrenics. You could, as the introductory editorial paragraph suggested, "louse up his dreams!"

Politically, science fiction stories are often closer—uncomfortably closer—to more pressing problems. In Robert Heinlein's "Solution Unsatisfactory," for instance, the problem of atomic control was taken up as early as 1941. The solution Heinlein reached, admittedly *unsatisfactory*, was a peace enforced by the first nation to develop an atomic weapon, here—in fiction as in reality—the United States. The U.S. ordered and enforced the immobilization of all aircraft and set up a commission of world safety supported by an aristocratic corps of world policemen armed with the only atomic weapons in the world. Eventually, because the U.S. has never had a firm, stable foreign policy and because of the uncertainties of American politics, a military dictatorship of the world became necessary. Unsatisfactory?—true; but in 1946 Campbell termed our answer to the problem—secrecy—as an unsatisfactory solution as well, how unsatisfactory we suddenly realized a couple of years ago (Preface 9).[35]

In the field of philosophy, science fiction has advanced some theories, also; an interesting example is Heinlein's "Universe," in which the author describes the psychology of a metaphysical philosophy that grew up among the descendants of original voyages aboard a self-sufficient spaceship. They were originally bound for Proxima Centauri but lost their history and destination through rebellion.[36] Another example is Fredric Brown's "Letter to a Phoenix," in which the author postulates great scientific cultures of the past that rose to heights of civilization beyond anything we have reached, which colonized the stars and then, cyclically, reduced themselves to savagery through disastrous wars. Other races in the universe achieve sanity with intelligence, but eventually they reach the limit of their capabilities and have no choice but death, since life cannot be static. But because of man's insanity he will live:

> Only a race that destroys itself and its progress periodically, that goes back to its beginnings, can survive more than, say, a hundred thousand years of intelligent life ... the human race will last. Everywhere and forever, for it will never be sane and only insanity is divine. Only the mad destroy themselves and all they have wrought. And only the phoenix lives forever [151, 153].

VII

One of the fundamental philosophic positions of modern science fiction is evident in this last quotation: change or death are the two choices of life—a neo–Darwinism, if you like. The position is not new, but many of its implications are. Most of the utopian writers of the past centuries, from Plato through Bellamy, were willing to assume the vitality of a changeless society, and many of our more orthodox modern writers, as we have noted, yearn ceaselessly for a static society. But H. G. Wells recognized the inevitable decay of such a society in at least one of his works, *The Time Machine*, and older authors, writing in the pre-modern science fiction tradition and imbued with the horror of the machine, were only too ready to predict collapse.[37]

For a time, coincident with and dependent, perhaps, upon the absolute faith in science described earlier, science fiction adopted the popular view of eternal progress—a naïve viewpoint that was soon modified to belief in the necessity of change.[38] The idea of progress was not entirely discarded, however; it was converted into a faith in the infinite capabilities of man. There is no limit to what man can do, the science fiction authors of today assert, if he wants it badly enough and will fight for it hard enough. A case in point is space flight, which, like atmospheric flight, men have dreamed of for centuries. Men learned to fly eventually, and engineers will tell you that they can build a ship today capable of carrying a man to the moon, with today's knowledge, today's fuel—if any person or any government has a few billion dollars to spare. One of the best fictional statements of science fiction's attitude is contained in George O. Smith's "Dynasty of the Lost": "Man's capability is as yet unlimited. To do, to think, to act, not one of us has ever tapped but the surface of our ability.... Life itself is strife; the willingness to fight against odds in order to bring about a better life is strife, and only upon that day when there is nothing left to fight against will the business of life cease" (37). True, half-true, or completely false, this philosophic belief has at least one merit: it is positive and it provides a basis for positive action. It is this that chiefly distinguishes the philosophy of science fiction from that of the Existentialists, with which it has much in common. The most significant theory, shared, for instance, is the doctrine of human responsibility. In both philosophies, this states that the human race is responsible for itself; upon it alone depends its fate—it can look nowhere else for help. But where the Existentialists draw from this nothing but gloom, it inspires science fiction to greater efforts. It is not oppression but liberation. In this sense one might call the philosophy of science fiction an optimistic Existentialism.[39]

In its stories of the future, science fiction extends this philosophical position to include the galaxy or the universe, of which man is conceived as the inheritor or trustee. This contains an element of the geocentric it is true, but that is not the entirety of the attitude. It is an effective basis for thought and action: the only road to success leads through the land of faith. Without faith in his own powers or his own destiny, man has incapacitated himself. And, in a certain limited sense, man is what he thinks himself; an attitude has a propaganda value. Science fiction aspires for man to be great, not merely in a technological way, though this colored much of early modern writing, but great in spirit and action. It dreams of the time when man will be integrated, within himself and within his environment, when he will reach some of the potentialities science fiction dreams of as his.

Science fiction justifies its belief in the possibilities of man's future philosophically, not sentimentally. That mankind is the inheritor of the universe (or, at least, must act as if it were until it is proven otherwise) is a workable, progressive philosophy—one under which mankind may grow. And, harking back to fundamentals again, the primary concern of life, racial or individual, is survival; before this consideration all others crumble

VIII

Science fiction sets three tasks for man before he can achieve true greatness. The first is the conquest of the physical universe (viewed variously as man's earthly environment, the Solar System, the galaxy, or the universe itself)—the material universe with its invariable, natural laws. The second task (sometimes concurrent with the first, sometimes following) is man's conquest of himself in a sociological and psychological sense. The third task, which is sometimes considered almost synonymous with the second, is the conquest of the non-material universe. The first task is that of a young, expanding ambitious race, the second that of an adult people; the third, from which one can smile at the first two as youthful exuberance, is that of complete maturity. It is a process of integration, the saga of man's conquest of life. Extracting the philosophic moral from this, science fiction says, in effect: one can conquer things without understanding them, but one cannot completely conquer life without understanding one's self. The final triumph is described in Campbell's "Forgetfulness," which pictures a peaceful race living in rustic simplicity on a gentle earth beside tremendous abandoned cities of shimmering, indestructible beauty and great machines that the race cannot even explain. But it is not a case of decadence; the race has grown beyond machines and cities—it has achieved the complete manipulation of the material universe by the mind and need search no longer. If this contradicts the statement about the inevitable decay of static societies, there is no help for it; there must be an end somewhere, and this is as good an end as any. It would, moreover, be undesirable and inconceivable that science fiction should be completely consistent.[40]

The ambitions of science fiction for man are great but not blind. Against threats to man's existence or dominion from without, from physical forces or alien races, man's survival is of prime importance, and if he is unsuccessful it is the raw material of tragedy. But, if man is incapable of rising to meet science fiction's challenge, he must give way to a better man— *homo superior, homo novus,* or what you will. Man's successor, however, is not Nietzsche's amoral superman but a superior man, and, in the science fiction philosophy, physical or mental superiority goes hand in hand with moral superiority, a theory based on the belief that morality is a function of clear thinking.[41] The means of change is usually mutation, either natural or induced by man's commercial or incautious use of radioactives.

The first instances of this theme, perhaps, were Olaf Stapledon's *Odd John* and H. G. Wells's *Star-Begotten*.[42] In the latter novel, a fascinatingly quiet study of a family's suspicion that cosmic rays are producing mutations, the first horror of change evolves into the belief that the change is beneficial. The theme was picked up again in modern science fiction's main stream, the magazine, by A. E. van Vogt in *Slan* (1940), a novel which influenced much subsequent thinking and writing about the subject. Almost standard, for a time, became the mutant's mental superiority aided by telepathic powers with, usually, some physical abnormality to denote his difference (in *Slan*, tendrils instead of hair).[43]

In these stories (told almost always from the viewpoint of the mutant), the logical and dramatic problem is survival again. In some cases the solution is conflict, open or hidden (as in *Slan*), in others one of securing tolerance. In Olaf Stepledon's *Odd John* such an attempt is unsuccessful and the unoffending mutants, desiring only a secluded life of their own, are wiped out by an intolerant human race.[44] In Lewis Padgett's (Henry Kuttner and C.L. Moore) "The Piper's Son" the mutants (distinguished by being bald) win slowly but with great effort to an acceptance of themselves, with their telepathic powers, as merely men with special talents. They buy safety for their species by minimizing their differences (wearing wigs) and giving up ideas of individual advantage, wealth, position—an interesting commentary, of course, on minority problems.[45] In still a third variation, the solution is one of camouflage as in Wilmar Shiras's "In Hiding," which suggests that the most difficult problem of a thirteen-year-old genius is to act like an ordinary thirteen-year-old boy.[46]

When the viewpoint shifts to the race of *homo sapiens* from which mutations have sprung or are springing, the effect changes to one of pathos, the sort of pathos inherent in the conscious dying of a species or an era. Illustrative of this pathos is such a story as Judith Merril's "That Only a Mother" or Poul Anderson and F. N. Waldrop's "Tomorrow's Children." In the latter story, the remnant of the U.S. Army that is left in an atomic-war-blasted world is slowly rebuilding a basis for civilization when it discovers that seventy-five percent of all births are mutations of one kind or another. There is no hope for the survival of man as a species; he must either destroy himself or learn to live with his mutant children while they gradually take over the world.

The latest thought of science fiction on the subject is that it doesn't take a great deal of difference to make *homo superior*; he doesn't have to have startling new abilities, such as telepathy, extrasensory perception, telekinesis, etc. All a tall man needs is an inch or two to be taller than anyone else and break whatever height records there are. One development that might make a successful and superior mutation, for instance, is reflex action a few fractions of a second faster. Or, as Robert Heinlein observes in "Gulf":

> "What is the one possible conceivable factor—or factors, if you prefer—which the hypothetical superman could have, by mutation or magic or any means, and which could be added to this advantage which man already has and which has enabled him to dominate this planet against the unceasing opposition of a million other species of fauna? Some factor that would make the domination of man by his successor as inevitable as your domination over a hound dog? ... What is the *necessary* direction of evolution to the next dominant species?" [57–58].

And the answer? To think better—just a little better.

Another possible successor to man is the machine, either generally or in the specific form of robots. This theme, however, does not have as much to bring to science fiction as that of the mutation. Science fiction is inextricably (and necessarily) tied up with mankind; a mutation may intensify and concentrate the best qualities in humanity, but a machine is fundamentally alien and can suggest few human philosophic answers. The theme of the machine can function in two ways only: as an example, extracting certain human qualities and satirizing or commenting upon them; or as a symbol of the relationship or conflict between man and his creations.[47]

IX

If science fiction has been successful in getting over its philosophic viewpoint (or, to put it another way, in securing the necessary suspension of disbelief)—and I think it has—it has been largely due to its adoption of a realistic form. About 1930, I have suggested, the realistic era of science fiction first began to assume the shape of a trend. It went hand in hand with the shift of viewpoint from anti-science to science; a necessary realism—for if there is any hope for our era it lies in a scientific attack on our multifarious problems. Science fiction assumed the duty of expressing and attempting to resolve what no other type of literature is attempting—the problem of our era, the relationship between man and his scientific creations. Other writers may deplore or condemn, but condemnation of the machine and the age of science is no solution. Man cannot turn back. The only way to go is forward, to a more sound and sane relationship between man and science (to the stars, if you will) or to a gradual psychological and sociological growth in man himself, both of which themes we have already noted.

Gradually the emphasis in science fiction changed from the fertility of the imagination in thinking up details of strange lands and customs to the fertility of the imagination in thinking up new and fantastic inventions and scientific experiments and explorations. As gradually, the latter element evolved into realism. The inventions became either logical extrapolations of known science or those already theoretically predicted. Campbell has summed up this trend, although he rather arbitrarily narrows the field more than he might, at another time, be willing to admit:

> Science fiction is a form of prophecy. Normally there is a lag of five to as much as a hundred years between the discovery of a fact in the laboratory and the application of that fact in engineering practice. Science fiction lives in that gap. Drawing its background material from the laboratory knowledge, it projects it to a time when the engineering applications will be effected ["Science of Science-Fiction" 97].

This sort of technical accuracy was a form of realism, but it was not enough alone. As an inevitable result, however, this emphasis on accuracy spread to the psychological and sociological aspects of the world depicted. Realism in character portrayal and dialogue came slowly; minds that delight in ideas do not easily turn themselves to such literary details. Even yet that refinement of realism has not been completely reached except in a sprinkling of better authors.

The basis, then, for a sound science fiction story today lies in exact scientific detail and the latest approved theory (i.e. of Einstein, Korzybski, etc.).[48] The modern reader wants not details to wonder at but a picture of life as it may (or possibly *will*) be today, tomorrow, or a million years in the future. That picture, made as vividly realistic as the authors can contrive, is one of the chief attractions of modern science fiction.

It might be noted here that stories with satirical or propaganda purpose cannot be the purest type of science fiction, because the manipulation of their material is too great. Thus Aldous Huxley's *Brave New World*, for instance, though it is science fiction in form, is too frankly satirical to be true to the modern genre.[49]

For science fiction, believe it or not, is a very serious business. It treats of serious topics in a serious manner. It is written by writers who take themselves seriously and read by readers who are more serious than those who study the editorial columns of the *New York Times*. Let one minor inaccuracy slip into a story and an editor will be deluged by protests. E. G. Ewing, vice-president of the Pacific Rocket Society, for instance, wrote the following objection to a statement in *Astounding Science-Fiction*:

Part One—"Some of Us Are Looking at the Stars" 57

> I hate to see a writer jumped on and pounded to a pulp for minor errors, but when he becomes the victim of a popular misconception and unwittingly perpetuates it.... The same (mistake) was restated succinctly and with improvements ... by L. Sprague de Camp when he said, "Moreover liquid oxygen is a dangerous material to handle; hydrocarbons like lubricating oil explode on contact with it—as for that matter they do on contact with pure oxygen gas." In the first place, liquid oxygen is about as dangerous to handle as so much hot water, and in the second place, we of the Pacific Rocket Society wish very fervently that it would cause hydrocarbons to ignite spontaneously on contact [158].

One of the interesting technical effects of the contract between the imaginative nature of the subject matter and the realistic quality of the writing is to set up a fundamental tension in the work as a whole. The imaginative is made real, science is made imaginative, and both are made dramatic. In a future, distant, or past world made tangible, one finds real people, the big and the little, facing real problems, and yet it is all as fanciful as a fairy tale—even if the problems are more pertinent. This tension may well be one of the primary attractions of the form.

Another attraction, too often lacking in other forms of modern writing, is a judicious use of action. Long recognized by writers of all types of literature as one of the most useful dramatic devices, it is currently scorned by our more pretentious literary contemporaries. But action, properly used, can reveal character and theme in a way no writing about the subject can ever hope to achieve. The early days of pulp science fiction, it is true, stressed action and plot almost to the exclusion of all else, and it is still a major ingredient of several magazines in the field. But action is slowly taking its proper place—and a good place it is—in the better science fiction stories and the magazines they are appearing in.

X

About the time realism became an important factor in science fiction, a group of authors came upon the scene equipped to write in the new form. They were predominantly scientists. Robert Heinlein, for instance, is an Annapolis graduate and a plastics research engineer. Isaac Asimov is a research chemist, recently employed by the Navy Research Library[50]; Norman Knight is also a chemist. David H. Keller is a doctor. John Taine is Dr. Eric Temple Bell, research mathematician and professor of mathematics at the California Institute of Technology. L. Sprague de Camp and L. Ron Hubbard are engineers, and John W. Campbell, Jr., was graduated from the Massachusetts Institute of Technology with a degree in nuclear physics.

That they paved the way and laid such a solid scientific foundation is the reason, no doubt, that one need no longer be a scientist to write science fiction, although it helps. Most of the basic technical theories have been laid down—of time travel, space flight, alien worlds, etc.—and one can start from there, knowing that his readers will presume that foundation if the story is well written and in the science fiction tradition. This has opened the field to a number of new writers without training in the physical sciences but with ideas that they feel can best be expressed within the science fiction framework.

These early scientists, however, some of them early on the scene, some of them coming to attention later, turned to science fiction for a variety of reasons, no doubt, but prominent among them, probably, was the belief that they could contribute something to an understanding of today's scientific world within the realistic structure of modern science fiction. They found there the freedom they needed in the most unrestricted popular medium of expression, barring none. There is no stereotyping in science fiction: any form that is well-handled is acceptable; no subject, no theme is taboo if it falls into the science fiction classification; no plot pattern is required or desired. Effectiveness is all that is required of form, and almost every possible form has been used. Unlike the national slick magazines, science fiction thrives on controversial subjects; they are its lifeblood. And as for plot, anything goes: a tragic ending, and inconclusive ending, no ending. In fact, if there is any pressure upon the writer it is that he must not, in the better magazines at least, write a stereotyped story. He must write something different, and the more different the better.

The result of the science and the freedom has been that science fiction has appealed to a particularized audience, one the authors might have hand-picked: a group interested in the problems of today and tomorrow and possible solutions suggested through an attack by means of the scientific method.

In science fiction magazines, scientists or their spokesmen are speculating on the effects of their laboratory work and dramatizing their hopes, fears, and ambitions. And, in an age whose fate and future may well lie in the research laboratory, science fiction commands a following of scientists and professional men probably unequaled in any other fiction field. Science fiction has become, in effect, what has been the crying need of the age—the conscience of the scientist. It asks not "what shall we create" but "what shall we do with what we create."

In a recent survey conducted by *Astounding* (which estimates that it has 150,000 readers), it developed that over 93 percent of its readers were male. The average reader was just under thirty, had a college degree, and had been reading the magazine for about eight years. The occupations held, in decreasing percentage order, were: engineering (14.7 percent), mechanical-electrical, sales and advertising, research, chemistry, professional, executive management, technician, clerical and secretarial, auditing-accounting, armed forces, writers-editorial, supervisory, architecture-design, civil service, agricultural.

This is the practical side of the science fictionist—and an interesting and worthwhile side it is. But on the other side, and what draws fully as many readers, is the dreamer. Today is an era of wonder—scientific wonder. Pessimists and lost, isolated modern souls to the contrary notwithstanding, today is an exciting era in which to be living. It is a platitude that humanity is at a crossroads, but it is no less true. Science is putting the stars within man's reach at the same time as it is placing in his hands the possibility of racial suicide. Life has changed beyond belief in the last fifty years; the next fifty are likely to see even more radical changes. The first man to leave the gravitational influence of the earth may represent for humanity not only a physical but a spiritual conquest; the first spaceship to the moon (as we have said, a physical possibility *today*) may well open up a new frontier and with it a new frontier psychology, one which presents to the human spirit the possibility that there are greater (at least, more urgent) conquests than those of fellow men. *Ad Astra per aspera*; to the stars is not an unworthy ambition.[51]

Science fiction today is written for and by the impatient. Everywhere are new possibilities for conquest: physical, sociological, psychological, philosophical. No one need weep with Alexander; everywhere are new challenges to the human spirit. Tremendous tradition-shattering and soul-charging things may happen in the not too far distant future. But the "not too far distant future" is too distant for science fiction writers and readers. They don't want to wait—and won't wait—fifty or even ten years for the first rocket to conquer space. They want to live the experience now—and the experiences of setting a foot down on an alien planet, of seeing the wonder of a spiral nebula or a blue sun, of meeting the challenge of a suddenly, wonderfully available universe.

PART TWO

"Through Caverns Measureless to Man": The Plot Forms of Science Fiction

> *The extent of the powers that may exist, we can never ascertain; and therefore we feel no great difficulty in yielding a temporary belief to any, the strangest, situation of things.*—Samuel Taylor Coleridge

Any universally accepted definition for science fiction is as difficult to arrive at as one for the novel or the poem—and properly so. A literary form that can be confined within the rigid limits of a definition has outworn its possibilities and has ceased to grow; science fiction is still vital, still amorphous, still something different to every reader. But attempts at definition have their purpose and their place; one of their places, surely, is in literary criticism and one of the permissible, possibly useful, purposes is to circumscribe the field without limiting it, something akin to the definition of the novel as a long piece of fiction.[1] The problem of circumscribing science fiction is, however, particularly complicated by the fact that it has so lately emerged as a literary type that its boundaries are nebulous, its domain is shifting, and its critics and analysts, without tradition or history to fall back upon, are in agreement upon only one thing—that there is such a thing as science fiction.[2]

The nature of the problem can be appreciated by examining a few of the definitions offered by various authorities in the field:

> Science-fiction concerns itself with the world of the future, a world whose political, social and economic life has been shaped by the expansion of scientific knowledge—Raymond J. Healy and J. Francis McComas [xi].
>
> Science fiction is fantasy wearing a tight girdle—Sam Merwin, Jr. [150].
>
> "Scientifiction" (a word coined by the magazines which do fancies based on current scientific hypotheses—rocket skips, fourth-dimensional stuff, and so on)—Phil Stong [9].

A piece of scientific fiction is a narrative of an imaginary invention or discovery in the natural sciences and consequent adventures and experiences. The invention must be imaginary at the time the romance is written, an imaginary airplane, space-flier, radio, rocket, atomic bomb, or death ray.... It must be a scientific discovery—something that the author at least rationalizes as possible to science—J. O. Bailey [10].

To be science fiction, not fantasy, an honest effort at prophetic extrapolation of the known must be made.... Prophetic extrapolation can derive from a number of different sources, and apply in a number of fields. Sociology, psychology and parapsychology are, today, not true science; therefore instead of forecasting future results of applications of sociological science of today, we must forecast the *development of a science* of sociology—John W. Campbell, Jr. ["Science of Science-Fiction Writing" 86].

Actually science-fiction embraces all imaginative fiction which grows out of scientific concepts, whether in mathematics or geology or nuclear fission or biology or any scientific concept whatsoever, whether already demonstrated or whether projected out of the writer's imagination into future space and time—August Derleth [Introduction, *Strange Ports of Call* n.p.].

It may be suggested that science fiction is composed of "supernatural" writing for materialists. You may read every science-fiction story that is true science fiction, and never once have to compromise with your id. The stories all have rational explanations, provided you are willing to grant the word "rational" a certain elasticity—Groff Conklin [xxi].

These seven men are discussing the same literary phenomenon, but their fields of exclusion and inclusion are often quite different. The utmost exclusion is achieved, perhaps, by Bailey, who is refuted by Campbell and Derleth; Bailey limits science fiction to a story of discovery in the *natural* sciences which must be *imaginary* at the time of writing, Campbell broadens the definition to include the sociological and psychological sciences, and Derleth admits any scientific concept even if already in use. Healy and McComas project science fiction into the world of the future, and Merwin is, to understate the matter a little, rather general. Everything considered, however, I believe that generality is the most satisfactory; for usage, not dictionaries or critical articles, determine definitions, and it is better to include too much than to exclude something generally accepted to be science fiction. As I have observed in the preceding section, I agree generally with Conklin—with the emphasis on the rational explanation.

The unsatisfactory nature of Bailey's definition requires further amplification, since his book is the only extended critical discussion in the field. Generally speaking, a definition in such a work serves as a convenient means of limiting one's material, a necessary device in a genre as extensive, as old, and as untouched by the critical pen as science fiction. As a device, it serves Bailey's purpose admirably, his "imaginary invention or discovery" desideratum forming an effective framework upon which to hang his historical survey. At the same time, unfortunately, Bailey's definition acts as an authoritative voice to limit not only the material with which he, as the author, wishes to deal but also the literary field itself. And an imaginary invention or discovery is not essential to a science fiction story, as a hasty inspection of any anthology or current magazine would reveal; a glance at Bailey's book itself would show that he has used as examples such books as James Hilton's *Lost Horizon*, Jack London's *The Scarlet Plague*, and so forth, works which include no imaginary invention or discovery. Nor, as Campbell pointed out, need the invention, if present, be in the natural sciences; nor is it necessary that the invention be imaginary (here again Bailey is somewhat inconsistent, for he includes such non-imaginary inventions as those described by Jules Verne's *Around the World in Eighty Days* or his *Five Weeks in a Balloon*.

The most significant objection to Bailey's definition and critical method, however, is that it is not functional, or, to be more precise, the nature of the invention or discovery contained in a science fiction work does not function as the most revealing aspect of the work—it is not the most significant ingredient of the science fiction story. That ingredient is plot or theme.

There are many ways of classifying science fiction stories, most of them useful; the only way of choosing between them, perhaps, is as to their degree of usefulness in the circumstances. Bailey, for instance, subdivides his book in the following manner:

A. The Wonderful Machine
B. The Wonderful Journey
C. Utopias and Satires
D. The "Gothic" Romance

Later in his volume he adds such classifications as "The Occult and the Supernatural," "The Historic Romance," "Crime and Detection," "The Cosmic Romance." It is, as I have said before, a satisfactory arrangement for a historic summary.

Groff Conklin, for the purposes of his first anthology, *The Best of Science Fiction*, classified his stories under six headings:

The Atom
The Wonders of Earth
The Superscience of Man
Dangerous Inventions
Adventures in Dimension
From Outer Space

In his second anthology, *Treasury of Science Fiction*, he added "Far Traveling."[3]

Campbell, as we noted in the preceding section, suggests three broad divisions: prophecy stories, philosophical stories, and adventure science fiction. This classification is of potential analytical value and could be the basis for a revealing discussion. Prophecy and philosophical stories, for instance, are principally "problem" stories, one of the favorite types of science fiction, which would be subdivided according to the type of problem presented, something like this:

1. The development of man
   a. Technologically
   b. Mentally
   c. Psychologically
   d. Sociologically
   e. Politically
2. The degeneration and/or self-destruction of man (with the same divisions as above)
3. The machine
4. Mutations
5. Aliens
6. Academic or purely philosophical problems

The possible value of such a classification is apparent: the problems, and the stories written around them, include, directly or by analogy, summations and perhaps solutions of current problems. "The development or degeneration of man" points out directions the human race may take and thereby presents possible answers to questions puzzling the world today. "The machine" discusses a problem that has been a matter of deep concern and debate since the inception of the industrial age. "Mutations" is a subject for our era—the atomic era with its dangers of mutating radiations—and, together with the stories on "Aliens," suggests answers to questions of minority and racial problems. "Academic or purely philosophical problems" has stories of no immediate application, perhaps, but which contain inherent possibilities of the abstract. The one great disadvantage of this basis for discussion is its lack of inclusiveness. For this reason or for others which I have already discussed the other systems of classification above are unsatisfactory as well for a comprehensive analysis of the breadth of modern science fiction. That type of analysis is most rewarding, I believe, on the basis of plot. Science fiction, as we noted in the preceding section, is a medium of ideas, and the only way ideas can work themselves out dramatically is in terms of plot.[4]

There are, basically, two main types of plots, in unspecialized fiction as well as the specialized form which is science fiction: plots in which the conflict is between man and his environment and those in which the conflict is initiated by a character's activities. The first of these I have called in the following outline *plots of circumstance*; the second, *plots of creation*. The significant differences between the two lie in the nature of the stories constructed around the plots. Under plots of circumstance there are the adventure story and the problem story, which depict characters battling against circumstances for which they are not responsible but from which they can extract themselves sometimes or over which they can exercise some control. Under plots of creation, there are the stories of the mad or incautious scientist described in the preceding section, the stories of the creative scientist, the stories of experimentation which turns out well or ill; in these stories the responsibility for the situation rests on the shoulders of the characters. These differences are vitally important in determining the nature of the story.

These two basic plot types, I suggested above, are as true for ordinary fiction as for science fiction; the difference lies in what Conklin calls "supernaturalism for materialists." To put it more explicitly, in science fiction something happens which should not, in the ordinary run of things, happen and this occurrence is reconciled to the ordinary run of things. The distinguishing mark of fantasy is that this reconciliation is not necessary and does not take place.

Editor's Note: In the original thesis, there are four pages of charts categorizing stories by type from the five major anthologies Gunn analyzed: *The Best of Science Fiction* (Conklin), *Adventures in Time and Space* (Healy & McComas), *A Treasury of Science Fiction* (Conklin), *Strange Ports of Call* (Derleth), and *The Other Side of the Moon* (Derleth). To mitigate the disruption of Gunn's narrative analysis, I have moved the distribution chart to an appendix at the end of the thesis. The stories themselves are identified in the narrative analysis which follows. However, at various times throughout the remainder of the thesis, Gunn does refer to the distribution chart and his headings and subheadings are structured from it; hence the need to keep the distribution chart in the present volume.[5]

Section One: Plots of Circumstance

Plots of circumstance are by far the most popular forms for science fiction stories; out of 145 stories analyzed, as shown by the distribution chart, 123 of them belonged to this major category. For a number of reasons, the distribution chart can lay no claims to any sort of statistical accuracy; principal among them is the reason inherent in the nature of anthologies, since the chart attempts to classify and total all the stories in five anthologies whose plot forms fall under the various divisions and subdivisions of the outline. Anthologies are, by definition, collections of the best and as such are limited in extent and cannot be considered as typical of the field as a whole. They are, moreover, the selections of one or two editors and inevitably are more representative of the individual tastes of the selectors than of the gamut of the genre. This shows up most clearly in the collections of August Derleth, who includes only one story under "plots of creation," and that a variant. Derleth is fondest of stories about "modern men in the modern world," as the distribution chart illustrates: twenty-four out of his total forty-two stories fall under this classification and nine of the remainder under "a being in an alien environment."

Despite the statistical deficiencies of the chart, its results are illuminating when they are as one-sided as those shown in the distribution between the two main types. The reasons why plots of circumstance are so overwhelmingly favored are not so hard to find. Plots of creation are limited and difficult to write; plots of circumstance provide an immediate dramatic suspense and identification with the characters: few of us are creators but we all know what it is to battle against circumstances. In this category the possibilities are unlimited.

The most important considerations in plots of circumstance are the protagonist and the environmental situation in which he finds himself. The protagonist can be in either his own environment or an alien one. If in his own environment, he can be, in relation to ourselves, only in the past, the present, or the future. There are, thus, four possible variations:

A. A being in an alien environment
B. Modern man in the modern world
C. A past being in the past
D. A future being in a future world

These subdivisions make up the plots of circumstance—with the addition of one more which could probably be classified under the categories above but which is given its own section because of its thematic importance and because, in the final analysis, environment in this type has little influence on its basic nature:

E. Mutations

There are two possibilities which it might be well to mention in passing: an alien in an alien world in the present and a dimensional being in another dimension. Since there is no contact with earth, the time element (earth time, of course) in the first is unimportant and would probably never come up; it is probable, moreover, that they are not science fiction at all, but fantasy, since there can be no rational explanation without some reference to earth or mankind.

It is possible that every possible science fiction story cannot be classified according to the outline I have suggested; there are perhaps some classifications which I have forgotten or which have not occurred to me. But I have not yet found a story that did not fit into one division or another. There is the additional danger of misclassifying or duplicating a classification, as, for instance, a story might be classified as either "an ancient being or primitive man in a modern human environment" or "modern man in the modern world facing problems introduced from the past"; another might be classified as "an alien in a human environment in the present" or "a modern man in the modern world facing problems introduced from another dimension or another world or space," still another as "a future being in the present" or "modern man in the modern world facing problems introduced from the future." In these cases the decision of where the story belongs must be made on the basis of viewpoint or, if that is shifting, of emphasis. The differences, not so obvious in theory, become readily apparent on inspection of the individual stories. Theodore Sturgeon's "Killdozer!" would, for instance, be a story of a modern man in the modern world facing problems introduced from the past rather than an ancient being in a modern human environment because the emphasis is always on what the men are going to do about it, whether they will meet the menace, conquer it, or survive.

Chapter One: A Being in an Alien Environment

Probably the favorite science fiction plot structure is that of "a being in an alien environment," a fact not so obvious from the distribution chart as it would be from a general analysis, although even on the chart the number of stories under this heading (43) is only exceeded by that under "a modern man in the modern world" (50). But at least nine-tenths of the lead novels in *Startling Stories* and *Thrilling Wonder Stories* are of this type;

there are as many, if not more, in *Planet Stories* and others of the magazines running more to the adventurous type of story. Almost every science fiction novel Edgar Rice Burroughs wrote belongs to this category (the *Tarzan* series is not science fiction, although it is close to the borderline)[6]; A. Merritt wrote only a few novels of any other type. And the list of the "elder statesmen of science fiction" who wrote almost exclusively in this classification might go on for several pages.

This is not the type of story that has secured for science fiction the reputation for prophecy. It is primarily an adventure story theme, although other and more significant uses have been made of it, as we shall see. It is, in the final analysis, the primal essence of science fiction, the earliest exciting breath which drew its first and still unwavering devotees. Its origins go back as far as the beginnings of science fiction and the pre-science fiction tales of wonder before; Poe, for instance, wrote many such stories. The fundamental suspense and drama of the plot type are the reasons for its popularity then as now; place one person or a small group in a completely new environment where they must solve the riddle of their circumstances, seek out in some cases the bases of the new civilization into which they have been projected, fight off singlehanded the menaces of an alien world—all these for survival, and you have a story of the greatest possible suspense potential. That this suspense can be used to carry something besides the story line or the reader's escapist interest is what has in the recent past and may in the future rescue this type from insignificance.

The alien quality of the environment depends, naturally, upon the identity of the character placed in it, and the four principal subdivisions of this classification are predicated upon that fact. One can have as one's protagonist: 1. A modern man; 2. An ancient being or primitive man; 3. An alien; 4. A future being. Except for the alien, these variations are based, obviously, upon a position in time relative to our own, and, again except for the alien, the protagonists listed are native to earth. Collectively, then, they bracket the field of possibility: a principal character can be either native to earth or alien; if native to earth, he can be native only in the past, the present, or the future.

The environments are not quite so all-inclusive. The alien is placed only in a human environment; presumably one could write a story about an alien in a non-human but still alien environment, but this belongs in the same category as the "alien in an alien world in the present" discussed above. It is possible but without significance. Somewhere along the line there must be some relationship to earth or earth problems to push the story across the line from fantasy to science fiction.

The modern man as protagonist carries the greatest potential reader interest, chiefly because there is the greatest potential reader identification or empathy. His one fault as a hero is that it is difficult to make his normal circumstances contain that ingredient of the strange that is basic to science fiction as well as fantasy. Ordinarily this defect is remedied by placing the scene of action only a few years in the future, where new things can happen or current trends can come to fruition. But the largest ingredient of the strange is supplied when modern man is placed in entirely different circumstances from those with which his readers are familiar. For this there are three possibilities: a. The past; b. A distant world, space, or dimension in the present; c. The future. How to make the transition to these circumstances plausible is the science fiction author's principal initial task.

A Modern Man in the Past

The past is the place for violent contact with nature, for evocations of the carboniferous era with its giant ferns and steaming swamps, pterodactyl and tyrannosaurus, or of the ice age with its cave men, mammoths and saber-toothed tigers. It is the place where man becomes the hunted, where it is he, puny and insignificant, against the harshness and cruelty of a primitive world, where survival is the problem set by nature for the individual and the species.[7]

The problem of reaching the past has been solved in various ways. One of them is to visualize a spot so isolated that it has had no contact with the outside world and evolution has passed it by; in effect this is the past although it may not be in reality. Another method is by passage through time via time machine or accident. Although time theories will be discussed in more detail below, these stories, it should be mentioned here, find it necessary to describe the shape of time in order to justify a passage through or around it. In some of the stories, time is pictured as a circle, spiraling like a spring, or branching like a fan or the limbs of a tree.[8]

In Conan Doyle's *The Lost World*, perhaps the first example of the plot type in science fiction, the first solution is used: a group of English explorers find in the depths of the South American wilds a large area which has been preserved from change by its position as a plateau surrounded by almost insurmountable cliffs. There they discover giant reptiles and primitive cave men, holdovers from the Jurassic period. Their problem is survival and escape, solved eventually by the construction of a balloon out of skins which is inflated with hot air and lowers them over the cliffs. There is, in addition, a literary mystery connected with *The Lost World*: Doyle suggests a sequel but this, like that to one of the Dr. Doolittle books of my youth (in which the doctor who can speak with animals is carried to the moon by a huge bird), I have never been able to find.[9]

A situation similar to Doyle's is found in Edgar Rice Burroughs's *The Land That Time Forgot*; a man is cast away on an island so protected and so far out of normal trade lanes that it has remained untouched for hundreds of thousands of years. The castaway finds there primeval conditions in which tribes exist in different stages of evolutionary development; his problem is to solve the riddle of the peculiar situation in its sociological and anthropological aspects and preserve his life.

Of a slightly different type is P. Schuyler Miller's "The Sands of Time," in which a physicist invents a time-traveling machine that takes him back to the Cretaceous era. His picture of time is that of a coiled spring, a two-dimensional surface twisted in a third dimension; ordinarily one follows along the spring from one day to the next, but if one cuts across the spring in the third dimension one can take a shortcut to the future or return to the past. In this case, however, the spring has sixty million years to the turn, too great for practical values. The inventor's purpose is to prove that he has traveled in time; as proof he brings back pictures, eggs, a reptilian bird, and he plants a box in the past containing quills of radium and his name. He proves his point, but he never returns from a last romantic errand to the past. As an archeologist acquaintance reads the last of the story from excavations in the sands of a Cretaceous beach, he was apparently killed by beings from another planet.[10]

Such is the standard story about modern man in the past. But there is an offshoot of this classification that deserves special attention because of its great popularity among writers and readers of science fiction.

Time is the playground of science fiction. When its authors tire of writing run-of-the-mill stories, they turn to the paradoxes of time for amusement. Almost every modern author in the genre has toyed with the idea for fun or bewilderment: van Vogt, Heinlein, Kuttner, de Camp—the list is almost endless. For, given enough time (as the saying goes) anything can happen. In science fiction it usually does.[11]

The classic theory of time envisions it as a fourth dimension in which we exist as well as in the other three. Or, to put it more explicitly, for an object to exist in our three-dimensional world it must have extensions in each of the three dimensions: breath, thickness, and length; a one or two dimensional object cannot and does not exist in our world (except in theory). But three-dimensional extension alone is not enough for existence in our world; an object must have an extension in time. It must have duration; it must exist for a certain length of time. And, if time is a dimension, one should be able to measure it, to travel in it, as one travels in the other three.

But time travel into the past has inherent paradoxes that would have made Zeno throw away Achilles and the tortoise in envy. Suppose, for instance, in a classic example, one travels into the past and kills one's grandfather before he sires one's father: that leaves the time traveler, to put it mildly, without apparent reason for being. Such a plot, however, is too old and hackneyed for use today. But in a variation by P. Schuyler Miller called "As Never Was" a grandson contemplates such a murder as he ponders over a mysterious knife brought back from the future by his time-pioneering grandfather. The knife is fashioned from a metal harder than diamond, which earth science cannot duplicate and which later time explorers can find no trace of in the future. The grandson eventually finds the spot in the future his grandfather had reached: the ruins of a museum founded as a memorial to his grandfather and as a repository for the mysterious knife his grandfather had found in those ruins and brought back. The knife, therefore, existed in a closed, three-hundred year circle with no beginning and no end: his grandfather found the knife in some ruins, brought it back, placed it in a museum, whose ruins he was to visit and from which he was to bring back the knife again. It was a simple paradox with only one drawback—the knife the grandfather brought back was perfect, but the physicists sawed out a notch for tests. Where in that circle was the notch restored? How was the knife created in the first place? And how can the circle be broken?

Another such circle is described in "By His Bootstraps" by Robert A. Heinlein. A code is necessary to understand any summary of this plot in which a Time Gate provides a doorway to a future world. A Man (One) steps through the Gate into the room of a student (Two) to persuade the student to step through the gate into the other world. Another man (Three), a twin to the first, steps through to persuade the student not to go through, but the student (Two) is knocked into the Gate in a struggle and wakes up to find himself facing an older man (Four) thirty thousand years in the future. The older man, the undisputed ruler of the world, persuades him (Two) to go back through the doorway to persuade another man to return; he finds he is acting out the role of the first man (One) to step through the Gate. Eventually he finds he is not only the student (Two) and the first man (One) but the objector (Three) and still another man who returns to the past of the future world and after searching vainly for the ruler for a decade or so finds that he (Two) himself has aged into the ruler (Four) he met when he first was propelled through the Gate. He searches curiously back through time for his own room and finds it, only to have a figure (Two) come hurtling through the Gate—and begin the circle anew. Again the question "how did the circle start?" remains a mystery and the plot a paradox.[12]

Classic time theories pretty well rule out time travel into the past. A possibility suggested in some stories is that time has a certain inertia which, like physical inertia, tends to damp out any disturbance which an intrusion from a future period would introduce. Another and more fertile possibility is that entitled "probable times" in which time is pictured as branching like the limb of a tree. In this theory, each possible action, no matter how small, creates a branch whose existence depends on its probability; using this theory two or more time streams can exist side by side and battle in the past for greater probability and insured existence. Using this theory a man can go back in time, alter some event subtlety, and return to another time stream; or he may leap time boundaries and reach another time stream where, for instance, the American colonies were defeated in their bid for independence.[13]

A story in this vein, with an interesting twist, is "Brooklyn Project" by William Tenn. A military press relations secretary is discussing an experiment in time with a group of reporters, ridiculing the idea that any change will occur as the experiment begins and disturbances are set up in the past. But as the mechanism vibrates back and forth through time, minute changes occur in the past which produces unnoticed changes in the group until, at the end, the secretary exclaims triumphantly that nothing has changed at the same time as he extends fifteen purple blobs. And this illustrates one of science fiction's thoughts about time travel: if changes were made in the past, one would change but would never know it, since that change would automatically become part of one's own history.[14]

A story based upon this concept is "The Comedy of Eras" (one of a series) by Henry Kuttner,[15] which sets the idea down in a light-hearted situation. The mind of the protagonist, in this story, is sent back in time to inhabit the body of a man of the Elizabethan age; purpose—to determine once and for all the authorship of those plays attributed to Shakespeare. While there, the hero hobnobs with Shakespeare, Jonson, and Marlowe (who were, probably, never together historically) and out of his memory of Shakespeare's plays suggests several plot turns and developments to the Bard. On his return to the present, the hero informs the scientists that Shakespeare had done his own work; he was then informed, in his turn, that he had inhabited the body of Sir Francis Bacon.[16]

All things considered, science fiction's use of time has made some interesting, at times dramatic, at times amusing, but seldom significant stories.[17] There is nothing of any thematic importance involved in concepts of time travel and in visits to the past. That the framework itself may be used to carry a theme of greater philosophical significance or that it may be used as part of some larger plot is here, as in other plots, an ever-present possibility, as evidenced in the recent Clifford D. Simak novel, *Time Quarry* [aka.

Time and Again], which will be discussed in more detail under plots of creation.

A Modern Man on a Distant World, in Space, or Another Dimension in the Present

If the plot form of a modern man in the past is basically an adventure theme, that of a modern man on a distant world, in space, or in another dimension in the present is even more so. In the former, the protagonist's surroundings are part of our earth, part of our heritage, but in the latter the environment is usually completely alien or when still on earth is so inaccessible and strange as to be almost divorced from modern experience. The form, consequently, is a perennial favorite of both writers and readers, since it is both easy to write and straight, uninvolved, suspenseful reading. The problems set by the plot usually involve physical difficulties and opposition, discovering the real nature of the environment, the old standby, survival, and finding a means of returning home.

The means of reaching the alien environment are so various that a complete summary is impossible. When the place is on earth, the protagonist finds it or is projected into it occasionally by foot but more often by machine. Space or another planet are usually reached by spaceship. Dimensions are almost always entered by accident, although sometimes ancient, forgotten entrances are rediscovered or dimensional beings trap humans for purposes of their own. Occasionally the means is mystical or mental in nature, and in that respect approaches fantasy.

The form is so old that its beginnings are lost in prehistoric mists: Lucian's works mentioned in the preceding section were of this type; myths often contained elements of it; medieval travel tales were basically plots of this kind; fictional utopian works—the list is endless. In modern science fiction, one could include almost all of Burroughs's science fiction stories in this classification: the story mentioned earlier, his *Pellucidar* series, and his novels laid on Mars and Venus. In the *Pellucidar* books, first entry into a hollow world inside the earth is made by boring through the earth's crust in a newly invented machine that emerges finally into a topsy-turvy world of innumerable strange tribes and beings. Later, Tarzan comes to the rescue by flying a zeppelin through a large hole at the North Pole. John Carter finds a similar if more involved situation on Mars, where the social progression is highly stratified by tribes, each tribe of a different color, and the civilization has degenerated from a previous peak. Carter gets his adventurous destination by concentrating his thoughts on the red planet.

Many of A. Merritt's novels are of this type. In *The Ship of Ishtar*, for instance, a mysterious rapport is established between the hero and an ancient, intricately carved, miniature ivory ship, and the hero falls into a fantasy world of gods, goddesses, priests, priestesses, soldiers, and slaves of a dimensional Egyptian world. In *The Snake Mother* and *The Face in the Abyss* the modern characters, travelling by foot and pack animals, come upon an isolated region in Central America inhabited by a half-snake, half-human woman, ancient gods or powers, intelligent spider-like creatures, and more or less normal humans. Another region is reached by foot, this time in the far North, in *Dwellers in the Mirage*; there the characters meet, in a mist-shrouded valley, peoples and places out of Norse mythology. In a final example, Merritt, in *The Moon Pool*, introduced his characters into a huge hollow world reached via mysterious ruins on a strange island in the Pacific. The modern humans find there, among more ordinary persons, a strange, seductively compelling life whose form is a swirling column of light, and an old and wise frog race.[18]

Two more modern examples are "The 32nd of May" by Paul Ernst and "Goldfish Bowl" by Robert A. Heinlein. In the first, the protagonist on the stroke of midnight stumbles between two mirrors in his host's living room and finds himself in another dimension, a strange, geometrical place with hexagonal plants and warring beings in the shape of two-dimensional circles and triangles; after many minutes he finds his way back and discovers that the final stroke of midnight is still ringing. "Goldfish Bowl" describes the efforts of two scientists to solve the mystery of two permanent waterspouts that have sprung up near Hawaii; one of the scientists ascends a spout in a converted bathysphere, and the other is carried away by an electrical ball of fire. They meet in a prison-like room above the pillars of water, never seeing their captors; they finally decide that their captors are superior beings native to earth, that (as Charles Fort suggested)[19] man is the property of some unseen race whose traces we notice in mysterious rains, disappearances, etc., but which science ignores. One of the scientists dies and his body is removed; but before the other dies he inscribes a cryptic message on the fore part of his body by continual scratching with his fingernail until scar tissue is formed. The message which, with his body, is found eventually in the ocean: "Beware—creation took eight days" (277).[20]

Alone, this plot type has resulted in nothing particularly important to science fiction or the world at large. It can only echo, thematically, Shakespeare's "there are more things in heaven and earth, Horatio..." As the carrier for theme or symbolism, however, it has served in the past on occasion and shows promise for the future, but the plot type, even without embellishments, will probably remain a standard expression of science fiction's escapist function.

A Modern Man in the Future

A modern man in the future has provided a plot type not quite so adventurous, although it has been used for that purpose on occasion. The stories of this classification, however, tend more to thoughtful or provocative analyses, to utopias and satires, to speculation about man's goal, possibilities, or destiny. A modern man enters the future with one primary question which both he and the reader demands to be answered: what will life be like? Upon the answer depends the protagonist's attitude toward the new world: will it satisfy all his desires and will he be satisfied to settle down and stay? Will there be something wrong which he can struggle to right? Or will the world be so fearfully alien or so irrevocably evil that he wants only to destroy it or escape from it?

Science fiction's view of the future through the eyes of a modern man has not been, on the whole, particularly cheerful. The utopia, generally, went out of style with Edward Bellamy's *Looking Backward*; since H. G. Wells's *The Time Machine* authors have taken, in such stories, the darker view of the possibilities of man's progressing toward any better life. There are reasons for this, of course, aside from purely philosophical ones. From the author's standpoint a perfect world is not good story material—nothing happens; a flawed or completely evil world provides a natural conflict and is thus much better for his purposes.[21] It is natural that he should choose to represent such a world when he decides to write about the future, since science fiction writers, like almost all writers of the past, are entertainers first and philosophers, if at all, second. And so, even when the world depicted has many attractive points in its favor, there are usually one or two strong drawbacks, most often culminating in the rebellion of the newcomer against the regimentation of a highly organized society. All this, by the way, does not hold true for stories built around "a future in a future world," where the characters have other problems than the nature of the society they live in and the viewpoint is quite radically different.

The future has been reached fictionally in many ways. In *Looking Backward* the hero was hypnotized and slept in a vault for over a hundred years; in other works suspended animation has been achieved by drugs, machines, or natural forces.[22] The use of the time machine is, of course, common, and occasionally a story uses a time "fault," natural passageway, or cataclysmic event to slip a character into the future directly.

One of the gloomy views is presented by Harry Bates in "Alas, All Thinking!" Here, a young genius is visited by an overly intellectual woman from the distant future and is taken forward with her, some three million years, to her own time. In mere boxes for rooms, the hero finds a few old, spider-like, mummified men, immobile and dusty, who, with their huge, supported heads, spend their lives in thought and contemplation and are fed by pellets shot by a mechanism into their mouths. Revolting against such a dusty prospect, the hero ends their lives one by one, thus closing the final chapter of the human race.[23]

A slightly less dismal picture is suggested by Frank Belknap Long's "A Guest in the House," in which a family moves into a new home and accidentally activates time-travelling machinery which a former experimenting tenant has left behind. Out of a gray fog which surrounds the house steps a scrawny gnome who informs the father that they are half a million years in the future and that his race, stemming from atomic-age mutations, is taking over the time-travelling machinery. The gnome's designs upon the past are foiled and the house is returned to its normal time by the nine-year-old son of the family, an atomic-derived prodigy of I. Q. 270.

This fictional form has not, outside of a few interesting exceptions, been particularly important in the history of science fiction or very popular with its authors, and its place will probably continue to be minor. The gap between the present and the future is usually too great to encompass anything significant for modern humanity, and the form lends itself too readily to satire. Science fiction today is essentially anti-satirical, anti-utopian; it is realistic, and both tendencies lead in the other direction. In spite of this, an occasional amusing or satirical story of note may be hoped to come from the type.

An Ancient Being or Primitive Man in a Modern Human Environment

The entrance of an ancient being or primitive man into our modern era is a plot type which has not often been used in modern science fiction and perhaps rightly so.[24] What little the form has to offer is in the nature of comparisons of primitive ways of life and possibly intervening history with our life and times. Even as an adventurous plot it has drawbacks, since there is, in the beginning, a difficulty in overcoming the tendency of the reader to identify himself with modern man and thus change it to a story about modern men in the modern world facing problems introduced from the past—since there is often only a subtle difference in emphasis separating the two types even though the effects are quite distinct.

One such story, however, which is successful, although a large part of its success is due to its surprise value and the theme it carries rather than any intrinsic quality in the plot itself, is Fredric Brown's "Letter to a Phoenix," which was discussed in the first section of this work. Another effective example, though for a different reason, is "The Gnarly Man" by

L. Sprague de Camp, which tells the story of a Neanderthal man who is discovered in a carnival by anthropologists. The principal attraction of the story is the recounting by the primitive man of his thousands on thousands of years of experience and the events and societies through which he has lived, enlivened, on the side, by an abortive romance with a frustrated female researcher among the anthropologists. The gnarly man's longevity was due to the mysterious accidental effects of a lightning bolt which struck close to him when he was a young man on a much younger earth and changed his structure so that he did not age. The Neanderthal man has survived so long because of his habit of effacing himself and moving to another region at regular intervals, before his agelessness is exposed; and this is what he does to escape his present predicament.[25]

An interesting variation of a number of years ago is Thomas Calvert McClary's *Rebirth*, in which the primitive characters are not brought from the past but created. In this novel, a scientist decides that drastic measures are in order to sweep away the world's corruption; he invents and puts in operation a machine which obliterates all knowledge from the minds of the world's millions, thus giving mankind a clean slate upon which to write—a rebirth. The situation in which the characters find themselves is one of perennial fascination in science fiction: the miracles of modern technology available for any who are ingenious enough to make use of them, civilization, with all the luxuries and conveniences it holds and which most of us have a materialistic yearning for from time to time, unowned and waiting. Any number of stories have been built around such a situation, and one of the primary essences of its appeal is the reader's vicarious delight in the unrestricted enjoyment of material possessions. In *Rebirth*, the situation enables McClary to comment effectively on the valuable arts of existence and the unnecessary excrescences of civilization. The experiment starts poorly, for mankind, without knowledge of fire, food, or any of the specialized knowledge necessary for urban life, reverts to the most primitive savagery. The remainder of the novel discusses man's rapid rise to a more civilized state.[26]

The form has never been seriously explored by modern writers; some of the technical difficulties we have already noted, and the results are seldom sufficiently rewarding to overshadow them. Like the former type, it is essentially satirical, and it is doubtful now, with the current realism in science fiction which has been largely responsible for much of its development, that anything significant will ever be done with it.

An Alien in a Human Environment

The plot form of the alien in a human environment has been used, like that of the preceding type, chiefly for comparisons, although there have been other, important philosophical applications. Satirists have turned frequently to the plot ever since its first application in Voltaire's *Micromegas* (1752) in which Micromegas (a native of the star Sirius) and a native of the planet Saturn visit earth, which seems as small as a meteor to them. Modern science fiction has found the type just as useful, and the distribution chart attests to its popularity. As a general rule, the stories are more thoughtful and less adventurous than the preceding types, their interest resting on bases more intellectual and less emotional.

Fundamentally, the alien is a character who is almost completely ignorant of earth's physical facts, the characteristics of its people, and the nature of its civilization. He is an outsider to whom everything is new and by whom nothing is taken for granted, from those truths we accept as axiomatic through our most deep-grained beliefs to the mores of our culture. Unlike the primitive being, he is an entity with a background of culture and possibly superior culture at that, if he is at times liable to short-sighted judgments due to his unfamiliarity with the situation.[27]

In modern writing the alien almost always reaches earth by spaceship, although occasionally writers hark back to Voltaire for such mystical means of transportation as light pressure or thought waves. The latest fad, in magazines that like to appear as current as today's newspaper, is the flying saucer.

AN ALIEN BEING IN THE PAST

Modern authors have not been particularly fond of placing their aliens in the past; there, possibilities of comparison are limited and satire is not as immediate or as pointed. When such a situation is used, it is usually tied in with human history or mythology to give the story an air of plausibility or a philosophical application. A number of stories, for instance, have tried to explain the presence or evolution of humanity by emigration and later degeneration of an alien race, or by alien experiments with sub-human life forms (usually in such circumstances as to suggest reasons for the springing up of legends of creation, paradise, heaven, Satan, etc.).[28]

A popular explanation of the mystery of Atlantis as the presence on earth of a pre-historic alien civilization is another example. The explanatory type of story has found places for all other ancient artifacts, ruins, and races as well—from the Minoans to the Egyptians, from the Chinese to the Mayan Indians. Anything the least strange or outlandish which has come down to us in legends or folk tales has been attributed at one time or another to aliens: the pyramids—built by aliens; magic—the misunderstood powers of aliens; mythological figures—the aliens themselves.

Such a concept figures in Oscar J. Friend's "Of Jovian Build," in which part of the action takes place in the past. Ancient Greek warriors find a spaceship from Jupiter and mistake it for a dragon before the Jovian within, misunderstanding their intentions, annihilates them. The Jovians, the remainder of whom are in suspended animation, have been reduced in size from their normal giant stature by a machine which condenses their cellular structure, but the failure of the artificial gravity machinery has fatally injured the pilot and he cannot revive his companions. Cadmus, founder of Thebes, arrives and courageously clambers into the ship, follows the instructions of the dying pilot in reviving the other Jovians, but then leaves in terror as he finds them increasing in size. The pilot realizes that the atmosphere is poisonous to his race and destroys the ship. Thus we have the explanation of the legend of Cadmus and the sowing of the dragon teeth.

Occasionally a plot of this type finds a place in a larger work. In *The Incredible Planet* by John W. Campbell, Jr., for instance, is an account similar to that above. Here, a spaceship crashes on earth with its crew of half-horse, half-man, centaur-like creatures; the crew, in an effort to repair the ship, impresses the labor of the surrounding, ignorant, scarcely human natives, but the attempts end in failure. One of the members of the party, with a name similar to Chiron, is sympathetic with the natives and over the years of his long lifespan endeavors to teach them the elements of civilization. So we have the legends of the centaurs and Chiron, the tutor.

Fictional explanations of another legend have been so frequent that such a story must be unusually well written to gain acceptance today: the legend—the fall of Adam and Eve in the garden of paradise. A fairly recent example is Eric Frank Russell's "First Person Singular," which tells the story of two pioneers from the planet Dise who are set down upon the primeval earth to care for and watch the native plants in a garden which had been carved out of the prolific surrounding jungle and protected by high, strong walls. The purpose is to see whether the flora essential to the welfare of the Disian race can survive on this primitive planet and whether the Disian pioneers themselves can live here unchanged—prior to a general colonization. There is only one admonition: that the pioneers eat nothing native to this world lest they become changed beyond acceptable limits. Between the six year visits of the ship, however, things did change; some plants died, some lived, all changed, but most of all the preliminary colonists themselves changed: in minute ways, as in the appearance of body hair, and in psychological ways, as in increasing aggressiveness and combativeness. Eventually, because of a natural cataclysm which destroys their garden, they are forced to rely almost entirely upon native food and they change too greatly. The ship offers to return them to Dise for treatment, giving up this world as hopeless at present; the man, Edham, and the woman refuse, and they are abandoned. They leave the destroyed garden they had called Para-Dise, and they take their place in the native earth. They have children:

> all of their own shape but none truly of their kind.
> The first was a murderer.
> The second, his victim.
> The fifth had a yellow skin and tilted eyes.
> Only the tenth had red hair.
> The twelfth was born black.
> But the seed of this seed subdued and mastered the stormy world which some call terra (103).

There is a basic reason why stories of this type have not contributed anything of importance to the development of science fiction and why they are unlikely to do more in the future. The stories partake of the nature of their material; in explaining myths, legends, folklore, and ruins, they are, in effect, myth's opposite pole. The most pertinent question science fiction asks is not the why of the past but the whither of the present and the future.

An Alien Being in the Present

The present is, as I intimated earlier, science fiction's favorite time for aliens to arrive on
Earth; there is an immediacy about the situation which translates itself into drama, suspense, and philosophical application. There is enough unexplained phenomena today, from flying saucers to mysterious disappearances, to provide a plausible basis for any number of stories about aliens in our society or even in our neighborhood; science fiction authors no longer feel the necessity of placing their aliens in secluded or poorly populated sections of the globe, although it is still done occasionally. Obvious satire is seldom present in modern versions of this plot type; satire, to repeat an observation made several times before, is not compatible with realism. Philosophical observations, when present, stem directly from the plot, and, unlike early stories, they are seldom stated overtly.

In one of the best examples of the type, Harry Bates's "Farewell to the Master," humanity's anthropomorphic blindness is exposed.[29] The story begins with the sudden arrival of a time-space machine in a large city at about the present time. From the machine step a metal giant and a man-like creature; the latter is immediately shot and killed by a fanatic. The robot-like being freezes into immobility, and it and the ship are placed in a museum. In the solitude of the night, however, the metal giant tries to recreate his human companion from the recordings of the man's speech made when he stepped from the ship—theoretically based, probably, on the suggestion that given one fact a good, philosophic mind could reconstruct in its entirety the universe from which it came. At last, with the materials for success at hand, over the misunderstandings and attempted interruptions of officials, the robot prepares to depart in the ship. He is asked to carry a message to his master, and the metal giant replies with what is one of the most effective lines of any story: "You misunderstand. I am the master" (815).[30]

A story suggesting a different kind of visitor is "Expedition" by Anthony Boucher, now co-editor of *The Magazine of Fantasy and Science Fiction*, which depicts the possibly disastrous consequences of man's native skepticism—a theme very common in science fiction recently, since several magazines have loudly championed the flying saucers and their extraterrestrial origin.[31] In Boucher's story, the insect beings of Mars, whose principal art form is the torturing and killing of other types of life, send an expedition to earth which lands in an American desert and meets a photographer specializing in desert photographs. After entering into communication, they are finally frightened away when the photographer shows them greatly enlarged pictures of an insect being killed by the huge hand of a man and thus convinces them that he is actually a dwarf specimen of his race.[32] After returning to our moon, however, the Martians realize that they have been tricked but are safe from discovery, since no one will believe the photographer even with his pictures. They can proceed to build up an invasion base on the other side of the moon, which is always concealed from man.[33]

This story introduces a factor in science fiction which is assuming the nature of a symbol: the use of Martians to represent any kind of alien. To refer to an unidentified alien as a Martian began originally as a convenience, a tendency probably tracing its origin from Orson Welles's radio version of H. G. Wells's *The War of the Worlds*, when the attention of the United States was focused on Mars as the most probable invader. Ray Bradbury has doubtlessly used this kind of symbolism to the best advantage in his Martian stories, but others have contributed to its growth and significance.

One story of this kind is Martin Pearson's [Donald A. Wollheim] "The Embassy," in which a detective is approached by a man who insists that there are Martians on earth and he wants them traced. The detective is skeptical but, being well paid, agrees to accept the assignment. The two track down the Martians in New York by finding a private house which subscribes to every major paper and magazine (a convenient way to learn a great deal about earth), but they are frightened by the death of an agent they have had watching the house. They get drunk and disagreeable and are finally slipped a doped drink. When they are searched for addresses to which to send them, the address of the supposed Martian house is found. Arriving at the house conscious but paralyzed, the detective watches the Martians attack his client with unconcealed sadism, exclaiming with loathing, "That Venusian!" (434).

An example that carries this tendency even farther is Henry Kuttner's "Don't Look Now," which builds a surprising amount of suspense out of the conversation of two men at a bar. The conversation is, however, unusual, to say the least: one of the men (most conveniently referred to as One) nervously begins the conversation by leading up to a discussion of possible alien presences (Martians) on earth and finally confessing that he is convinced that there are such beings here. They pass as humans, he says, but actually, through their hypnotic powers, control almost everything that goes on. Their identifying feature is a third eye in the middle of their forehead, which is undetectable except when they think they are not observed. The other man (Two) is amused at first, then incredulous, and finally, after his objections have been explained away, convinced by a picture One has snapped of a Martian in an unguarded moment. He admits, then, that he has had suspicions of such things for some time but has feared to mention it, not knowing who might be a Martian or under Martian control. They set a time for a further meeting, and Two gets up to leave. One, who had begun the conversation, opens his third eye in the middle of his forehead and stares after him.[34]

There have been a number of stories in recent years built around alien invasions or reconnaissances of earth in which the aliens are defeated by forgetting or neglecting to take account of one minor fact. Such a story is Edwin James's "Paradox,"[35] in which the first human to reach the moon happens to be an ignorant, superstitious petty thief who drives the aliens encamped on the other side of the moon, supposing that he is representative, mad with his twisted, inconsistent mind.[36] Murray Leinster's "Nobody Saw the Ship," suggests a one-being survey of earth, which is foiled because the being ignores the insect population and takes off with good news for his race only to find that the ship is ruined and his mission can only end with his death. A final instance is Eric Frank Russell's "Exposure," which describes an invasion by a race of aliens so malleable that it can imitate anything; the spaceship descends in a poorly populated district and the aliens proceed to imitate some of the humans they find. But when they go out into the world, they are quickly picked up. They had set their ship down in a nudist colony.

An element of satire still remains in occasional stories of this type as evidenced by Ross Rocklynne's "Jackdaw"; its characters are members of the oldest, wisest race of the universe, and their reason for being and greatest delight in life is the solving of puzzles of all kinds. They send their spaceships throughout the galaxy to seek out new puzzles and problems and prefer them complicated artificially, if necessary. (Which is to say that man's noblest aspect is his thirst for knowledge; what is, after all, man's attempt to understand the natural laws of the universe, himself, and the nature and purpose of life but an effort to solve the greatest puzzle of all?) One "recreation ship" returns with a problem encountered on the third planet of a small solar system; there, they found the cities in ruins and one lone survivor in an airplane, a survivor with a toothbrush mustache and hair that falls down over his forehead, who, after attacking the ship with robot planes, finally crashes his own into it in a last suicidal mission. The exploring party which returns to the planet to solve the riddle applies several psychological axioms to the problem in order to translate the language, such as: "the ultimate and even the direct purpose of all intelligent creatures is to solve puzzles" or "all intelligent creatures seek intelligently that relaxation of mind and body which is known as recreation and happiness," but neither of these works. The researchers play their trump card: "all intelligent creatures seek happiness by devoting themselves to the happiness of others entirely, forgetting themselves" (781–82). Using this axiom, the situation translates itself into a planet divided into sectors, each with a Captain of games; from time to time one sector would wage a game with another sector, not for its own enjoyment but for the enjoyment of others, and everyone would joyfully join in turning out materials for both sides. The last survivor had started the biggest game in history—but there the translation falls down. The old and wise race had to give up the problem in failure, commenting in the end on the vanity of a jackdaw that stole a jewel to glorify its nest.

This type of story, together with that following, seems to have an assured future in science fiction; it is dramatic and capable of great variety, and its flexibility makes it adaptable to any number of thematic messages. The one difficulty—and it is a large one—is making convincing the description of alien psychology and thought processes.

An Alien Being in the Future

There is little difference in plot form between an alien in the present and an alien in the future. Most of the comments that apply to the preceding classification apply to the present one, except that the stories concern themselves more with future problems and the element of immediate application to our modern problems is not so often present. The type itself probably originated in modern fiction.

The principal thematic trend in stories of this type is a glorification of humanity—not in its present state but in a possible future state of perfection, which it has reached by long struggle. The philosophical position is, then, not anthropomorphic, but one which points out to mankind the way to a better life. A current attribute of humanity, usually minor and unnoticed today, is occasionally singled out as important in preserving mankind or establishing its superiority in the universe. Whatever the reason, these stories, unreasonable as it may be, have the effect of leaving the reader with a warm glow of satisfaction in belonging to the human race.

The perfection reached by humanity in Campbell's "Forgetfulness" has already been discussed in the first section of this work. A. E. van Vogt's "Resurrection" is a story of a similar nature, which begins with an expanding alien race landing an expedition on a ruined earth. The scientists, who have a means of reconstructing a living being from a piece of the skull, revive three men from remains in a museum; as soon as they have learned all they need from the men, they kill them. The fourth, however, disappears as soon as he is revived; he has almost complete mental control of matter, just as did Campbell's characters. The human race was destroyed, he later tells the aliens, by a vast nucleonic storm from space, ninety light years in diameter; the race had dispensed with spaceships, and, in any case, the only star with planets that had been discovered was in the path of the storm. The most important discovery of the alien race—and that by accident—was a machine for locating stars with planetary systems, an absolute necessity for a stellar civilization in a galaxy where (so our astronomers theorize) only one star in 200,000 may have planets. This locator and the resurrection machine were the first missions of the revived human when he disappeared; with them in his possession, he could not only resurrect the rest of the human race but it would make possible the galactic civilization the race could not found before. The aliens remain a menace; they can bring down destruction on earth before the race is ready if they can get the news back. But the man tricks the aliens into leaving and finally destroying themselves in the belief that they are keeping their devices from him.

A slightly different type of story, one that might best be described as gentle satire touched with sentiment, is Robert Moore Williams's "Robot's Return," which describes an expedition of robots to a desolate earth and its attempts to solve the riddle of the death of the world in an effort to discover the mysterious origin of the robots themselves.[37] Anthropomorphism gets a few subtle digs in the robots' efforts to find metal forebears and their attempts to trace a line of descent from simple machines to themselves, but finally they are forced to the conclusion that chemical life must have built them.[38]

Arthur C. Clarke's "Rescue Party" contains the greatest amount of that somewhat illogical glow of pride in humanity described above. The author postulates a galactic civilization, led by a race that has been lords of the universe since time began and composed of every race, of sufficient civilization, in the galaxy. These races have constituted themselves as guardians of life in the galaxy and inspect each solar system once every million years. But in the "incredibly short time" of 400,000 years, intelligent life has appeared on a planet of a sun about to become a nova. A huge spaceship is sent to rescue what members of the race remain, but they arrive on earth to find the land already burned to a crisp, the world completely deserted—nothing remaining but an enigmatic tower apparently broadcasting aimlessly into space. They leave, just before the sun's explosion, still puzzled about the absence of people. Not until they are deep in space does it occur to them that the tower might have been broadcasting television pictures of the nova and its results to remnants of the race who have escaped in ships. Incredible as this sounds to the members of the rescue party, who have never heard of any race achieving space flight in less than three thousand years after the discovery of radio waves—much less in two centuries, they follow the line of direction of the radio beams and find thousands of huge reaction-rocket spaceships. The attempt to cross interstellar space would take centuries and only the descendants of the original voyagers could hope to reach their goal. The leader of the rescue party turns to his second in command:

> "You know," he said to Rugon, "I feel rather afraid of these people. Suppose they don't like our little Federation?" He waved once more towards the star-clouds that lay massed across the screen, glowing with the light of their countless suns.
> "Something tells me they'll be very determined people," he added. "We had better be polite to them. After all, we only outnumber them about a thousand million to one."
> Rugon laughed at his captain's little joke.
> Twenty years afterwards, the remark didn't seem so funny (517).[39]

The scope of the type is limitless, and so are its possibilities. If at times the stories seem somewhat inconsequential and without great meaning to our modern day, it is not because they have to be so. If science fiction's future lies anywhere, it lies in the opposite direction, toward greater meaning, greater significance. In this respect, the present type has, at least, great potentialities.[40]

A Future Being

The plot form of a future being in an alien environment has the advantage of wider scope over the other three main subtypes of this category (with the possible exception of that just preceding, an alien in a human environment in the future): there are more environments conceivably available to a future being than to one in the present or the past (the word "being" is used as more inclusive—in most cases translate "man"). Science fiction, with its lack of restrictions, can, of course, make all environments available to modern man, but the realistic tradition of modern writing in the field has cut out many such possibilities in recent years. To offset this advantage, however, there is the disadvantage of lessened reader identification: the farther the protagonist is removed from modern man the more difficult becomes the problem of securing the necessary empathy. This can be, and usually is, remedied to some extent by skillful writing, but it can never hope to achieve the completeness of that secured when modern man is the subject. It is, nevertheless, a form which is coming into more and more popularity because of the scope and opportunities it affords.

A Future Being in the Past

The past (our past) has seldom been used as an environment for a future being and for good reasons: little can be gained by using a future being when modern man would do just as well. Bypassing the modern era entirely, making that much more difficult the always difficult problem of securing empathy, can only be justified by results that more than compensate for the drawbacks. The usual reason for such plots is to place the story in a period in which time travel is more plausible, but it is doubtful if that reason alone is sufficient justification. There have, consequently, been few stories for this type in modern science fiction, and those which have been written have been principally attempts at wringing humor from interference in historical events of the past.

Such as series of stories by Noel Loomis, under the pseudonym Benj. Miller, ran for a time in *Thrilling Wonder Stories* a few years ago, describing the adventures of a reporter for a newspaper which specializes in stories and pictures of the great events of the past.[41] The reporter is assisted by a robot whose chief function is to act as an advance agent; he is supposed to organize the event for greatest effectiveness, but he usually achieves only confusion by introducing anachronisms and commercial enterprise. One such story was "Monster from the West" in *Thrilling Wonder* February 1949. The series was not particularly effective.[42]

Other stories written apparently around this plot type have actually derived much of their interest from the paradoxes of time travel.

A Future Being in the Present

A future being in the present has been a favorite plot for satire as long as the concept of time travel has been accepted. Olaf Stapledon's *Last Men in London*, a companion volume to his *Last and First Men*, is an example of the satirical use of this type. The viewpoint is that of a future man on Neptune who projects his mind into that of an English child about the time of World War I and grows up with him. The future provides an excellent vantage point for judging the manners, mores, and civilization of modern man.[43]

But stories of this type are not necessarily satirical; in some, using the theory of probable times, men of the future come back to the present to insure the occurrence of some event upon which their time stream or their personal existence depends. In others, a man who is living a few years or decades in the future is projected, usually accidentally, into the past, which is our present. He attempts to change the sequence of events that led up to his catastrophe, but, like Oedipus, he finds that his efforts to escape his fate only make it certain.[44]

One story which eschews such a fatalistic attitude is H. Beam Piper's "Time and Time Again," whose protagonist is a man injured in an atomic explosion in a war in 1975. He suddenly finds himself in 1945 as a boy again; after discarding the idea that he has been dreaming, he works out the theory that a man is totally existent throughout every moment in his life span and that in unconsciousness the mind moves backward or forward to some prior or subsequent moment, forgetting when it wakes or having the memory buried in the subconscious. Somehow the subconscious barrier didn't work in the hero's case. He discovers that the future is not immutable; if it can be changed, the hero, with his knowledge, determines to prevent World War III. Funds can be raised with his memory of future sporting results and then:

> "About 1950, we start building a political organization, here in Pennsylvania. In 1960, I think we can elect you President. The world situation will be crucial, by that time, and we had a good-natured nonentity in the White House then, who let things go till war became inevitable. I think President Hartley can be trusted to take a strong line of policy. In the meantime, you can read Machiavelli."
>
> "That's my little boy, talking!" Blake Hartley said softly. "All right, son: I'll do what you tell me, and when you grow up, I'll be president.... Let's go get supper, now" (341).[45]

In still other stories, modern man's inability to understand until too late the aims and psychology of visitors from the future is stressed—his inability to comprehend or appreciate the mental patterns, the culture, even the physical differences which have molded the human race into something altogether different from modern man, so different, in fact, as to be almost as alien as visitors from Mars or Sirius. One such story is Henry Kuttner and C. L. Moore's "Vintage Season," in which the problem is first of all to fathom the origins of strangers who have come to rent the house of a modern man and the origin of other strangers who fight for possession of the house. They seem to be typical tourists except that the objects of their curiosity are unknown and without interest to others; their dress is odd, their furnishings and amusements odder. Once it has been determined that they are visitors from the future, the question changes to why. The answer, when it comes, is shocking: the visitors from the future are tourists, touring time while they tour earth, sampling the most perfect seasons ever found—autumn (Chaucer says April) making the pilgrimage to Canterbury with Chaucer, winter at Charlemagne's coronation in Rome in 800, May in the present. But the last tragic revelation is to come—the month ends with the falling of a meteor on the town, followed by a virulent plague, a work of destruction for which the house is a perfect vantage place. There must be something wrong with a race, the protagonist, dying of the plague, reflects, which can treat such a disaster as a spectacle, which is satisfied to do nothing but tour time as mere onlookers. He painfully scribbles a note, warning others of these visitors, hoping that sometime they can be caught and forced to change the probabilities, but the house is dynamited in an effort to halt the spread of the plague.[46]

This type of story has great potential power, some of which has been revealed in Kuttner and Moore's work. What has the future to say about the present? What has the present to say about the future? In the answers to these questions lies drama and significance. Can the past be changed? Can the future be altered? Here lies a fundamental philosophic question which the past has speculated upon and science fiction can present in a dramatic and memorable fashion for the first time or solve fictionally. The possibilities are endless and important, and they have never been plumbed to the depths. There seems, consequently, promise for better stories of this classification in the future.

A FUTURE BEING ON A STRANGE PLANET

A future being, as we have observed, has a wider scope than a modern man, even in science fiction, and it is more believable that a future being should reach the planets and the stars beyond the planets. There have been stories in which modern man achieved this, but it strains reader credulity that even the adjacent planets should be available in the near future. But the sky is definitely not the limit for a future being—neither the sky nor the solar system nor the galaxy.

Stories of this classification range from the purely adventurous through descriptions of strange life forms and cultures to reflections on human nature in contact with a strange environment. Some of the worst and some of the best stories in science fiction are of this type, and the best include some that have shown the most promise for the future of science fiction.

Eric Frank Russell, who seems to take great delight in writing about strange life forms, has a story of this type in "Symbiotica." In this work, an exploratory mission is sent by spaceship to a planet whose inhabitants have followed the vegetable rather than the animal path of evolution; the efforts of the crew to solve the riddle of the situation form the structure of the story. They find, finally, that the life forms of the planet are symbiotic, each being sharing in the life of the others, contributing something and gaining something.[47]

A favorite menace of the future is the alien race with strange, almost incomprehensible powers, which mankind meets as it expands across the galaxy. One remnant of such a race is found in A. E. van Vogt's "Black Destroyer," a creature with several extra senses who lives on a certain life substance associated with bone phosphorous. It is telepathic and can control and broadcast energy—powers which would have made his race masters of the universe except for one thing: its planet was the only one in its system and the jump directly to interstellar space flight was too great to accomplish unaided. But with the coming of the expedition of human scientists, an advanced spaceship is available, and the creature, acting with all the cunning of its cat-like being, gets taken aboard ship. Once there, with his incredible powers, he soon gets control of the engine room, and, when the ship takes off, constructs a small spaceship and escapes. Without experience in the strange, new environment of space and without knowledge of its laws, he experiences some baffling, frustrating phenomena: the speed he is making back toward his own planet is not sufficient to overcome the momentum imparted by the speed of the original spaceship away from it, and he sees the planet and even the sun dwindle and disappear. Van Vogt also presumes that earth science has developed a force of "anti-acceleration," a means of neutralizing acceleration; when the humans apply this to their ship, it appears to the cat being that their ship has disappeared (as it stops in space and the small ship continues outward) and then appeared beside his own. It is too much for the already strained powers of the creature; he commits suicide.[48]

Ray Bradbury's Martian stories are an example of something different in the plot form and in science fiction itself, something which, if they are as influential as they deserve to be, presages the start of a new kind of character exposition and development in the genre. His stories, somewhat unrelated in their original form, have been given a continuity in their collected version which tells, in its entirety, the story of man's conquest of Mars and the mutual effects of man on the planet and the planet on men.[49] Although

Part Two—"Through Caverns Measureless to Man" 89

his total output seems somewhat uneven and he occasionally lets his enthusiasms and his mood pictures carry him to excesses or in unproductive directions (as in his latest series on the banning of fantasy and the burning of books in the future, "The Fireman," which turns his unusually—for science fiction—lifelike human characters into abstract allegorical symbols),[50] Bradbury's Martian stories are almost uniformly good, and they form, perhaps, the most significant single contribution to science fiction in recent years.[51]

To cite one example, Bradbury describes, in "—And the Moon Be Still as Bright," the fourth expedition to Mars and the first that was successful; the crude, earthy reactions of the crew in the presence of the strange silence, the fairy cities, and the recently dead, peaceful civilization of Mars; and the effect on one sensitive man, Spender, of the crew's irreverence. The news of the finding of Martian bodies, dead of chicken pox caught from the first expeditions, is received by the crew with nonchalance, but it strikes Spender with sudden melancholy, and he watches with disgust the crew getting vulgarly drunk. Spender finally walks off into the hills and stays until he can read the Martian language, until he has become saturated with Martian culture, philosophy, psychology. Then he comes back:

> "Well," said Spender, "I've found a Martian."
> The men squinted at him.
> "Up in a dead town. I didn't think I'd find him. I didn't intend looking him up. I don't know what he was doing there. I've been living in a little valley town for about a week, learning how to read the ancient books and looking at their old art forms. And one day I saw this Martian. He stood there for a moment and then he was gone. He didn't come back for another day. I sat around, learning how to read the old writing, and the Martian came back, each time a little nearer, until on the day I learned how to decipher the Martian language—it's amazingly simple and there are picture-graphs to help you—the Martian appeared before me and said, 'Give me your boots.' And I gave him my boots and he said, 'Give me your uniform and all the rest of your apparel.' And I gave him all of that, and then he said, 'Give me your gun,' and I gave him my gun. Then he said, 'Now come along and watch what happens.' And the Martian walked down into camp and he's here now."
> "I don't see any Martian," said Cheroke.
> "I'm sorry."
> Spender took out his gun. It hummed softly. The first bullet got the man on the left (79).

Spender hopes to kill off the crew in order to delay indefinitely man's conquest and inevitable vulgarization of Mars, but he is finally tracked down and killed, dying with the realization that, though he does not regret them, his actions were only a gesture.

The fictional exploitation of the totally strange environment of another planet has only just begun. The trend is away from the acceptance of a strange planet in its purely physical effects as merely a convenient and exciting new stage setting for adventure or as a transplanted earth for acting out purely human dramas. A strange planet will have sociological, psychological, philosophical effects on its human conquerors, effects whose implications are probably far more significant than those of any physical difficulties or limitations and which can cast a valuable light on the basic nature of humanity itself. Bradbury has shown some of the possibilities implicit in the plot type, and other authors have ventured recently into this hitherto almost untouched field. But the plot type is just opening up; it is wide open, and the results may be the most rewarding of any story type in science fiction.

A FUTURE BEING IN SPACE

Space is, of all environments, perhaps the most difficult to write about, for the simple reason that space is, by definition, the absence of environment. It is—emptiness; it is the most complete isolation possible. There is only nothing and not-nothing, and the not-nothing is, like the planets set like jewels upon the breast of infinity, the universe. But where the planets have the protection of miles upon miles of atmosphere to soften the harsh blackness of nothing to a soft, innocent blue, man in space has about him only a barrier of, at best, a few inches or feet of steel. Which is why, no doubt, there have been few stories in which the central plot factor has been man as an alien in the environment of space.

That there have been a few underscores the courage of science fiction to tackle anything; that there have been few successful attempts underscores the difficulty of the problem. As a general rule, space, in stories of space travel, is treated like any other medium through which, over which, or under which men have been transported; it is recognized as a different medium, it is true, and efforts are made to give it an illusion of difference. The descriptions are usually stock, however: the velvet blackness sprinkled with unwinking myriads of stars, the sun undimmed splendor with all its prominences and spots visible to the naked eye, the dim, dark reaches of infinity. Only on occasion has something new been offered in the way of response to this most difficult of all environments.

Usually, too, space as an environment is offered as only a part of a work. Something significant is offered in this way by Jack Williamson in *Seetee Shock* with a description of a single, space-suited man seated on a small machine in space:

> The void leered. Implacable hostility flattened itself against the frosty dark, waiting the time to strike. Shocking danger fled away from him into the sucking emptiness, and cunningly eluded him, and ruthlessly returned. Timeless peril watched forever, with the cruel, cold eyes of the stars...

"Back little man—better go back!"

The only sound his ears could hear was the faint hiss of oxygen from the regulator valve under his jaw, but his private hopes and terrors turned that thin susurration into a warning voice, whispering unceasingly out of the airless, soundless spatial night.

"Back, human being," it jeered. "Your place is Earth. You weren't designed for space. You and your puny kind are too feeble to exist here, and far too foolish to use the deadly toys you're grasping for... [3].[52]

Another contribution is made by Robert Heinlein in "Universe," in which the isolated aspect of space travel is translated into a concept of cosmogony and a huge spaceship becomes, for its lost generations, the universe in its entirety. The tearing down of that cosmogony, and the theology and society that grew up to support it, is the work of the main part of the story, and the first look at the stars outside with the accompanying realization that the universe is not measureable, not enclosed within steel walls, is an event of soul-shaking significance.[53]

There have been too few of such sensitive reactions to the possibilities of such an environment; the plot type has great potentialities, and its exploitation will result in stories of perhaps permanent literary value. The environment is infinitely provocative because it is, of all environments the most completely alien.

In the next three main subdivisions of "plots of circumstance" the characters are in a familiar environment—their own.

Chapter Two: Modern Man in the Modern World

The plot type of "modern man in the modern world" is a favorite of current science fiction, its popularity assisted by the distribution chart, which shows that more stories (50) fall under this classification than under any other similar category. One does not have far to look to find the reasons why this should be so. There is an immediacy about such a situation which translates itself into heightened reader identification and consequent interest; the world described is a familiar one, and the problems presented are often as real to the reader as they are to the characters. It adds up to peculiarly effective realism when well done; it presents a fictional problem, whether with a counterpart in the physical world or not, as urgently as possible. It is the form which is best adapted to political, social, and psychological observations and analyses.

The popularity of the type was greater a few years ago than it is today: in the interim authors almost wrote the vein out. From the period beginning in the late 1930s to about three years ago, the plot form, the world situation, and the growing realism in science fiction combined to give these stories their power and appeal. While doing so, they also gave science fiction a reputation for prophecy through its pre-Hiroshima stories of atomic fission (a reputation which will be discussed at more length under the second subsection of this classification, "a modern man in the modern world facing problems raised by new technology." After Hiroshima, however, there came such a spate of stories of atomic bombs, atomic cataclysms, and atomic wars that the editorial ban described in the first section of this work was clamped down upon the type. The flood diminished, although a well-written story on the atom will still find a place in any magazine, and other themes under this classification go on with relatively unchanged vigor.

The type presents a minor writing problem in that, if the time is strictly today, the lack of common knowledge of the event described must be explained in some way. Sometimes this is done by placing the event in some secluded section of the world, such as the polar regions; more often, by ascribing some reason for lack of circulation of the news, such as a need for secrecy, the disappearance of evidence, or the natural incredulity of the human species. Most often, however, the problem is solved by placing the occurrence just a few years in the future, when trends whose course is now undetermined have come to a point of decision—the stories become, in other words, prophetic fiction.

It is obvious from this discussion that the phrase "modern world" has a certain elasticity; plus or minus a few years, the story still falls under this classification. It should be recognized, as well, that older stories whose fictional time is contemporaneous with that of the author are also of this category. The decision as to whether a story belongs to this type, however, or to that of "a future being in a future world" must be made more on subjective grounds than on a strict time basis: if the setting is substantially as we know it today, if there have been no inventions or industries impossible to our science or engineering ability today, the story is modern.[54]

The subdivisions of this classification have been selected on a different basis than those of the preceding major type—"a being in an alien environment." There, the nature of the environment changed and became the most important single element in determining the nature of the story; here, the environment is constant and the nature of the problem is varied. On that basis the classification was subdivided into—modern man in the modern world: 1. Facing a continuing problem; 2. Facing a problem raised by new technology; 3. Facing problems in the mental and social fields; 4. Facing problems of a new war; 5. Facing problems introduced from a. the past, b. another dimension, c. another world or space, or d. the future; 6. Facing a change in natural conditions; and 7. Facing new natural phenomena.

These divisions are, of course, open to argument. Although an effort has been made for all-inclusiveness, there may have been a few problems overlooked, or there may be a few stories which will not classify properly. All subdivisions, moreover, do not carry the same theoretical weight and some seem to include a wider field than others, but each covers a segment of the field which seems individual and distinctive. This much seems certain, however: the "problem" line of attack appears to be most productive and significant.

Facing a Continuing Problem

A continuing problem, in this case, is used in the sense of a problem which has its roots in human nature or in a tendency to apply an old answer to a new problem—or which stems, in fact, from any of the human traits of thought or emotion which have been responsible for the less praiseworthy aspects of our world. All stories dealing with human characters must contain it is true some elements of these human problems, but the decision must rest upon whether these elements occupy a significant position in the story. Usually these factors are allied to those of some other type to make a composite story, although occasionally the "continuing problem" portion is so strong as to completely overshadow the other. Often the human trait is tacked on to the end as a reflection—as in the frequent observations on over-skepticism in modern humanity, as in Boucher's "Expedition" above.

One example in which the "continuing problem" is strong is Clifford D. Simak's "Lobby." The aspect of human nature that presents the problem is the power hunger of entrenched interests or, to put it another way, the desire of those in power to stay in power, by illegal means if necessary, despite the public welfare. In the not-too-distant future, the story develops, a strong power lobby is fighting the development of atomic power. No help can be expected from the limited strength of a world committee. In an effort to discredit atomic experiments, the lobby blows up the experimental atomic plant, killing a hundred men. The problem is presented: armed with proof of the lobby's part in the explosion, should those concerned try to bring the lobby to justice and make it pay for its crimes? The story insists that this would solve nothing. Instead, the criminals are permitted to go free after they make restitution, turn over existing power installations, and permit atomic power to be given to the people. (This is, of course, an example of science fiction's pragmatism: results are the only sound criteria; ethics are only valuable when they secure the desired results.) At this point the world committee can step into real authority with the administration of atomic power, giving the committee time to build gradually toward a government in which men trained in governing and who make a profession of good government can run the world scientifically. The conclusion, of course, may not be altogether sound, but the principles upon which the story is based may be argued with some justification.

A story discussing the atomic problem from a slightly different viewpoint is Philip Wylie's "Blunder," which points out one of the possible disastrous consequences of the worldwide answer of secrecy to the atomic question—the answer that Campbell has called "unsatisfactory."[55] In "Blunder," two scientists, necessarily working alone since publication of atomic speculation is forbidden or endlessly delayed, prepare to conduct an extensive experiment in the fission of bismuth to produce usable power. They set off a chain reaction bismuth bomb in a secluded and abandoned Norwegian mine, which is close to the sea; they expect it to last for centuries, the sea water producing superheated steam which may be harnessed to generate cheap and abundant electricity. But, thousands of miles away, the experts who could have pointed out the errors in the experimenters' equations are just reading their paper, long delayed, and before they can overcome secrecy, regulations, and censorship, the experiment has begun and in less than one-nineteenth of a second the earth is an expanding sphere, heated to trillions of degrees.

Such stories as these are, of course, mixtures; they are not pure. A year ago I would have said that I had yet to see a completely pure example. I would have said that I don't know exactly what it would be about, but I know what it would be like. It would have no new inventions or new uses of present inventions. There would be no wars or threats of war or any other unusual circumstantial occurrence. The story would deal completely with human impulses and the human mind. Ray Bradbury has come closest to this in some of his work, but his stories are placed in the future. Perhaps the story cannot be written, I would have said; perhaps, if it were written, it would not be science fiction. But if someone were to overcome the difficulties and write such a story, it might be a tremendous influence on the development of science fiction.

Now, fortunately, I cannot say these things with complete justice. Fritz Leiber's "Coming Attraction," while not completely a pure example of the type and while it does not fulfill all the requirements described above, comes closer to being what I called for than anything yet written. While being true science fiction and in the true science fiction realistic tradition today, it concentrates on the exclusively human factors of the story almost to the exclusion (in effect, at least) of all else and brings to science fiction those techniques of characterization and symbolism which it has needed to make it richer and more communicative on all levels.[56]

"Coming Attraction" tells the story of a visiting Englishman in a New

York which has been hit but not destroyed by a hydrogen bomb attack in World War III. The war is over but the armament race between the two crippled giants of the world, the United States and Russia, continues. They are both trying to establish bases on the moon from which they can launch guided missiles. All this, however, is merely background; the story concerns itself with the emotional and psychological effects on the citizens of New York, which manifest themselves in various symbolic mores and fads. The guilt and insecurity of the people expresses itself in the following ways: The women mask their faces and leave other parts of their bodies bare, so that a bare face seems indecent. Youthful gangs in turbine-powered cars roam the streets and cast out hooks to catch women's skirts. Religionists sing anti-sex songs; advertising signs, which have been forbidden the use of female face and form, use sexually suggestive lettering. Small, wiry men wrestle large, young, and attractive women in public exhibitions; the male wrestlers are idolized, and their masculine admirers don't want them to have a girl. But they are often beaten, and they must have girls upon whom to work out their sadistic frustration.

The Englishman becomes fascinated by a masked girl, infatuated by the beauty he feels must lie behind the mysterious mask. She is entangled with one of the small wrestling men and pleads for a passport with which to go to England, but it is all pretense. In a final scene she lashes out at the Englishman with her dagger finger caps,[57] cuddles her little wrestler, and croons that he will be able to hurt her afterwards. The Englishman tears her mask away:

> I really don't know why I should have expected her face to be anything else. It was very pale, of course, and there weren't any cosmetics. I suppose there's no point in wearing any under a mask. The eyebrows were untidy and the lips chapped. But as for the general expression, as for the feelings crawling and wriggling across it—
> Have you ever lifted a rock from damp soil? Have you ever watched the slimy white grubs?
> I looked down at her, she up at me. "Yes, you're so frightened, aren't you?" I said sarcastically. "You dread this little nightly drama, don't you? You're scared to death."
> And I walked out into the purple night, still holding my hand to my bleeding cheek, No one stopped me, not even the girl wrestlers. I wished I could tear a tab from under my shirt, and test it then and there, and find I'd taken too much radiation, and so be able to ask to cross the Hudson and go down to New Jersey, past the lingering radiance of the Narrows Bomb, and so on to Sandy Hook to wait for the rusty ship that would take me back over the seas to England (85–86).

This story is an isolated example, of course, and its significance has probably not been generally recognized. But this single short story and Bradbury's Martian stories represent two of the most hopeful and pregnant possibilities of the future of science fiction. If the lines of development they have pointed out are followed up as they should be, science fiction will become not only a medium of significant content and comment but a literary medium for literary critics to reckon with.

Facing a Problem Raised by New Technology

From this type of story, as we noted above, science fiction derived the name of prophet, a title which Groff Conklin thinks is undeserved. The science fiction authors' ability to write about atomic fission as far back as 1940, he says, "only proves that they read the right science journals, in which the coldly scientific possibilities of the atom were described with accurate detail for them to pick up and embroider" (xvi). But Conklin wants to stretch the word "prophet" too far; it does not necessarily imply the possession of any mystic powers. That the science fiction authors had some scientific grounds for their stories is true (if they hadn't, the stories wouldn't have been science fiction); that they took these grounds and showed with a considerable amount of accuracy what they might develop into is prophecy. A great many persons, some in high places, could have read these early speculations on the problems, as well as the uses, of atomic fission with profit not only to themselves but also to the world.

Science fiction is engaged, in one segment of its personality, in the business of prediction, just as it indulges in flights of fancy and considerations of the fictional possibilities of relatively improbable events. It is the same sort of prediction as that produced by the Navy's gun directors, with an input of the known factors of the target's position, course, and speed, these directors compute mathematically the target's future position at any given time. This is prediction, and, subject to change in the target's course and speed, it is accurate prediction—its accuracy increased in recent years by the development of radar and other means of detection. Campbell suggests that there are, basically, two types of prediction:

> You can predict long-term trends; what man wants hard enough, somebody will eventually figure out.
>
> You can "predict" short-term trends by, actually, simply discussing a laboratory phenomenon as an engineering practice. Atomic bombs and radar, robot bombs, and radio-controlled planes, were all perfectly predictable. The function of science fiction is to consider what those inventions can, or could, do to people [Preface viii].

The remarkably accurate predictions of Robert A. Heinlein's "Solution Unsatisfactory" have been described in the first section of this work. This story was published in 1941, before the entry of the United States into World War II and several years before the start of the Manhattan Project. Cleve

Cartmill's "Deadline," published in 1944, created a different kind of stir. Written about a war on a mythical planet, the story describes an effort to capture or neutralize an enemy atomic bomb, a description so complete that it aroused the interest of the Military Intelligence. As a publisher's note to the story observed:

> "Deadline" appeared in the March 1944 issues of *Astounding Science-Fiction*. Within a few days agents of the Military intelligence approached the author and the office of the magazine demanding to know who, on the Manhattan Project, had been talking. It was explained that the technical data was based upon principles published in technical papers in 1940. As the Smyth Report says, "Looking back on the year 1940, we see that all the prerequisites to a serious attack on the problem of producing and controlling atomic power were at hand." The Military Intelligence was persuaded that to suppress such discussions of atomic energy as had consistently appeared in this magazine would be more of a give-away than to leave them alone (*Best of Science Fiction* 67).[58]

Another story of atomic fission, this time not of atomic bombs or atomic wars but of a power plant using atomic fuel, is Lester Del Rey's "Nerves," published originally in early 1942. The story describes a runaway experiment that threatens a cataclysmic explosion, told from a medical viewpoint with the careful attention to detail and accuracy which makes the contrast between the subject matter of science fiction and its realistic technique so effective. The story line itself is too long to summarize, but the picture of the exploding section of the large plant with its semi-molten mass of radioactive material, the desperate infirmary measures, the surgery, is presented with almost reportorial clarity and detail. Again, perhaps, prediction.[59]

The technically prophetic type of story seems firmly established in the science-fiction repertoire. It is doubtful if there are any significant advances in the type, but it already has been well exploited—its beginnings reaching back at least as far as Jules Verne—and its form is settled. There will, very likely, be many more stories in this vein, although they will seldom (with the exception of the general interest magazines, the movies, and the radio which are trying to catch up with the science fiction field) have atomic fission as their central issue. They will be about something else, some phenomenon, as Campbell suggests, still in the laboratory or just reported in the scientific journals—if secrecy does not mutilate the pages.

Facing Problems in the Mental and Social Fields

The mental and social fields have been lumped together for two reasons. The first is that they are, after all, closely connected. Psychology is the science of the individual mind; sociology is the not yet perfected science of the group mind. But there is a better reason: the mental and social fields, although favorites of early fantasy writers, have been largely neglected by modern science fiction authors until recently—so recently that Groff Conklin was complaining in 1946 of the death of stories of this type.

Even more recent anthologies have included no pure stories of this classification, as is shown in the distribution chart, but they are gradually beginning to appear. It is not entirely necessary, contrary to what Campbell suggested in his definition quoted in the early pages of this section, that a science of sociology be developed. Advanced in our knowledge of psychology or sociology, new applications of present knowledge, or steps toward the development of a science are sufficient. Two such stories appeared in the August 1949 *Astounding Science-Fiction*.

One, John D. MacDonald's "Trojan Horse Laugh," combines psychology and sociology into a story about a new kind of war sabotage. A group, calling itself "Happiness, Incorporated," has developed a method of adjusting individual emotion cycles so that they are similar to and coincide with those of their family, social and community group. It is supposed to eliminate all types of emotional conflict and make family and industrial planning possible, with the knowledge of when everyone is going to be happy and when everyone is going to be mildly depressed. The group is ostensibly conducting an experiment in a number of test communities throughout the country, and, for a brief time, everything seems to work well—until fifty-one percent of each city is adjusted. Then it is found that the adjusted emotional cycles reinforce each other so that the happy moments become manic in their frenzy and the gloomy moments become suicidal, a condition affecting by contagion the unadjusted members of the community. It is just at that moment, with urban centers all over the country populated by uncontrollable manic-depressives that the enemy whose plot this has been chooses to strike.

Peter Phillips's "P-Plus" puts the emphasis on psychology in a story about the effects of the invention of a machine which increases the potency of the personality until it becomes as magnetic as those of the great men of history. The "pep pill" which makes a rabbit the equal of a wolf is produced "by electronically reducing the resistance offered at the synaptial junctions to the spread of activation of behavior patterns, thus more closely integrating the personality and realizing potentialities previously confined to cerebral processes" (119). The process is startling in its effects—formerly ineffective personalities becoming irresistibly successful in any undertaking. The difficulty arises when the process has become so widespread that almost everyone has been treated—and the wolf has taken a "pep pill," too. The situation has returned to what it originally was. Phillips seems to be fond of this sort of story; his "Dreams are Sacred," describing a method of curing schizophrenia by injecting the mind of an outsider into the mind of the patient to "louse up his dreams," has already been discussed in the first section of this work.

The mental and social fields are, at this time, wide open for exploitation. Their surfaces have merely been touched, and, as appreciation of their possibilities grows along with possible increase in scientific knowledge of the workings of the individual and group minds, many more stories along this line can be hopefully expected. It would be an interesting field for an author who is also a psychologist, a sociologist, or an anthropologist, and, indeed, the August 1950 *Astounding Science-Fiction* contains a story by Dr. Bernard I. Kahn (an anthropologist?), called "A Pinch of Culture," which describes a savage, unethical civilization whose fictional genesis was the description of the Doubian culture (Dobu Island, off the southern coast of New Guinea) in Ruth Benedict's *Patterns of Culture*.

FACING PROBLEMS OF A NEW WAR

Wars are the eternal theme of science fiction (even if they are in a temporary and mild decline due to an overabundance of war stories following World War II), just as, it seems, they are the eternal theme of the world itself.[60] Wars or the threats of wars or the memories of wars are never long absent from one or the other, especially in the last decade. Fictional wars have the added attraction to the writer in that they provide the epitome of effort and interest; there is nothing larger or more fraught with general peril except a bigger war. Wars, consequently, grew bigger and more widespread in science fiction as the genre developed. The type began with nation against nation and grew in geometric progression from a planetary war to planet against planet, solar system against solar system, star empire against star empire, until it reached almost its ultimate in E. E. Smith's galaxy against galaxy in his *Lensman* series. All that remains is universe against universe. Weapons grew with the wars until in the largest conflicts mere planets were destroyed with a single bomb or were maneuvered as projectiles, greater and greater energy weapons were "invented," greater and greater energy shields were developed to counteract them: tractor beams, pressor beams, negative matter bombs, negative space bombs, vibration, gravity, light, time, mind, sub-atoms, super-atoms, and so on *ad infinitum*—all these were developed as weapons and thrown into the struggle.

But these pleasant devices belong to the future and the modern world, even in science fiction, must limp along without them. The fictional wars of the near future have developed along more tangible and more successful lines. Questions of an atomic war have been seriously and soberly debated, although aggression without atomic weapons has had its share of stories. In these stories some very pertinent things about the world situation have been said; they have, in effect, provided a public forum on the atomic question. In almost all of them an attempt has been made to find some solution to the problem of power politics, armed aggression by a superior enemy, and survival in an atomic age.[61] They are a far cry from earlier pictures of war as a possibly undesirably but unendurable state of affairs.

One of the most cogently reasoned stories of a possible future situation is Chan Davis's "The Nightmare," published in *Astounding* in 1946, when some sort of atomic control still seemed possible. In a world a few years in the future, Davis supposes, the Security Council has been given supervision over all atomic piles, plus sizable military intelligence forces; all nations have atomic knowledge and facilities. Sabotage bomb attack is the only possibility until open warfare breaks out, at which time the Security Council would be defied and rocket-atomic war would start. One answer is decentralization of industry and population, but the terrific inertia of our civilization would not permit one nation to compete economically with the rest of the world if it undertook such a step—and while it was in the middle of such a process, it would be easy prey to a sudden attack. So, city-wide radar screens and atomic search procedures are instituted to prevent atomic materials from being slipped in and a bomb assembled. In such a situation, guards come upon evidence of the preparation of such a bomb and foil the attempt just in time. But—again in science fiction's pragmatic approach—they allow the saboteurs to escape rather than capturing them and making identification of the responsible nation—and war—inevitable. The situation must remain as it is; decentralization now would so disorganize things that such a sabotage attempt would be unavoidably successful. The situation is a "nightmare"—but there is no other answer.[62]

Robert Heinlein's "Solution Unsatisfactory," discussed in the first section of this work, belongs in this category, as does Theodore Sturgeon's "Memorial," which describes the efforts of a scientist to initiate a chain reaction which will create a huge, radioactive pit lasting ten thousand years as a warning to mankind against atomic warfare. But the explosion results in immediate suspicions that the country is being attacked; the atomic war begins and the human race is destroyed.[63]

Will F. Jenkins's [Murray Leinster] "Symbiosis," while belonging under this classification, is a story of a slightly different nature. Jenkins envisions the bloodless conquest of a small European country whose citizens have been completely immunized so that they are able to establish a symbiotic relationship with the entire series of diplococcic germs. The germs are then spread among the conquered people who, though immune themselves, become carriers of a deadly plague to which the enemy soldiers fall easy victims.

One of the best of the atomic war stories is Theodore Sturgeon's "Thunder and Roses," which gives a thoughtful answer to the question: what should this country do if suddenly attacked and almost completely destroyed by atomic warfare? The country has more bombs than the rest of the world put together, but the sudden attack so poisons the atmosphere with radioactive carbon that the population of the whole hemisphere is doomed to a slow but certain death, a death which will spread as well, if not as completely, to the rest of the world. Should the United States retaliate in such a case? The answer Sturgeon gives is "no": it would be an act of useless vengeance that would completely sterilize the earth so that not a microbe or a blade of grass would grow. If the United States does not retaliate, a few sparks of enemy humanity will remain to possibly build again. And thus pragmatism may bear the strange fruit of mercy.[64]

This type of story has had an interesting, provocative, and possibly significant and important role in the recent past. After the temporary fatigue of the type has passed away, it will, doubtless, be of importance again—potentially of even greater importance when its possibilities become realized generally. And, of course, the general interest magazines and publications will regale their readers with many such stories—as, indeed, they have already begun to do.

Facing Problems Introduced from the Past

This classification differs from "an ancient being or primitive man in a modern human environment," whose stories may sometimes be confused with the present type, in the viewpoint of emphasis. In this case, the center of reader interest and identification must be the modern man or man as they face the problem from the past.

Several methods have been used for making credible the entry of the past into the present. A frequent device is suspended animation of one sort or another, induced by sudden freezing, by enclosure in an energy sphere, by burial in the earth, by chemical means, by machine, and so forth. Occasionally a time machine figures in the story or an accidental passage through time, and eternal life for the visitant from the past has been used.

The problem from the past can be in the form of a man, a machine, an animal, an ancient being of strange form and powers, a plant, a seed—the list is endless. Almost without exception, the visitant is a menace to modern man; his or its unknown powers must be battled against in order to preserve the lives of the characters or the future of mankind itself. The thematic attitude expressed is, perhaps, that the past has had its opportunity and that the attempt to get a second chance and thereby rob humanity of its opportunity, however little it has made of it, is an act of horror and almost impious defiance of fate or the laws of nature. The necessary struggle, therefore, presents a fictional opportunity to reassess humanity, its advantages and disadvantages, its merits and demerits.

In one such story, P. Schuyler Miller's "The Chrysalis," archeologists find in Adirondack pre-ice remains, in a long shrine, the golden figure of a beautiful woman of a race like none that has existed in recorded history. On close examination, the scientists discover that there is no opening in the perfect figure: there are no pores, the mouth is sealed to the teeth, the hair blends into the scalp—but it is not a statue. Then the scientists try X-rays, and the figure splits, out of it coming a black humped form with shimmering, blazing wings. It kills four of them, although it is invisible in normal light. Then it flies from the room, leaving the survivors to wonder if it will die or breed in some strange way and return, mold once again its chrysalis in the shape of a beautiful woman, and scourge the earth.

H. P. Lovecraft's works were chiefly of this type. Although his stories tended to be more fantasy than science fiction, there almost always was some explanation, either stated or implied, even though it was often not credible. Lovecraft's modern world is a strange, sinister place of half-remembered superstitions and horrors, of decaying New England houses and degenerating New England families. And the conflict is always between the formless or indescribable, terrifying Elder Races (who were thrown "outside" a long time ago and are still trying to get back in to resume their dark pastimes) and modern men, who get their necessary knowledge from ancient, forgotten books of black magic and mythology. Lovecraft built up an entire mythology, half-old, half-new, to serve as a background for his stories and was one of the few to succeed in such an attempt. Shaver's "Mystery" is an example of what happens when the attempt fails.

Theodore Sturgeon in "Killdozer!" unearths a different holdover from the past when he describes the efforts of an eight-man crew to carve, as an experiment, all but the paving of an airstrip out of a Pacific island during the war. The men, supplied with a million dollars' worth of machinery, barely start work when they accidentally release a being confined millions of years in a perfect insulator built by a long-dead race as a weapon against an invading race of organized electrons, sentient and intelligent cloudforms. The being possesses intelligence, mobility, and a will to destroy, but little else. Its natural habitat or life medium is metal, and it invades and takes control of a bulldozer. The remainder of the story tells of the suspenseful efforts of the men to destroy the "killdozer" and its inhabitant, a battle between huge machines like carboniferous dinosaurs.

A final example is Campbell's "Who Goes There?" which was touched upon in the first section of this work. Here, in one of the most dramatic stories science fiction has produced, a scientific expedition chips a frozen monster from Antarctic ice—a monster which has the ability to absorb any kind of protoplasmic life and imitate it down to cell structure and thought. Refusing to believe that any highly organized being could survive millions of years of such freezing, the scientists melt the extraterrestrial monster from the ice. Only to have it come, horribly, to life. To its ability to eat and imitate any kind of protoplasm, it adds, they find, the ability to have as much matter left over as it began with, an ability which would enable it, if able to reach the populated sea, to conquer the world and people it with itself. At the moment, it is winter at the South Pole and there is nothing alive but the men and their animals (the latter are quickly killed), but when spring comes, birds will be flying in from the sea. The monster has imitated one or more of the men, they discover by a blood test which they hope will be definitive; the blood serum from the dog they have tried to immunize against human blood has been contaminated by monster blood, and one of the two men contributing to the test are surely monsters. The problem: how can these pseudo-men be detected? The tension builds as they glance sidelong at their neighbors, wondering if they are monsters, if they will spring now or sneak up in the night. They finally devise a test that works: any blood drawn from a monster becomes a separate entity and tries, selfishly, to crawl away from a hot needle, thus revealing that the owner of the blood is not human.[65]

There have been many excellent examples of this type of story in the history of science fiction, and there will probably be many more. It provides easy reader identification, suspense, drama, and it is well suited to many purposes, not the least of which is a philosophical consideration of mankind's position and future in relationship to his world and the universe.

FACING PROBLEMS INTRODUCED FROM ANOTHER DIMENSION

Dimensional intrusions into the modern world are not so common in science fiction as those from the past. Dimensional explanations, especially when men are not projected into the strange place, are always difficult; what explanations there are consist usually of suggestions and horrible hints that do no more than sketch in a shifting outline. Occasionally devices are used to effect the transfer, but usually it is done by some natural power peculiar to the dimensional being. The dimensions are seldom numbered; the source is not the fourth or fifth dimension but merely a strange place outside the ken of man. A favorite authority for this type of adventure is Charles Fort, with his accounts of mysterious happenings and strange visitations.

One such visitation is described in George Allan England's "The Thing from Outside," in which a party of Americans discover strange footprints in the far northern regions of Canada. Although they never see anything except the prints, which are etched in rock and eternally cold, they die one by one, killed by a "thing," they suppose, which uses their minds as men use the fur or bodies of animals. Only two of them escape, and of them, only one remembers.[66]

Donald Wandrei relates a story about another being from outside our world in "The Monster from Nowhere," which depends more on conventional notions of dimension. An exploring party (a favorite device of earlier science fiction stories, the reader will have realized by now) to a plateau in upper Peru discovers a thing that changes its shape as it sends apparently unconnected arms and objects into our three-dimensional world from its world of four. After killing three of the party's members, it is captured by the survivor, who manages to insert a metal pin through one of the pseudopods and bring it back to the United States. When the thing is revealed for inspection, however, it pulls loose, grabs the survivor of the party, and disappears with him.

A very effectively told story of entirely different emphasis is Henry Kuttner and C. L. Moore's "Call Him Demon," a quietly horrible tale of a household in which a "wrong uncle" is accepted by the adults as always having been there, while the children all realize that he is only acting. The children know that the uncle is only an imitative shell, an extension of a blood-hungry dimensional beast who "lives" in the cellar and whom they feed on raw meat to pacify in a strangely exciting new sort of game. In lieu of a better name, Kuttner suggests, "call him demon." But the youngest boy gets tired of the game and decides to end it. Knowing nothing of the reality of death, he skips the regular feeding of the beast when left alone in the house with the "wrong uncle" and his grandmother. The beast's hunger gets overpowering, and the only food available is the grandmother. The police come, as the boy knows they will, and take the uncle away where he—and his source in the cellar, unable to break the link—starves to death. The story ends: "No adult would have done what Bobby did—but a child is of a different species. By adult standards, a child is not wholly sane. Because of the way his mind worked, then—because of what he did, and what he wanted—Call him demon" (243).

This type of story does not have the possibilities of the problem from the past; dimensional beings, supposedly, have always been with us and able to encroach upon us. The danger is nothing new, therefore, and it can make but little comment upon the nature of mankind. It can suggest little more than that man is not the apex of creation that he considers himself, that there are now and always have been greater worlds and superior beings. Its use is fairly well limited, then, to stories that terrify, that suggest nameless horrors like the "things that go boomp in the night" of the old Scotch prayer. The type is, nevertheless, good for its purpose, even though that purpose borders closely on that of fantasy.

Facing Problems Introduced from Another World or Space

The plot form of the problem from another world or space has been an extremely popular one in recent years; the distribution chart shows seventeen stories in this minor classification. Scarcely a magazine comes out today which does not contain one or more of these stories in it. The reason why this should be so is fairly obvious: though the environment is familiar and thus secures immediate reader identification, the variety of problem which can be brought from other regions is unlimited. An immediate contrast is secured and an immediate alignment of conflicting forces. This type of story is more effective than that of the preceding two sections, problems from the past or another dimension, or the following section, problems from the future, because the means are more credible. The problem, the intruders, usually arrive by spaceship, a means of travel which science fiction—and a good section of the general public as well—believes is not only possible but, to a limited extent, probable in the next ten to fifty years. It is not the same with time travel, dimensional travel, suspended animation, and so on. The stories carry a touch of conviction which has, very likely, influenced the recent speculations about flying saucers.

Earlier writers, Voltaire in *Micromegas*, for instance, have used this plot for satirical purposes; occasionally science fiction does the same thing, but the use is not too frequent. Usually the type inspires one of a few recurrent themes. The first is the sense of wonder, exploited in other plot types as well: the "more things under heaven and earth…" sort of thing, the "that this should be true!" exclamation. Science fiction is, of course, practically committed to the belief in life on other worlds, although not necessarily, life on the planets of our solar system besides earth. It justifies its belief on mathematical grounds: it was Sir James Jeans, I believe, who computed that if planets were formed by the most coincidental means (the theory of the collision or near miss of suns) about one out of every 200,000 suns would have planets, which, with the uncounted billions of stars, would leave several million planetary systems scattered through the universe.[67] Surely, science fiction reasons, even if life itself is an accident and not a natural development, somewhere in those millions of planets the accident will have been repeated, probably a number of times. And, if so, some other races will be in advance of us, will have conquered space; what is more natural than that they should visit earth?

The second theme is one we have already encountered several times: man's over-skepticism. Science fiction has a natural hatred of skepticism—that type of skepticism, at least, which refuses to admit the possibility of any happening out of the ordinary; science fiction feels that it is that type of skepticism which refuses to take the genre seriously, that earthbound imagination which scoffs and will not willingly suspend its disbelief for the sake of a good story. Some stories exposing the dangers of over-skepticism concentrate on that factor alone, as in C. M. Kornbluth's "The Silly Season," which describes a series of unexplainable visitations of mysterious objects (like the flying saucers) every summer until the public and the newspapers refuse to put any credence in them—at which time the invaders strike. Other stories carry this theme over into an attack on man's provincial geocentricism, blasting it with the most unflattering comparisons possible.

The geocentric approach often leads into the theme of a community of worlds, a galactic federation, or what you will, a theme which envisions an earth on trial before it can join the superior, enlightened civilizations which roam the star fields at their pleasure. Earth usually fails the test because its social and psychological knowledge and control have failed to keep step with its scientific progress. Such a story is Morton Klass's "Invitation from the Stars," which includes an explanation of flying saucers and a decision by the galactic judge to purge the earth of its deadly impulses.

Occasionally invaders from other worlds are neutral or friendly, but most often they are ready and willing to take over the earth for their own purposes. One example of a friendly intruder is offered by Raymond F. Jones in "Correspondence Course." A visitor from another world is stranded on earth in a ship it cannot repair without outside help; by means of a correspondence course it imparts the necessary knowledge to a mechanic, who is then persuaded to join in a mutually beneficial symbiotic relationship in exchange for the gift of the power of space flight to mankind. A not-so-friendly invasion is described by Theodore Sturgeon in "The Sky Was Full of Ships." A man on trial for murder, in this story, tells a strange tale of being led, by the scientist he was supposed to have murdered, to a cave in which there was a machine for measuring atomic fission activity and a radio for transmitting the information into space. It had recorded and transmitted, they decide, the information about the first atomic bomb to a race on another planet so that they could interfere before man got too technologically dangerous. If that were the case, the coroner jokes, they—whoever they are—should be here by now. And they go out to find that the sky is full of ships.

Visitors from other planets come in all shapes and sizes in science fiction. In a story which belongs, properly, in the following subdivision (since it happens in the distant future), Raymond Z. Gallun's "Seeds of the Dusk," a spore drifts to earth from Mars, and, developing into intelligent though vegetable Martians, it conquers earth.[68] In Frank Belknap Long's "The Flame Midget," the alien, a microscopic, man-like creature of great powers, easily baffles efforts to destroy it after it announces that it is only the forerunner of its race from a distant planet. A visitor the size of a walnut and the shape of a tortoise, incredibly heavy, comes from beyond Sirius in John Russell Fearn's "Wings Across the Cosmos"; it is a female, the last of its race, and by means of cosmic rays, which it absorbs and wields, it converts a man into its own shape to be its mate.

The list could be extended indefinitely. The form itself is one of the best developed in science fiction; interesting, effective, and occasionally significant stories have been written in this form, and it has promise of even greater merit if it develops its thematic possibilities along new and perhaps more productive lines.

Facing Problems Introduced from the Future

From the future come all manner of things. Men of the future occasionally return to the present for various purposes: research, sightseeing, influencing a probable future, and so forth. But the most common problem to enter the modern world from the future is an object or a machine—of strange properties and incomprehensible design. These objects, used or misused by modern man, are usually projected into the present by accidental use of a time mechanism or inadvertent use of some other means of transportation that acts in such a way that a time displacement is affected. The most frequent story to result from such an accident is a grimly humorous one—the kind of grim humor which was largely originated and developed by and was the most common stock-in-trade of the late *Unknown Worlds*, the erstwhile and long-lamented companion fantasy magazine to *Astounding*.

Such a story is William Tenn's "Child's Play," which begins with the delivery of a mysterious box to a struggling lawyer, a box which opens and closes on command and which is stocked with jars of liquids and solids and unlikely looking machinery. The box, an instruction booklet informs the recipient, is a "Bild-A-Man" set, which carries the slogan "only with a Bild-A-Man can you build a man!" The table of contents for the set, which is intended for children between the ages of eleven and thirteen, is worth quoting:

I—A child's garden of biochemistry.
II—Making simple living things indoors and out.
III—Manikins and what makes them do the world's work.
IV—Babies and other small humans.
V—Twins for every purpose, twinning yourself and your friends.
VI—What you need to build a man.
VII—Completing the man.
VIII—Disassembling the man.
IX—New kinds of life for your leisure moments (249).

Such a table of contents is illustrative of one of the better techniques science fiction has worked out for giving a great deal of background material, exposition, and comment in as brief and subtle way as possible. The implications of the quotation above are so extensive as to call up a world, to evoke a different and rather frightening civilization—not completely, of course, but sufficiently to provide a logical basis for the existence of such a set (which is all the plot of the present story requires) and to imply comments upon it.

The lawyer begins experimenting with making simple living things, progresses to manikins, finally twinning a baby, while he discovers that the manufacturer listed on the set does not exist. He speculates about its possible origin in the future and hears reports of a tall, dark person looking for him. The girl he wants for himself chooses another person; he decides to twin her, but first he practices by twinning himself. The twin, however, rebels and insists on staying alive instead of being properly disassembled. At that point the dark stranger arrives and informs the two that he is a Census Keeper (what image does that evoke of a world in which such an official is necessary?) from the future. The package came from there by mistake, and one of the two must be disassembled. Each of the twins insists that he is the original; the Census Keeper decides in favor of the twin and begins to disassemble the lawyer.

Henry Kuttner and C. L. Moore have two stories of this type. In "The Twonky" a workman from the future hits a "temporal snag" and falls, dazed, into a modern factory that makes console radios. He begins to make his usual product, a twonky, camouflaging it to look like the radios being built around him; when he has finished, he remembers what has happened, finds the temporal snag, and returns to his own time. The twonky, however, is delivered to a couple who ordered a radio, and it begins to do strange and wondrous things. It first analyzes the psychological patterns of the husband, lights cigarettes, washes dishes, selects appropriate records, censors reading matter and diet, neutralizes imbibed alcohol, and generally acts as a monitor for all activity. On being threatened, it remolds thought processes and wipes out memories. In desperation, the couple attack the machine and are destroyed. The story ends with a new couple renting the furnished house, complete with twonky.[69]

"Mimsy Were the Borogoves" begins with a time experiment by a scientist in the far-distant future, which has mastered the art of crossing over to the fourth dimension to live. He sends back two loads of the toys his son had used to educate him to the crossing and now needs no longer; they are handy objects, and he needs something by which to determine the era to which they returned. Unfortunately, they do not come back; the scientist forgets about them, but the household in which the second load arrives does not. The two young children of the house begin to play with the strange toys, one of which is filled with little figures that perform activities dictated by the thoughts of the holder, another a tesseract strung with beads that can be maneuvered into another dimension. The toys are educational, but the education is not exactly what the parents would have asked for their children. The toys teach the children the things the future child needs to know: the ability to transfer himself into the fourth dimension. Eventually the toys are taken away, but it is too late; the minds of the children have already been conditioned. They find a mathematical formula for translating themselves into the fourth dimension in the first stanza of "Jabberwocky"; for Lewis Carroll (perhaps science fiction's favorite author for quotations) didn't invent *Through the Looking Glass*—he transcribed it from the stories and songs of the girl who found the first box of toys.[70]

This type has seldom been used for stories of particularly serious or significant nature, although there have been exceptions and there is no essential reason it should not be. When the object from the future precipitates a crisis, small or great, in the modern world, something very worthwhile may come out of it. In C. M. Kornbluth's "The Little Black Bag," for instance, a moral decision must be made as to the use and disposition of a bag of perfect, automatic, self-replenishing medical instruments and supplies from the future—and the wrong decision results in the deaths of the users and the withdrawing of the bag's powers.[71] On the whole, however, the plot form is now—and will perhaps continue to be—the basis for stories written and read for pleasure alone.

Facing a Change in Natural Conditions

A change in natural conditions is not a popular plot type in modern science fiction; such a change requires too great an upheaval or too great a coincidence. Two trends militate against the type: the realistic tendency we have noticed before and the desire of science fiction to keep the probabilities as high as possible. A change in natural conditions is neither realistic nor probable. Earlier authors had no particular desire to be realistic and probability was far from their minds—there are many stories, particularly novels, of this type in early science fiction; the same is true today of the adventure type of science fiction magazine, although to a lesser degree (they prefer, usually an active and animated antagonist).

The kind of change the older writers preferred was the cataclysm. The "rogue" planet which wanders through to a collision or near collision with earth,[72] the comet with its tail of poisonous gases, the great new flood that again covers the earth, the sun exploding into a nova or growing cool, the onset of a new ice-age or a new era of volcanic-earthquake activity—all or any were sufficient to set off an epic tale of courageous humanity battling against incredible odds. The form is a little too flamboyant, a little too grandiose, a little too indiscriminate for modern taste. The epic is out of style.[73]

One such cataclysm is described by Philip Latham in "N Day," which tells of an astronomer's discovery that the sun is going to become a nova in a few days and the reaction of the world to that discovery. A slower catastrophe is provided in H. F. Heard's "The Great Fog." In producing an edible mold, men slowly find that they have released a rampant growth which controls its own atmospheric conditions, collecting moisture around itself until first the valleys and then all the world is filled with a thick fog. The air separates out: below into a saturated atmosphere, above, where only peaks appear, into a cold, black world where unfiltered sunlight and cosmic rays make life impossible. In the dank but livable regions things rot and rust and normal civilization is impossible, but the fog turns out to be something of a blessing after all. War is impossible as well, the mold provides abundant food, and new arts and a gentler life are created. The Fog was a second flood to protect mankind from its own destructive impulses.

The form is decaying but persistent. It has served its purpose and might as well die a natural death, but it is as hard to kill off as Heard's mold, with all its natural appeal of great events and struggle epitomized. And so it will probably continue to exist in one form or another as long as science fiction is written and read.[74]

FACING NEW NATURAL PHENOMENA

There is a distinct resemblance between this type and the preceding one—but also a significant difference. New natural phenomena we have always had but have not recognized until now; it is not a change but a recognition. Scientists are engaged in this sort of activity constantly—unearthing new facts that reinforce their theories or cause them to revise or discard their old ones. A change in natural conditions is a different matter; it is something that upsets the entire scheme of things.

Most natural phenomena available to modern man in the modern world have been fairly well observed and reported in the last few centuries of scientific curiosity. If a science fiction author wishes, then, to suggest something new which has been missed, he must offer some reasonable explanation of why it has not been noticed before—not always an easy job. The usual method is to place the phenomenon in a not completely explored medium, such as the depths of the sea, the upper regions of the atmosphere, or secluded regions of the land surface (often bolstering this solution with folklore or superstition). Another method is to discuss phenomena which is still on the periphery of public or scientific acceptance, such as spiritualism or the little understood powers of the mind. Parapsychology (the "science" of using the mind directly to procure a result instead of working through the body) is the latest development to come into common use. In writing such stories, science fiction authors, as Campbell suggests in his definition, often predict the time when the branches of knowledge will have been developed into sciences.[75]

In "Magic, Inc.," for instance, Robert Heinlein predicts, in a slightly fantastic vein, a short time in the future when the secrets of magic will be rediscovered and its use will be common in business, government, and so forth.[76] A more classic example is H. G. Wells's "The Remarkable Case of Davidson's Eyes," in which a man is struck blind in our world and sees instead events which occur on the other side of the world, events which later prove to have actually happened.

Stories of this type are usually more successful when cast into the future (not falling under this category). There have not been too many of this type, then, as they often tend more toward fantasy than science fiction should. It is, all things considered, not too fertile or possible a field for stories whose scenes are laid in the modern day.

Chapter Three: A Past Being in the Past

This classification covers all stories in which the character or characters are in their own environment which itself is in our past. This does not include stories that are not in our past but were in the present at the time of writing. It does not include, either, stories in which time travel figures; most stories of such travel into the past naturally takes the viewpoint of the travelers, and the paradoxes of time travel have been covered under "a modern man in the past." Although it should, theoretically, include stories of the recent past, there is not much incentive to write such stories; I do not recall ever having read one. Recorded history is fairly complete; a writer would have to scratch hard to come up with an event of science fiction nature for which he could construct a plausible theory of why it is not common knowledge, an event, moreover, which could not just as well be placed in the present with, consequently, greater reader identification. The most common procedure, then, is to insert the story into a period in which recorded history is incomplete or non-existent, where mythology and folklore can be cited as partial evidence, where mysterious archeological remains or historical situations can be explained.[77]

The plot form as a whole is not particularly popular, especially among the better writers. Only one story was included in the five anthologies studied. It is not a fertile field, except when allied with some other plot type or when used as a part of a larger story of another type. Alone, the form has a tendency to degenerate into adventure for its own sake.

Plot subdivisions used in previous classifications must be discarded for this type: the past being, as we have noted, is in his own environment, and the problems he is concerned with are not those of advancing scientific knowledge. There are three basic reasons for writing a story of this type, other than that of entertaining. The first, and perhaps the most significant, is to describe a point of crisis in the development of the human race or of some other species native to earth.[78] The second is to describe a problem faced in the past that duplicates or casts light on a problem we face today. The third, and least important, is to describe a problem that has little or no bearing on our history or our present existence. These considerations seem to be most influential in determining the essential nature of the story, and this classification has been divided, consequently, into the following sections: 1. Facing problems important in the history of the race; 2. Facing problems similar to those faced today; 3. Facing problems of no significance to the modern world. These seem to be the most significant criteria.

FACING PROBLEMS IMPORTANT IN THE HISTORY OF THE RACE

The really important crises in the history of the human race occurred thousands of years ago—and by important I mean those decisions and discoveries that determined whether mankind was to become the dominant life form on earth or was to remain so. Decisions in recorded history have not been so crucial: they have determined occasionally whether man will become more dominant, more often whether he will dominate his fellow man. (One of the chief drawing cards of science fiction, of course, is that it can, logically, present such important crises in a fictional form.) The magnitude of other decisions, though more nebulous than man's dominance, cannot be exaggerated—such decisions as: the combination, through some as yet undetermined agency, of chemicals into a one-celled body possessing life; the development of that cell into multicellular life and so on through the fish; the decision, forced though it may have been, of a fish or group of fish to use their fins or flippers to crawl out upon dry land, to develop lungs, and so forth through the gamut of the animal kingdom until *homo sapiens* appeared on the scene. The decisions of mankind which have determined his development seem minor in comparison, but they can be and have been dramatized in science fiction: the discovery of fire and the bow and arrow, the decision of early man to abandon the hunt and till the fields, the domestication of wild animals, the discovery of the wheel, and so forth. Although there have been no such critical points in the recent past, there may be some in the future. But that belongs to another section.

One example must suffice to illustrate the type. Cleve Cartmill describes in "The Link" the moment of crisis in the affairs of humanity when a certain hairless ape straightened up, picked up a club, and discovered that he was different from his fellows. That difference is sufficient to get him expelled from his tribe, which hates his pink body and his strange, new smell, but it is also enough to enable him to reason, to find a mate, and to choose a cave as a dwelling instead of a tree.[79]

Is there any future for the plot type in science fiction? It is difficult to say, but it does seem apparent that the decisions of the near future are more pressing than the recollection of those of the past, that science fiction is turning more and more toward stories of the future. Science fiction is more interested, we might say, in where man is going than where he has been, in his fate than in his history.

Facing Problems Similar to Those Faced Today

There is one large drawback to stories of this type. The problems around which the stories are built can be treated more adequately in the present or the future. I cannot think of a single example, although there have undoubtedly been some since the inception of science fiction. The difficulty in writing such a story is that the problems must be essentially human ones, and human problems, unless allied with something else, are not different enough usually to bring a story into the realm of science fiction. There have been occasional stories of lost civilizations (Atlantis is usually chosen) which, though they are not good as a rule, fall under this category. A much more popular vein is the following.[80]

Facing Problems of No Significance to the Modern World

Stories of this type are almost exclusively adventure. The recipe is as simple as one for making a cake: take one savage or uncivilized world, throw in a strong hero with stirrings of nobility, add a dash of romance in the form of a strange girl from another tribe, chop finely a multitude of villains, wild animals, and rampant nature, season freely, pot-boil for a few minutes, and serve on a strong plot line garnished with many simple adjectives. These stories are written only to be forgotten as quickly as possible, and with me they have succeeded only too well. Though there have been many of them, especially in the science fiction of the late 1920s and earlier, they are lost now in dust and decay. Edgar Rice Burroughs's Tarzan stories are mainly of this type, although they take place in the present. *Amazing Stories* prints this kind of story now and then, and *Famous Fantastic Mysteries* occasionally delves into its files of the old Munsey magazines to reprint a classic example. Among recent instances is Robert E. Howard's republished *Conan the Conqueror* (*The Hour of the Dragon*), although the setting is more mythical than historical.

Nothing good can be expected from this type, although, if it is any mitigation, nothing bad either, I suppose.

Chapter Four: A Future Being in a Future World

The future, as we have observed before, is wide open; anything is possible. This is not to say that any flight of the imagination into the future will make a science fiction story; credibility is still a prime consideration. But any logical extension of present activities or present knowledge can be used, and that establishes boundaries broad enough for almost any theme. With such range, science fiction authors are probably the freest writers in general publication today. The only important consideration is writing a good and credible story; and with the unlimited future to roam, the word "credibility" can be stretched a long way. That freedom is perhaps one of the strongest attractions to the science fiction field for the author; nowhere else in the literary spectrum, with the possible exception of fantasy (which is closely allied but has little significant thematic matter to impart), can it be equaled.[81]

Earlier science fiction writers abused this form probably more than any other. They used the freedom it gave them to wrench the future into any shape they liked—utopian writers the foremost among them. They set up unlikely characters doing implausible things in absurd places; the plot form was undisciplined and chaotic. The rise of realism rescued it from worse than mediocrity. Readers demanded probable futures and the authors responded. Readers asked for suitable action and significant themes; they received them. Readers asked for subtler characterization and realistic dialogue; they are just getting them. There is, of course, a large inertia in science fiction (as in other regions); there are eddies and undertows in the publishing field, and many magazines are still publishing the stories of twenty or thirty years ago. Some of this may be attributed to the readers, part of whom are young and love action for its own sake and part of whom have never outgrown their earlier tastes. But the greatest responsibility lies at the door of the publishers and editors, who dislike the prospect of the greater effort a realistic science fiction requires or who hate to retire a moderately successful horse.

This type is probably the major plot form of present and future science fiction. Its scope is almost unlimited, and its possibilities are broad. It can recreate any mood, dramatize any situation or idea that the mind can conceive, make concrete any philosophy. Its appeal is immediate: everyone would like to know the future, and, barring an authentic glimpse into what is to be, they would like to know what someone else thinks the future will bring. To some it's a great day coming; to others it's Armageddon. To all it is fascination.

Stories about future beings in their future worlds could be subdivided into as many sections as those of modern man in the modern world and, perhaps, with profit. But it would not be profitable enough to justify the time spent on it. Basically, the significance and nature of the stories depend on the same factors which determined those of a past being in the past: either the story has something to say to us, directly or indirectly, which casts some light on our present world—or it doesn't. The subdivisions here, consequently, are much the same as those of the preceding sections. The stories concern themselves with future beings: 1. Facing problems similar to those faced today; 2. Facing future problems; 3. Facing problems of no significance to the present day.

The three broad divisions of science fiction that Campbell suggests (as discussed in the first section of this work), prophecy stories, philosophical stories, and adventure stories, are similar but not identical. They cover the same general ground, but there are important differences. As a general rule, however, most philosophical stories fall under section one, although there are a few under section two; the reverse is true for prophecy stories. Almost all adventure stories belong to section three.

But let us turn to what those whose business it is to peer into the future have to say about the worlds to come. It would be well to keep in mind, however, that the primary concern of these authors is to write an interesting story with only one restriction: that it seems possible. They are not utopian writers; they have no compulsion to prove anything; they are not, primarily, propagandists or satirists. They do not say, either, that the world they describe will necessarily exist in the future; they say that the situation they depict may well come to pass if the present tendencies continue. They are the guides to the worlds whose portals open magically at the sound of the word *if*.[82]

Facing Problems Similar to Those Faced Today

The most frequent type of story found in this category, as we have observed, is the philosophical story, in which the author uses science fiction as a stage setting in which to present his philosophical idea dramatically. Occasionally, a prophecy story, in which the author tries to predict the effects of a new invention, falls under this classification. The distinguishing mark for this type of plot must be whether the problem concerned or the invention described presents a problem—immediate or in prospect—in our day.

A. E. van Vogt's "The Weapons Shop"—one of a series of stories placed in the same situation—takes up the question of political oppression. He envisions a world 7,000 years in the future, a world in which a ruthless imperial tyranny governs in a cloak of paternal benevolence and propaganda. The problem is how to fight such widespread oppression, under which man has no power, privileges, or redress. The solution suggested by van Vogt is the Weapons Shops, set up to act as an incorruptible core of human idealism, devoted to relieving the ills that arise under any form of government. Master of science, the Shops do not interfere in the main stream of human existence, realizing that people always have the kind of government they want. But they right wrongs and act as a barrier between the people and their more ruthless exploiters and also sell incomparable guns with which men may defend themselves. The Weapons Shops have turned their science to the one path of salvation—the manufacture of weapons that are invincible.[83]

Two stories by Isaac Asimov belong to this category. "Blind Alley" discusses the problem procuring a desirable result in a galactic civilization bound up in red tape. The government, incredibly extensive in order to administer the affairs and populations of hundreds of worlds, has on its hands a race of intelligent non-humans—the only one ever discovered in galactic history. The non-humans are carefully tended, placed on a world which satisfies their every want (whereas before they were fighting a losing battle against an almost sterile planet), but they are dying out because they refuse to breed. They must not be allowed to commit racial suicide nor can they be allowed to go free, to seek their own life among the stars. A capable administrator, wise in the ways of government by bureau and concerned more with the fate of the race than with official regulations or technical legalities, works through the desires of others to enable the race to escape, keeping himself from any blame by being strictly correct in his own paper work—the only real bureaucratic evidence.[84]

"Nightfall" is a story with a difference, one which builds up a world to demonstrate a philosophical concept. Asimov begins with Emerson's observation: "If the stars should appear one night in a thousand years, how would men believe and adore, and preserve for many generations the remembrance of the city of God!" Would they really? wonders the author, and, translating Emerson's speculation into practical, material terms which can be handled, he imagines such a planet, around which six suns circle. Only once in every 2049 years is there a total eclipse, so that the whole planet is cast into darkness. The scientific mind concentrates upon Emerson's poetic idea and asks itself what will happen when complete darkness falls upon this people who have never known anything but light and when there appears in the sky what the religious mystics refer to as "stars." History is no help to them, for their archeologists have discovered remains of nine previous civilizations which climbed to heights comparable to their own and approximately every two thousand years were destroyed by fire. The people of such a world will not adore, will not preserve the remembrance for generations, Asimov says; they will be driven mad by claustrophobia, by fear of the dark, and by the sight of thousands of stars in the blackness of the sky. In their insane desire for light, they will burn everything. Their civilization will end in ashes, and the only memory remaining will be that in the minds of the blind and the drunk, the younger children, the insensitive, and half-mad morons. In this story, however, is more than the exposure of a poetic fallacy; here is a comment on the nature of knowledge and the emotional potency of the unknown.[85]

Murray Leinster in "The Ethical Equations" supposes a time in the future when mankind has achieved the ability of spaceflight within the limits of its own solar system and has just made a beginning in the development of ethics into a science. A space patrol discovers, floating beyond Jupiter, an alien war ship, disabled but potentially more powerful than human science can hope to achieve, its crew in suspended animation until its screens are sufficiently activated by solar energy. Should the crew be destroyed and the ship be taken back to earth for investigation as common prudence would seem to indicate? A young man, placed in a peculiar temporary position of authority, decides against it, preferring to disobey instructions rather than the dictates of the ethical equations which state, in part, by mathematical proof, that probabilities and ethics are interlinked, so that admirable results cannot be expected from unethical beginnings. Disconnecting the ship's screens, the young man investigates and takes pictures of the entire alien ship and all its devices; he then supplies the ship with fuel and sends it back toward its own sun. The ethical equations turn out to be right, for the ship was made up of isotopes of elements which do not exist on earth because, at normal temperatures, they explode with planet-shattering violence.

A story of prophetic nature, Robert Heinlein's "Blowups Happen," is found under this section for two reasons: it deals with a problem, atomic power, that is before us today, and the world described contains devices (chiefly solar power and moving roadways) which are not likely in the near future, thus keeping it from being classified under the "modern man in the modern world" section. In this future world of Heinlein's, an atomic pile is supplying an appreciable percentage of the U.S. power supply. A slight slip, a miscalculation, will result in an explosion which would wipe out millions of lives. The psychological pressure on the men responsible for the working operation of the power plant is overpowering; the engineers, the administrative personnel, become increasingly liable to psychological breakdowns. They must be watched constantly, which adds to the tension, by psychologists who, themselves, are not immune. The solution to the problem is a technical one. The atomic pile is used to make a safe atomic fuel, and the fuel makes possible a spaceship and an artificial satellite. The pile can then be transferred into space when danger can be minimized and fuel can be shipped back to earth as needed.[86]

This plot form has as promising a future as any in science fiction. Not as easy to write as the following, it holds the greatest rewards in the shape not only of effective fiction but of significance.

Facing Future Problems

Future problems are those which have no immediate bearing upon the modern world, but in order to avoid classification as "of no significance to the modern day," the next section, they must cast some light on our lives. This light can be upon human nature, man's place in the universe, man's future—if that future carries any meaning for us, or any of an almost endless array of other observations on problems which the coming ages may bring. It should be recognized, however, that the line between the preceding section and the present one is thin; the immediacy of a problem, after all, must often be a matter of subjective decision.

A frequent type that falls under this classification is the academic story—by which I mean a story based on theoretical points long discussed among scientists, science fictionists, or laymen, a story whose situation is extremely unlikely but which gains acceptance through its theoretical interest.

One such story is "First Contact" by Murray Leinster, an example of a work inspired by science fiction discussions. Science fiction has pondered, fictionally, the question of alien contacts for a long time; if, for instance, the alien race is of equal or superior technology and scientific attainment, the decision has always been that the location of earth should not be revealed, that no matter how trustworthy and friendly the alien race seems there would be no assurance that it would not wipe out earth and the solar system just to be on the safe side. But, on the other hand, the benefits of a peaceful contact between two races and the exchange of separate technologies would be incalculable and might well result in an enormous spurt in the development of both. On such a nice point, with variations, Leinster bases his story. The chief variation is that two spaceships, one from earth and one from an alien planet meet, by the most inconceivable coincidence, in the Crab Nebula. They cannot take a chance on attempting to destroy the other—it might be better armed; they cannot go home for fear of being trailed and revealing the location of the home planet. They temporize for a moment by exchanging valuable technical information, which makes it even more imperative that they get home with all they have learned. The situation seems impossible until a perfect solution is at last hit upon: the two crews trade ships, destroying their own weapons and tracing devices, and arrange a future rendezvous at the nebula—possibly paving the way to future friendly intercourse.[87]

Harry Stephen Keeler's "John Jones' Dollar," a similar academic story, is based upon a different type of theory, one current in less select circles to explain the marvels of progression and compound interest. In such explanations, it is premised that if one had deposited a dollar in a bank at compound interest at the time of Christ's birth (presuming the presence of dollars and banks), one would now have a nearly incalculable amount of wealth. A man named John Jones did such a thing in 1921, Keeler presumes, directing that the accumulated principle and interest go to his fortieth descendant in the line of the oldest child of each generation. As the centuries went by, the dollar grew until in 600 years it had reached $47,900,000, when a special bank and board of directors was created to care for and invest it. During succeeding years, the life span was lengthened and the planets colonized, but John Jones' dollar went on. In 900 years, the dollar was worth $332,000,000,000; in 985 years, the thirty-ninth descendant was engaged to be married. If he had a child by the thousandth year, that child would inherit $6,310,000,000,000, but the directors computed that the entire solar system, including a decent valuation for the sun's remaining heat per calorie, was worth only $6,309,525,241,362.15—a disastrous situation. The engaged couple, fortunately, had a lover's quarrel, never married, and the Interplanetary government stepped in, took possession, and established a socialistic and democratic regime. The professor of history who has been telling the story ruminates on the wisdom of the old socialist, John Jones the first, who chose this as the only way to establish socialism, and on how close his plan came to failure if the fortieth descendant had been born.

Two stories by Robert Heinlein take up different types of problems men may face in the future: the technological and the psychological. The first type is described in "The Roads Must Roll," which pictures a world in the not-too-distant future whose principal method of transportation is by transcontinental moving roadways. The dramatic interest of the story lies in a breakdown in the system caused by a Functionalist engineers' revolt and the exact engineering detail with which it is described.[88] "The Green Hills of Earth," published originally in the *Saturday Evening Post*, dramatizes the psychology of the future spaceman, the engineers, the deck hands, and so forth, through the story and songs of a blind balladeer of the spaceways (a la Robert W. Service) and the latter's final heroic end singing his song of the adventurers' homesickness:

> We pray for one last landing
> On the globe that gave us birth;
> Let us rest our eyes on the fleecy skies
> And the cool, green hills of Earth [364].[89]

This type will probably remain the most popular form for "a future being in a future world." Although it does not carry the potential power or significance of the first section of this classification (since problems of the far future can never be as pressing nor as important as immediate ones), its freedom and drama, its opportunities for realistic escapism, its ease in writing, will keep it near the top among science fiction's authors and readers.

Facing Problems of No Significance to the Present Day

This plot form is analogous to that discussed under "a past being in the past facing problems of no significance to the modern world." Within this classification fall the slight stories of the future: the adventures of the moment, the domestic and personal crises, the internecine space wars, the battles between space pirates and the space patrol, the million and one inconsequential events which are fictionalized for a moment's amusement, a moment's escape. Inconsequentiality is not a sin—but it is a quick road to oblivion in science fiction. The future road of science fiction[90]—if it is not to end, after all, in a blind alley—is toward greater and greater significance. A story must have something to say, and science fiction's hope must be to be able to say that something better than it can be said in any other form.

The stories that say nothing are numerous, but they do not often find their way into anthologies. One story that did is Wallace West's "En Route to Pluto," a slight thing about an earth space pilot who elopes with one of the few remaining bird women of Mars and takes to space to escape pursuit.[91] The two land on Pluto, are attacked by intelligent clouds which can control temperature and bring it down to 250 degrees below zero, and finally beat them off with their own weapon.

Further discussion of this classification would be profitless. Anyone desiring additional examples need only pick up any current science fiction magazines (with a few exceptions) and he will find a sufficiency of them—and more. Publishers who print these trifles justify their decision by pointing out that these shallow or meaningless occurrences are as much a part of the future as events of greater significance and are even more probable. They are a proper part of the domain of science fiction, they say. True, perhaps—but they are the poorest part, the arid, unproductive part, and the part that, with its Buck Rogeres and other comic-strip material, in print or picture, is largely responsible for science fiction's common reputation as a purveyor of paltry and poorly written escapism.

Chapter Five: Mutations

The problem of mutations fits into no set pattern of environment and protagonist. These considerations are, at best, secondary. It matters little whether the mutation is in the past, the present, or the future, and by the very nature of the situation the only alien factor present can be those qualities which distinguish the mutant. Wherever or whenever the mutation happens, the problem is essentially the same: are the mutations to become dominant? So important, moreover, is this theme to science fiction that the type has been given a classification of its own.

The theoretical basis for stories of mutation is, of course, the theory of evolution, in one form or another.[92] Evolution is a long process, but it is also, many persons suspect, an inexorable one. There is no logical reason to suppose that *homo sapiens* is evolution's ultimate goal or that mutating forces, independently or help along by artificial means (conscious or unconscious, human or alien), may not stimulate the birth of a new race tomorrow or a thousand years from now. When and if that time comes, unless some new principle of conduct has or can be found or an old one revived, conflict will be as inevitable as if a second rooster were introduced into a hen yard. The meaning of that conflict to both sides, the attitudes it would call forth, and its final resolution are significant elements science fiction deals with in considering plots of this type.

There are two kinds of mutations discussed by science fiction: of man, and of animals or insects. The latter type was very common in the early days of science fiction, but in the last decade or so mutations of man have almost completely supplanted it as a popular plot form. Several reasons account for this shift, some of which will be taken up later, but, basically, the greater significance and interest of the theme of man's mutation is reason enough. The rise of a new race of animal or insect life to threaten man's dominion over the earth can be used for adventurous, satiric, or ironic purposes but little else. The changing of the human race or the springing from it of a superior race of beings has almost limitless possibilities, those which the animal mutation theme possesses and more important ones as well.

Mutations of Man

The idea of the changing of men into other forms, their ennoblement or degradation, strikes deep into man's eternal subconscious hopes and fears. Mythology contains many instances of mortal men being raised to divinity or semi-divinity (Hercules, Ganymede, Aeneas, and so forth) and many more of men and women being changed into animal or vegetable forms of life or forms even more grotesque (Arachne, Narcissus, and innumerable others). Here were summed up man's aspirations to surpass his apparent limitations and his fears of losing the powers that were already his. Christianity translated these hopes and fears into religious ideas; philosophers, culminating in Nietzsche, spoke of them in terms of the moral or unmoral. Then, beginning with Darwin, scientists began discarding moral considerations and philosophical optimums to speak, instead, of necessity and of blind, careless forces, heedless of human emotions or aspirations. They spoke of evolution and of the long climb from the unicellular sea organisms to the more and more highly organized beings which needed increasingly specialized conditions. They spoke of environment, natural selection, the survival of the fittest—of mutation. As research continued, they spoke of natural mutations and artificial ones, of cosmic rays, or X-rays, of radioactivity. The search, that is the search for the origin of life itself and the reasons for its specialization, continues. Life has changed, say the scientists. Life changes, they add. What is the next change? asks science fiction.

The older authors, H. G. Wells among them, ventured a few answers, but the question did not come to real prominence until about the middle of the 1930s. Even then, it was not until 1940 and later that the question received careful, thorough consideration. During these years the possible effects of natural and man-made rays and radioactivity on heredity were being brought to popular consideration. And with the atomic explosion over Hiroshima—the explosion that opened the eyes of the world to vast, new worlds of possibility, great or horrible, and blasted the prophetic speculations of science fiction into the public eye—with that mushrooming cloud, heavy laden with death for the individual or the species, came the avalanche of stories dealing with the prospects of atomic war, atomic power, and atomic mutation. As was the case with atomic war, stories of mutations became so common for a time that they fell into disrepute with editors and readers alike.

The means for racial suicide were at hand, science fiction saw. On one side was a world flaming in a chain reaction or so radioactive that all life was impossible; on the other side—and only slightly less horrible, perhaps— was a world in which radioactivity had so altered human germ plasm as to render man's survival as a species impossible. Between the two worlds lay a third, in which man and his mutated cousins had to live, for a time, side by side. Science fiction saw in this prospect two ways the road of mutation could take: up the heights to superman or down into the depths of degeneracy and the grotesque.

The plot form itself is relatively simple and relatively constant. By some force, the unsolved one of natural mutation (the mysterious cosmic ray is under suspicion here) or the more recent, more overwhelming one of atomic power or explosion, a change in the human shape and/or powers, individual or widespread, becomes evident. In the individual cases, it represents dramatically a family tragedy or, in extrapolated form, the first indications of the passing of the human race. In its more universal appearance, it suggests, even more strongly, that the dominance of *homo sapiens* is approaching its end, mourned or un-mourned, that humanity's climactic struggle for survival is at hand, or that the theoretical equality of men is no longer even a subject for debate and that man must learn to live heterogeneously, must learn the impractical virtues of tolerance, sympathy, and generosity, if he is to live at all.

Here, perhaps for the first time in literary history, authors could deal realistically, in a realistic form, with the question of changes in shape and powers of the human race; "realistically" because of the liberation of form, subject matter, and the imagination that science fiction, through the medium of scientific knowledge and speculation, brought to the literary scene in the third decade of the twentieth century.

Superman

Two primary considerations faced authors who speculated about the emergence of a race of superior beings from the human race: what constitutes significant superiority and what would be the attitude of a superior race to the parent race. These questions, in addition, of course, to the means of transformation, became the principal factors in the development of the theme and the most important influences upon plot distinctions with the type.

Early realistic presentations concentrated upon considerations of changes of form by chemical or mechanical means. In 1897, H. G. Wells considered the disadvantages of invisibility in *The Invisible Man*; in 1906, Jack London discussed two means of attaining invisibility, by complete transparency to light or by complete absorption of all light, in "The Shadow and the Flash." In Wells's "The New Accelerator" a third method, increase of speed beyond the point of visibility, is described.[93] But a serious consideration of the essential nature of the conflict between the new and the old was not introduced until Wells's *The Food of the Gods* suggested that ordinary men would resist, with violent prejudice against a difference in size, the efforts of a few benevolent, giant sons of man to improve the general lot; even here, the romantic and satirical elements differentiated this story from the modern realistic treatment.[94] All of these changes were effected by chemical means, as was the tremendous increase in strength described much later in Philip Wylie's *Gladiator*, a story very similar in treatment to *The Food of the Gods*, which describes the inability of vastly superior strength to live in a world of comparative weaklings.

The first two modern considerations of the superman theme came in 1936 and 1937, Olaf Stapledon's *Odd John* and Wells's *Star-Begotten* respectively, both starting from the basis of natural mutation.[95] *Odd John* introduced into modern science fiction a number of new concepts. The first of these was a slow maturation rate for superior beings, derived from an extrapolation of the difference in maturation rates between less intelligent species and humanity. Another concept was immediate perception allied with a superior logic, which enables the hero, whose career Stapledon traces from birth, to grasp almost instantaneously the essential nature of things and to form these conceptions into a logical, consistent, ordered whole.[96] With clearer thinking, Stapledon says, comes new and truer social and ethical values and a rejection of old and worn-out forms and prejudices for a truly humanitarian viewpoint. This viewpoint cannot be consistent with an attitude of snobbish superiority toward the great mass of ordinary humanity; in the end, when the group of young superior beings has retired to an island and is threatened even there by destruction when its powers are discovered, the members decide that they cannot destroy the civilized world even to preserve themselves and the future of their species.[97]

Star-Begotten takes a smaller aspect of the theme of mutation. Set to thinking about the possibility of mutation instigated by cosmic rays, the hero decides first that perhaps Martians are bombarding the earth with rays in order to develop a different type of humanity, then that this might be, all things considered, a good idea after all—that perhaps the great and good men of history, the brilliant men, the intuitional men have been such mutations. He looks at his family and thinks he detects signs of mutation in his son and wife; a wave of depression sweeps over him when he thinks that perhaps they belong to the new race while he is of the old. When he tells his wife, however, she laughs with relief; she has been thinking that he, and not she, was "star-begotten." The question of attitude toward humanity is not considered significantly in this novel.[98]

A. E. van Vogt's *Slan*, appearing in *Astounding* in 1940, brought the concept into the main stream of science fiction (the magazines, which have formed, developed, and exploited the technique and philosophy of the genre) with a story about a boy whose mother is killed and who finds the power of the civilized world against him. He is a natural mutation, his difference accentuated by a physical characteristic—in this case, for it was a facet much duplicated in later stories, tendrils instead of hair. Besides a greater intelligence, the mutant has certain telepathic powers and others of a similar nature. Upon reaching young manhood, the hero finds that he is not alone; the other mutant slans have migrated to Mars, where they have developed a tendrilless variety. The attitude of the mutants, conditioned by the efforts of ordinary humanity to stamp them out, is that they are a new race, that *homo sapiens* must step aside.[99]

A few years later, van Vogt was to consider a variation of the subject in *The World of Null-A* and *The Players of Null-A*. Although the primary philosophic consideration is of the merits of non–Aristotelian logic, the protagonist is a surgically constructed superman, a man with a second brain. The superman develops startling new mental powers through a process of education for his extra brain and through use of the techniques of null-A, among which is instantaneous mental self-transportation without physical limit, provided that the physical characteristics of the destination has been memorized to a specific and extensive number of decimal points. With only one such super being in existence, the question of attitude toward the rest of the race does not arise.[100]

The normal (to science fiction, at least) attitude of the new race to the "parent stock" is one of the same sort of contempt (tolerant or otherwise) that mankind has for the ape. The old race is done, thinks the mutant; evolution has condemned it to share the oblivion of the dinosaur and the dodo, its job done, its day in the sun at an end.

Such an attitude is exemplified in Nelson Bond's "Conquerors' Isle." In this war-time story, related by a pilot shot down with his crew over the south Pacific to a medical officer of the hospital to which he is taken after his rescue, a description is given of a tropical island near which the airplane landed in a storm. The pilot and his crew are captured there by a race of superior beings, natural mutations, who have gathered together by telepathic communication and isolated themselves to prepare for the time when they will be ready to take over the world. Their powers are great; they have an intuitive sense of what ordinary man struggles to learn and their studies are beyond ordinary comprehension. A sample of their power is an ability to move through a solid wall by a mental adjustment that recognizes the solidity of matter as only an illusion, which realizes that there is a great deal more of empty space in a wall than there is of matter. The new race does not plan to destroy mankind but to protect it, to act as guardians over wards, to be as masters to pets, until, inevitably, mankind dies out. The pilot escapes, casts himself adrift in a raft, and is picked up, delirious and raving, weeks later. He tries, frantically, to make the doctor believe him so that humanity can act in time, but the effort is useless. And the doctor (in an example of science fiction's dramatic technique—perhaps pragmatic in origin—of proof through demonstration), on leaving the pilot, walks through the wall.

In other stories the question of attitude is left undetermined or is not considered. In Robert Heinlein's "Gulf," for instance, the author suggests that there is a narrow but unclosable gulf between humanity and the superior beings. He adds, as well, some new facets to the question. His supermen are not mutations but natural variations who have but one added ability, that of thinking a little better. All through human history, he says, men like these have appeared and to them has been due almost all of mankind's progress, but only recently did they recognize themselves as essentially different, did they begin to separate themselves from *homo sapiens*, to nurture their talents, to educate themselves in a true sense, and to intermarry in order to make their variation into a race.[101]

In Wilmas Shiras's "In Hiding" and its sequels[102] the question of attitude of the atomic-explosion-bred-mutants, distinguished only by superior intelligence, is almost completely obscured by a preoccupation with the question of a number of these child geniuses keeping their mutation and exceptional minds and talents from coming to the attention of normal humans around them. Lewis Padgett in "The Piper's Son," on the other hand, takes only a partial consideration of the general question in dealing with the problem of a group of atomic-war-created mutations whose one exceptional talent is telepathy and whose distinguishing mark is their baldness. The situation requires mutual acceptance and tolerance between the mutants and humans and on the mutants' side a sacrificing of ambition and a policy of self-effacement in order to gain that acceptance and tolerance.

These stories have all taken place in the present or near future, and the resemblance of not only their themes but also their plot forms is apparent.

The same is true of stories placed in the past, as we have already noticed in Cleve Cartmill's description of the mutation from the near apes in "The Link." Going back even farther into the past is a part of Murray Leinster's "The Lost Race," whose action all takes place in the distant future when men have conquered interstellar space. Everywhere in the galaxy the human explorers find the ruins but no survivors of a former star-roving race; it becomes the great, unsolved mystery of space until a few skeletons are discovered on a remote planet. The Lost Race, the characters decide, found that its use of atomic power had converted all their children into monsters; unable to face the future, it destroyed its civilization and committed suicide. The monster-children? Men. In all such stories of mutations, the time element, the when, is unimportant.

The plot form as a whole is one of potentially great significance and one that has already been widely exploited. Too many stories of the type followed the end of World War II and jaded the public appetite, but the subject is so fundamental to the thought and emotional processes of mankind that a few years will have overcome that handicap. Even today, a really good story, of more novel or more thoughtful content, will find a place in any magazine. The form, the theme, is too provocative and too worthwhile to completely ignore.

Grotesque

The possibility of grotesque mutation is the Janus head looking in the other direction. Natural mutations of the externally abnormal kind are not only an inextricable part of folklore, even, indeed, of that segment of folklore which is still whispered in an age which prides itself on its lack of superstition, they are of such daily concern that every mother's first thought after delivery is the one that has plagued her throughout pregnancy—is her child "all right," does it have all its arms and legs, fingers and toes, and not too many of any? Tales of horrible divergences from the norm continue to be the subject of gossip: children with six or more fingers and those whose fingers and toes are webbed are the least important deviations.

Accounts of abnormal births are only slightly less numerous in folklore and mythology than tales of changes in form. Minotaurus, for instance, was the child of Pasiphae; Caliban was the son of the witch Sycorax. Throughout literature, one type of punishment for sin has been to give birth to a "monster." And the idea of sin is peculiarly appropriate to the modern possibility of grotesque mutations; the sin of uncontrolled atomics may well result in a great increase in such abnormal births.

Perhaps the earliest modern use of the grotesque, in the sense, at least, in which the parents were concerned, was in horror tales; almost every other story contained, in the cellar or turret of the dark, damp castle, an idiot and/or deformed son. H. P. Lovecraft was fond of such themes—the alien child, fish-like or bearing the stamp of the evil "Elder Things," allying it to his terrifying cosmology of old, half-remembered powers who have been thrown out of control on earth but who are always trying to get back. A significant use of the plot form did not begin, however, until the means of mutation became obvious, and it did not come to its full power until it became apparent that mankind faced a possibility of altering its own heredity.

As a whole, the spate of stories concerned with grotesque mutations which just followed, or preceded by a few years, the dropping of the atom bomb over Hiroshima was an outburst of horror at the possibilities implicit in an atomic age, particularly in one in which the atom was uncontrolled. It was a horror that struck deep. On one hand, it was the deadliest threat to what man has ever held most dear—the normalcy of his offspring; on the other, it represented the ultimate depths to which man could sink—complete self-destruction, or, rather, a destruction which did not need to be complete to end man's brief spell of earthly domination. As outbursts of horror, most of the stories faded quickly; only a few remain still vivid after the theme ran its course and became, as the editor of *Astounding* observed recently in reference to the broader theme of atomic wars, "like a bad joke we've heard before it wasn't funny the first time" ("In Times to Come" 150). Three stories will serve to exemplify those which have lasted.

Grotesque mutations is only a secondary theme in Robert Heinlein's "Universe," but the story embodies one of the first significant uses in modern science fiction. The story itself, published in 1941, has already been touched upon in the first section of this work, with its description of a self-sufficient spaceship lost between the stars and the myth-filled, superstitious history and cosmology which grew up to explain the strange circumstances. Cosmic rays, however, had introduced widespread mutations among the remnants of defeated rebels who had been driven generations before to the outer, and less protected, regions of the ship. Heinlein lends some extra significance to the theme by placing the "mutie" forces, led by a likable and brilliant two-headed mutation named Joe-Jim, on the side of the protagonist and a true picture of the ship's situation, against the forces of stubborn reaction. The outcast, the pariah, the different person, the author suggests indirectly, has nothing to lose by insisting on the truth, while those with vested interests have nothing to gain.[103]

Perhaps the most vividly realistic picture of possibilities of such mutations on a widespread scale was presented by Poul Anderson and F. N. Waldrop in "Tomorrow's Children." This story postulates an atomic-war-blasted world in which the U.S. Army has retained some organization and is slowly rebuilding facilities and some civilization. But seventy-five percent of all births are mutations, of which two-thirds are viable and presumably fertile, not including late-maturing characteristics or those undetectable by naked-eye observation or mutated recessives. Eradication or sterilization of mutants and parents is impossible, not only as a physical fact but because everyone was affected by the colloidal radioactive dust and bomb byproducts. Man is doomed as a continuing species, the authors say, but men and mutants must try to live and work together. "The impractical virtues, tolerance and sympathy and generosity, have become the fundamental necessities of simple survival" (38).

A simple domestic story with significant implications is told by Judith Merril in "That Only a Mother." Related entirely from the viewpoint of the mother, this story pictures a pregnant woman as she waits for her baby to be born into a world in the midst of an atomic war. The child, when born, is precocious, talking at seven months, and the mother writes ecstatic letters to her atomic designer husband about the child's beauty and normalcy. And when her husband returns on leave, he finds that the child has no arms or legs—and the mother doesn't know.[104]

Grotesque mutations still figure occasionally in stories today, though seldom in the place of prime importance. When they do appear, it is usually a case of realistic detail rather than theme. The theme itself never attained the significance of the superman; its meaning was necessarily limited. But what it attempted, it did well. More novel treatments of the theme may yet appear, and entertainment mediums of more general interest, untouched by the satiety of the science fiction field, may be expected to go in for the theme more or less extensively once they realize its possibilities.

Mutations of Animals or Insects

The animal or insect mutation theme, as we noted earlier, preceded the mutation of man upon the science fiction scene. The reason for this is intimately connected with the psychology of the era and the gradual development of science fiction's philosophy. The gradual disillusion of idealists and utopian writers began about the turn of the century and grew to a peak in the period between the two world wars. It developed an attitude that said: if man cannot be great and good, let another race of beings take over the supremacy of the earth. Eventually, modern science fiction changed it to: if man cannot be great and good (although the moral question was greatly subordinated as being too variable and basically incapable of exact measurement), let a better man supplant him. The change was inevitable; the earlier theme had only two variations, and they were extremely limited. There is danger, the first suggested, that man may not always be supreme on his own planet. Good enough, said the second; man is bad and deserves to be replaced.

The theme itself is not too popular, as evidenced by its frequency in the distribution chart (only two). It is very similar to the theme in "Goldfish Bowl" by Robert Heinlein and *Sinister Barrier* by Eric Frank Russell, which suggest (taking the idea from Charles Fort) that man is property. Instead of presuming, however, that mankind has never been supreme, even on earth, the mutation theme presumes that mankind is supreme but that he is only an evolutionary stage, a step in the ascending ladder of life or a blind alley.

One of the first instances of this plot form was in Guy de Maupassant's "The Horla" (1887), which has been often reprinted in anthologies and reprint magazines of fantasy and horror.[105] The narrator becomes aware of an invisible presence in his hours and gradually connects it with stories of similar beings in Brazil. After pondering whether the thing developed in the South American jungles, invaded the planet from another world, or evolved to supplant man, he tries to destroy it by burning down his house. But it is useless; the Horla remains to pursue the narrator.

Such was the beginning of the theme. In the few pages of this story, it could not come to any definite conclusions about the nature or result of the possibly impending conflict. Fundamentally, however, these considerations determine the nature of the story: is there a battle and, if so, who wins? "Mutations of animals or insects," therefore, subdivides into the following sections: a. With whom man battle for possession of the earth; b. Which take over the supremacy of the earth; c. Which cooperate with mankind. In most cases, the scope of the story will not permit an epic account of a planet-wide warfare; events are foreshadowed, usually, by a small-scale engagement of forces. It should be noted, moreover, that the term "animals or insects" denotes only the most common mutations treated; the plot form covers, generally, changes in any life form which raises it to a position as equal or superior to mankind. This would include even plant life, if it is endowed with some sort of intelligence.

The favorite type of being treated, early in science fiction and late, was the insect, specifically the ant and the termite. Writers, as well as others who have thought upon the subject, have always been impressed with the industry, organization, tenacity, and relative civilization that they have demonstrated. It has been a matter, perhaps, of projecting human problems onto the smaller scale of the ant hill and finding the problems more easily solved or of no significance; it has been, on the other hand, an admiration of the truly static society, where every being has its place and duties from which there is no hope of escape and, perhaps, no desire to do so. Given, thought the science fiction writers, a little more intelligence, a little more ambition, a little more cooperation between ant-hill communities, a little greater knowledge of the greater world and the possibilities of conquest, the ants could become the new masters of earth, the termites could, in a very literal sense, undermine the foundations of man's civilization.[106]

Animals or Insects with Whom Man Battle for Possession of the Earth

Two stories of H. G. Wells describe the insect menace. "The Valley of the Spiders" tells about an attack on a party of men in a desert by huge spiders, with bodies half as large as a man's hand and webs that carry them through the air like sails. The theme is better developed in "The Empire of the Ants." A Brazilian-government gunboat, sent to investigate a great upsurge in ants on the upper Amazon, finds the ants highly organized, some of them carrying poison. They have seized a steamship, killing the crew, and conquered a village. The ants have a knowledge of metals, fire, and engineering, tunneling under a river wider than the Thames. And with that threat the story ends.

A story that falls almost between this section and the next is Guy Endore's "The Day of the Dragon," which presents a fascinating but terrible possibility. A scientist, suffering under the scorn of his colleagues for writing popular and sensational articles about the marvels of science and nature, evolves a theory to rehabilitate his reputation. The reptilian heart, he is aware, is an incomplete organ, only half-cleansing the blood of its poisons because the wall between the ventricles is not complete. He operates on alligators and, after many failures, learns to repair the perpetually invalid condition. The alligators' appetites increase enormously and their size increases proportionately. Their movements grow quick; they develop deeper chests, necks, ridges on the spine, long, serpentine tails with flat, sharp arrowheads on the ends. The ridges on the back keep growing until they become—wings. The alligators become, in fact, dragons. Once they escape, the conclusion is foregone. They multiply rapidly, and, with their incredible appetites, they begin to sweep earth clean of life, human as well as animal. Attempts to exterminate them are useless. The story ends with a few remnants of humanity huddling in New York, hiding in subways, and wondering how long they can survive.

Suitable chiefly for satire and commentary, the form and its very definite limitations have been adequately summed up above.

Animals or Insects That Take Over the Supremacy of the Earth

The plot of the animals or insects which take over the supremacy of the earth does not readily adapt itself to dramatic presentation, lacking as it does a great deal of reader identification and presenting a state of affairs already accomplished. The form has, however, been used successfully in a few instances, resulting usually in a story which comments satirically or sympathetically on humanity, its pretensions, and its future.

Two such stories have been written by L. Sprague de Camp. *Genus Homo* is a work of recent vintage written in collaboration with P. Schuyler Miller[107] that sends a busload of passengers into the distant future—from which man has eliminated himself and in which intelligent apes and beavers run the world—doing a better job of it than humanity. In an inversion of the theme, the passengers manage to resume control for the race. "Living Fossil" tells of a world dominated by a mutated race of capuchin monkeys. Two of them, a zoologist and a biologist, find remains of a previous civilization, that of man, in a North American forest. They find, moreover, what was, perhaps, the one remaining tribe of the hairless monkey they know as their predecessor, and they go to great lengths to protect it for study.[108]

A post–Hiroshima story, Edward Grendon's "The Figure," is based, indirectly, on time travel, but its theme is more serious. The experimenters had worked for the U.S. Army on the problem of great insect mutations in spots where atomic bombs had been set off. Their time machine reaches into the distant future and brings back a figure, a small statue on a pedestal representing the globe of the earth. The figure appears intelligent and seems to represent aspiration or a religious theme. It is majestic. But the figure is that of a beetle.[109]

Animals or Insects That Cooperate with Mankind

It is a kind of romanticism that suggests that mutations of animals or insects can cooperate with mankind; the natural tendency of the new is to do away with the old, of the slaves or the downtrodden to wipe out the erstwhile masters. As romanticism, therefore, it is fundamentally at odds with one of the strongest elements in modern science fiction, realism. Occasionally, however, it finds a place, if an uneasy one, in current stories. Yet even the sentimental urge cannot justify the idea of cooperating insects; animals are the usual thing and the favorite, of course, is the dog.

Clifford D. Simak in "Aesop" (one story of a series)[110] describes a world in which man, or a few of the wisest, educated the dogs and then sealed himself in a city in order to let them build a better world than he himself was unable to create.[111] And the dogs built a better world in which there was no bloodshed, no hatred, instead a confraternity of all life—a theme which Simak was to pick up in a larger and more effective form several years later. In "Follower" by Eric Frank Russell, an alien spaceship lands on earth in the distant future, and the pilot, in return for help in leaving the planet (which is in the domain of a feared master race), agrees to take one of the natives to a point where he can join that race. The native regards the members of the master race as gods, who formerly ruled the earth and helped the natives but who had to leave them behind when they took to space because the natives could not stand a space journey. The native thinks that the changes the eons have made may enable him to survive. He is right, and when he arrives at his destination he meets with great affection the master race, the gods. They are man, and he is dog.[112]

Conclusion to Plots of Circumstance

Such are the plots of circumstance, the most fertile field of science fiction. Stretching from plots of pure or not so pure adventure to mature considerations of subjects of great seriousness and significance, they range the far reaches of the galaxy, the unplumbed depths of the past, the unlimited eons of the future.

In the preceding discussion, we have seen that the most important considerations in plots of circumstance are the protagonist and the environmental situation in which he finds himself. We have examined, therefore, the various types of protagonists possible in science fiction and the various kinds of environments in which they could find themselves, noticing the molding effect each plot type has upon the stories that are written under it, the advantages and disadvantages of each, how these plot types have worked out in fictional practice, and what possibilities each type holds, what promise it had for the future of science fiction. We have considered: A being in an alien environment; Modern man in the modern world; A past being in the past; A future being in a future world; and Mutations. These divisions may not be all-inclusive nor mutually exclusive, but a hard and fast classification has not only not been the aim of this work, it may be, in fact, impossible. The divisions have been set up for the purposes of convenient discussion, and if it has proved profitable the means have been justified.

The preceding stories have dealt with the conflict between man and his environment, a type which we have observed is the most popular in science fiction. We have seen the adventure story and the problem story, the prophetic story and the philosophical story—the stories which present characters battling against circumstances for which they are not responsible but from which they can sometimes extract themselves or over which they can exercise some control.

Now we turn to plots of creation.

Section Two: *Plots of Creation*

The distinguishing mark between plots of circumstance and plots of creation lies in the degree of responsibility of the characters for the problem with which the story is concerned. The word "degree" is significant. In few stories have the characters had no hand in the shaping of the situation in which they find themselves; in still fewer have they completely determined the nature of their own predicament. The criterion must be whether their responsibility is primary and substantial. This would imply, of course, that one cannot place with any absolute certainty a story either in one of the two major categories or the other. That is correct. On the dividing line are stories which can fall either way according to a judgment which must be, in the final analysis, subjective. The basic distinction, however, is worth making for the light it sheds upon the themes that are peculiar to the classification.

In plots of creation, then, the actions of one or more of the characters establishes the problem that it is the function of the rest of the story to resolve. Plots of circumstance, we have noted, divide themselves primarily between the adventure story and the problem story; they depict characters battling against circumstances for which they were not responsible but from which they can sometimes extract themselves or over which they can exercise some control. Plots of creation, on the other hand, fall into stories of the mad or incautious scientist, of the creative scientist, of experimentation that turns out well or ill. It is experimentation and not any other form of activity that initiates the action because only in experimentation are other elements (human factors, circumstance, environment), which tend to influence the situation, removed from significant consideration, and because—more importantly—it is science fiction. Experimentation creates the problem, and in plots of creation the responsibility rests on the shoulders of the characters. They create their own problems.

The distribution chart shows that there are relatively few stories based on plots of creation (20, as against 125 for plots of circumstance), and that fact holds true in the field as a whole. There are good reasons why this should be so. There are no boundaries for the imagination in plots of circumstance, but plots of creation are necessarily limited. The keynote of science fiction is reason (as contrasted with fantasy), and there is a limit to the things a person can reasonably create. Once those things have been fictionally created, there is nothing for science fiction authors to do in this form but retrace ground already covered, to try to plot a little deeper or to sow a more fertile seed. The limit was reached, for instance, in a story whose title and author I have forgotten but which was published in *Astounding* some ten or more years ago. The protagonist discovered that existence depended on his belief or disbelief; he began to disbelieve in one thing after another, and the things blanked out until the protagonist finally lost belief in his own existence—and the universe was an empty void.[113] Almost on the other extreme is a novel by A. E. van Vogt entitled *The Weapon Shops of Isher*, in which a man set swinging back and forth through time develops so much "time-energy" that he explodes in the remote past, creating the planets of the solar system. In still other stories the universe itself has been created by man. Between these extremes, far apart as they seem, the gamut has been largely run.

Plots of creation, when carried too far (as they tend to be), soon reach the borderline of fantasy and, too often, tumble over. Early modern stories of the type usually fell into that trap, although, to be perfectly just, at that time the line between fantasy and science fiction was thin and wavering. Scientists constructed machines right and left in these stories, with little purpose beyond a desire to construct something or to prove their point in some dispute over "pure" science. Out of once-read piles of garish pulps—now so dusty, yellowed, and tattered as to be unreadable if they were not burned to ashes long ago—I can dredge memories of fabulous machines: machines to rid the earth of all dust or to stop the earth's rotation.[114] Almost all were ridiculously simple devices. Almost all were disastrous.

The entrance of realism into science fiction put a stop to many of these plots. The realistic tendency demanded not only a reasonable creation but also logical motives and even more logical theoretical possibilities. And naturalism, which hit science fiction late, turned authors away from the idea that men controlled their fates and toward a consideration of environment and circumstance.

The final reason—and perhaps the most important—for the scarcity of plots of creation in the last decade is that they are inherently difficult to write. The author must find, first, a reasonable creation which has not been thoroughly exploited before, and he must keep that creation realistic. Having gone so far, he must face a loss of reader identification, for few of us are creators in any unusual or dramatic sense, while we all know what it is to struggle against circumstance. And finally, having overcome these handicaps, he must realize that he is still being romantic at bottom: science is not, primarily, a process of invention but one of investigation and discovery. The great strides of science have not been made by inventors but by those theoreticians who have perceived a new truth in their environment or have pieced together an underlying unity in nature.

Despite its disadvantages, the plot type has several merits which are seldom found in plots of circumstance. Limited, plots of creation may be—also romantic, unrealistic, and difficult to write—but at best they concentrate on man rather than on his environment. They present a dramatic analysis of certain aspects of man's psychology: his drives, desires, weaknesses, and strengths. But even more important, they deal most significantly and most satisfactorily with the problem that is, perhaps, *the* problem of our age: the relationship to man and his creations. What is man to create? And, more vitally: what is man to do with what he creates? Between these two—and there is a large number of important questions between them—the themes of plots of creation fall. If the plot type can suggest answers to these questions or, at least, present the questions in a new, a clearer, and a more dramatic form, it has more than justified its existence.

Plots of creation divide themselves into two main classification: the creation of life has been one of man's eternal dreams, for it implies what fathering or giving birth to a child does not, a comprehension of the basic processes which build up living matter out of inanimate substances, if not of the fundamental nature of life itself. Even the earliest civilizations had their myths of the creation of life, basing them often on a belief that inanimate objects are continually being vivified—a belief which continued in popular superstition very close to our modern age, if it does not survive yet (cf. the horse hair in water turning into a snake, the barnacle-goose, etc.). Jason sowed his dragon's teeth and reaped soldiers; Deucalion and Pyrrha repeopled the world by throwing stones, the bones of their mother, over their shoulder; Pygmalion brought his ivory statue, Galatea, to life with his love and prayers. The theme was brought into science fiction for the first time, probably, by Mary Shelley in *Frankenstein*.

Experimentation in other fields is largely the technological dream of the scientific age. The machine era with its continually bigger and more complex machines suggested that a machine or a technique could be developed to do anything; and while those who believe in that suggestion are, perhaps, a little naïve, the research and inventions of the last few decades have given them a talking point at least. The type of creativity exemplified in this type is that which tries to minimize environment; its goal is a completely self-sufficient race. Whether this is for the best, in specific instances and in general, is often the point in question in these stories.

Creation, especially of something new and significant, has always been considered a dangerous activity; through folklore and mythology to philosophy and literature, it has usually been thought safest and often best to be satisfied with the old and accustomed, to fear the new and untried. The attitude is closely allied to superstition: creation is a power reserved to godhead; those who presume to encroach upon that power may be endangering not only their own lives and souls but those of their family, friends and neighbors. Daedalus invented wings and his son was killed; Faust's thirst for knowledge led him to Hell. There are things man should not do or know; and there are always many to inform the world that God did not intend man to travel faster than twenty miles an hour or one hundred miles an hour or faster than the speed of sound. Creation has often been viewed as Pandora's box; there is no telling what evils research and invention may release upon the world. The ways of our fathers are best; they are tested by time and found sound. Let us not tamper with forces which we know nothing. Such is and has been the attitude of the world. Particularly is this true of the creation of life; there is nothing, says superstition, more sacrosanct.

This attitude has found unexpected support in recent years. Philosophers and sociologists, authors and columnists have asked themselves—and the world—if we have not, in our search for knowledge and our ever-greater inventions, outstripped ourselves, if we have not built higher than our present moral and sociological state is capable of supporting. The atomic bomb, of course, intensified this self-questioning until the matter has become one of popular concern. Even the scientists of today are given to public breast-beatings and are reaching a near-neurotic state of indecision, starting at shadows, skulking in darkened laboratories. This is not to dismiss all this alarm as without foundation; but alarm itself can do no good when there is no practical way to turn back, when the only way to go is forward.

There are only two primary roads that plots of creation can take, the same two roads that man's thinking about creation has worn smooth: creation is either good or bad; experimentation can turn out either well or ill; creation and experimentation can aid mankind or get out of control. That they should turn out poorly is the older, time-hallowed way of thinking, as we have seen. The technological dreams initiated by the industrial revolution brought in the hopes that experimentation and creation were the stepping-stones to a better world or rungs in the ladder of man's conquest of the universe. Today there is a mixture of the two. The older view has been reinforced by the current situation, but optimism buoys up the dreamers. In the following analysis, we shall see these two attitudes working themselves out in fictional practice.

Chapter One: The Creation of New Life or New Forms Thereof

Man has dreamed of creating two kinds of life; both dreams have long histories, stretching back into the ultimately unfathomable depths of folk and fairy tales and mythology. One of these, and perhaps the one with the greatest potential psychological appeal, is creation of chemical life—that which is based upon a mysterious substance or quality which distinguishes the organic from the inorganic, the living from the dead. It is a creation that implies an answer to that eternal riddle of existence: why do some things grow and reproduce and adapt to environment? Man has not yet solved the riddle; he has not yet created chemical life. But there is another type of life man has dreamed of creating which does not grow not, perhaps, reproduce. That is mechanical life, and authorities are arguing today whether man has succeeded in creating it in the last few years (cf. the electronic brains and the new science of cybernetics).[115] Early folk and fairy tales contained such creations, even though they were usually endowed with life by some sort of magic. One of them is described in the Squire's tale from Chaucer's *Canterbury Tales*: the flying horse of brase; another was the enigmatic brazen head (brass was a favorite material) fashioned by Friar Bacon. The vivifying principle was magic, but that is not as far from our modern methods as it seems; magic is, after all, only a force whose origin or workings are concealed or not understood. Earlier civilizations would have considered our scientific methods even more magical than theirs and I am not sure but what many of us do not feel much the same way.[116]

The final difference between creations of mechanical life and creations of chemical life, which must determine the classification in which the stories which deal with them are placed, is not one which can consist of a black line drawn carefully and definitely between the two. One can say, for instance, that chemical life is built up of organic compounds and mechanical life of inorganic compounds. But organic compounds, when analyzed, are only unions of inorganic ones with nothing left over for the chemist to weigh or measure; chemically speaking, they are compounds of carbon, but there is nothing in carbon itself which can impart the life principle (which is the only difference between the two) to unloving substances beyond the fact that it combines into complex molecules. No, the difference here, again, is one of degree. Chemical life is vitalized in the cell; mechanical life is vitalized in the "mind" and power center. The smallest living unit of chemical life is the cell; the smallest living unit of mechanical life is the power-mind-body combination.

I. Chemical Life

Chemical life is also divided into two classifications—or rather one principle type and another which lumps together the rest. Science fiction has chosen the word android to designate the first of these. Android means, of course, manlike; anthropoid would have done just as well, except that the term is used in more specific terminology by biology and its more specialized branches. The "other forms created or converted" covers all forms which are not manlike, including everything from amorphous masses of protoplasm to highly organized shapes, animal or vegetable—seldom mineral. The first division is the more popular; when man has dreamed of chemical creation, he has dreamed, usually, in anthropomorphic terms.

Androids

The primary question the creation of androids brings up—and one which every author of a story about them must answer to the reader's satisfaction—is: why create them? There are many reasons for creation of anything; all of them have been applied at one time or another to the creation of manlike forms. The most usual reason has always been usefulness, but there is also creation for the sake of beauty and the ultimate creation—that for the sake of creation alone. The last reason has always been the most compelling one; it was the reason, most poets assume, for the creation of the universe. When man creates in such a fashion, his motives are godlike; at the same time he is indulging in the most dangerous of activities. When man presumes to divinity, he is endangering his life and his soul. Man is not a god. His vision is not so clear; his comprehension of the factors involved is not so complete; his control of his creation is imperfect. So folklore insists, and we are often tempted to agree. Such creation, science fiction agrees as well, usually ends in disaster. While this type of creation is the most compelling and often the most pregnant with theme and meaning, it is in another sense the weakest because it is the most unrealistic. Man usually has more understandable and more practical motives.

Creation for the sake of beauty is the artistic purpose. It is not often used in modern science fiction, but there have been several good stories based upon this motive. It often follows the Pygmalion pattern up to but not including the happy ending, ending usually in failure of one sort or another.

Creation for usefulness is most common. It is the motive usual for other types of creation and the one most readers are likely to sympathize with immediately. But, of course, it brings up the question: why should a manlike creation be better than man himself? There are a number of answers, some qualified and some not. Androids could, for instance, do menial and other unpleasant work for which man is rapidly growing to feel himself unfit. Androids can be made to fit specific jobs; they can be constructed stronger, more resistant, tougher than man. They can be given special skills, quicker reactions, additional talents. They can, in the end, be made better than man. In certain cases, they may be needed to swell the ranks of humanity—which will be stretched thin when the conquest of space begins. Their chief limitation is usually that they cannot reproduce themselves biologically.[117]

Such useful creation may occasionally go away or develop new problems, but most often it becomes an aid to mankind. In these cases, however, the problem of the creation of androids is seldom central to the story; there is no drama implicit in the idea of building something which works. Drama is conflict; without conflict there is no drama. The only case, then, in which useful creations can be the central theme is when the android is constructed over the opposing desires, protests, and struggle of others. In most instances, it must be, therefore, peripheral.

- *Androids That Aid Mankind*

Androids which are an adjunct to the protagonist or his forces are encountered every so often in science fiction. The most familiar example to science fiction readers is Otho, one of the Captain Future ménage. Captain Future, originated by Edmond Hamilton a number of years ago, pursued his planet-shaking career in a magazine of his own prior to World War II; after the war he was revived for a time in regular novelette form in *Startling Stories*. His group of friends, so similar to those of Doc Savage (the leading character in one of the now-defunct Street & Smith adventure pulps) as to raise a suspicion of imitation,[118] consisted of Otho, the android; Grag, the robot; and Simon Wright, the human brain kept alive in the self-powered, mobile metal case. These three (the first two constructed by Simon and Captain Future's parents) raised the boy to young manhood after the death of his parents and then began to roam the galaxy looking for wrongs to right.

A more central use in a much more significant work was made by Clifford D. Simak in his novel *Time Quarry* [*Time and Again*].[119] Simak pictures a world of the future in which humanity has conquered the galaxy. It is a precarious conquest, however, for man has had to spread his forces thin, even with the help of androids and robots. Returning to earth after a mission on which he was gone twenty years, a man resolves to write up the philosophy he has learned from his experience on a strange planet of dying but being reborn in a rather mystic fashion by the help of certain "symbiotic distractions" which form symbiotic unions with every living being in the universe. They form a kind of destiny that tries to guide the being upward, sometimes succeeding, sometimes failing. The protagonist returns to earth to reveal this, to set it down in a book for everyone to read and know that all living things are equal, all have their "destiny." In the future, however, where the book has already been written, where it is the most important single document, there are men determined that it shall not be written or that it shall be changed so that only man is revealed to enjoy this symbiotic partnership. Dreaming of the great things that man can do if his thin line of domination in the galaxy is unchallenged, these men fear that the spreading of the idea of equality of creation will result in a rebellion of the other beings of the galaxy who greatly outnumber man. By the aid of their time machines (using the theory of probability time), they try to interfere in the past. They are opposed by the androids, who are human except for their inability to reproduce biologically and are distinguished by tattooed identification marks on their foreheads. The androids try to insure that the book is written as planned. Such is one way science fiction deals with the theme of intolerance, and in this case it is a particularly mature way.

The plot type itself has never been exploited as fully as it could be. Although the difficulty of making interesting a story about a helpful creation is always a problem, the type offers an opportunity to say some very significant and worthwhile things about the positions of a creator and his creation, about the attitudes and duties of each, about the emotions of an obedient but equal or superior creation.

• *Androids That Get Out of Control*

Although there are instances in mythology and folklore of a manlike creation getting out of control, the first example in which the android was created by scientific means—or, at least, means rationalized as being possible to science—was Mary Wollstonecraft Shelley's *Frankenstein*. The familiar story tells of a young scientist who fashions a manlike shape from materials taken from graves, vivifies it, and has it turn upon him finally. Such is the result of divine creation—that for its own sake.

Another example of such godlike creation—and an interesting variation—is contained in Nelson Bond's "The Cunning of the Beast." On a far-distant world, the author relates, lived a race of incorporeal creatures with great intelligence but little strength. They fashioned themselves metal carriers to assist their movement and work and to protect themselves from the deadly elements, but these were imperfect and liable to failure. One of the race, Yawa Eloem, decides to create animal servants whose bodies could resist the elements. First, he creates a male being and installs him in a pleasant garden. He creates a mate for the male, but he destroys her when she proves unsatisfactory and creates another. He forbids the two only one thing: entrance to his laboratory and library, where his knowledge is stored. The female, however, induces the serpent in the garden to slip through a grill and open the door, and she and the male learn enough to build themselves carriers and to blow up some of the domes that protect the race. On discovery of this, the elders of the race, forbidden to destroy any creature with a soul, put the two creatures and their creator into a spaceship and send them off into the unknown. Such are the dangers of creation, and such is the punishment for transgression.

A third example, "Black Thirst" by Catherine L. Moore, one of science fiction's most skillful woman authors, illustrates a type of creation which seems artistic but is actually, in a sense, utilitarian. An adventurer, introduced into a mysterious source of incredibly beautiful and charming women who are sold to the highest bidder, the Minga castle on Venus, meets the cloaked, dark owner and is rendered powerless by a hypnotic spell.[120] He is taken on a tour of the premises while the owner relates the history of his own race: how it was born in the slime on another planet, came to Venus when it was old and bred the race over the ages for its own purposes while it sold the poorer specimens as a means of avoiding suspicion. Now, at the apex of its work, the slime-race has bred out a distillation of pure, blinding beauty; on this ethereal element the race lives, vampire-like. The adventurer is shown exhibits, one woman more beautiful than another until his mind reels close to madness. The owner attempts to devour the adventurer's male beauty, coarser fare though it is, but the protagonist is able to overcome the spell. He kills the owner, who relapses back into his original slime, and escapes. All this made possible by the revolt of one of the lesser Minga creations, a woman who has not had bred out of her the courage which overpowering beauty usually obliterates.

The plot form of the android that gets out of control is probably the most pregnant of the plots of creation. It has possibilities of theme, depths of meaning and symbolism, and dramatic opportunities as yet unplumbed; it appeals to the deepest creative impulses of man, and through the working out of this ultimate of creations can be revealed the nature of man in this peculiarly significant activity. That creations should revolt is perhaps inherent in the nature of creation, but why this should be so is a question that might inspire a large number of stories and elicit some fundamental truth of existence. Tending toward the unrealistic, the type yet embodies so much of the eternal dreams of mankind that it strikes an immediate responsive chord. The great story of this type (as perhaps it should be) has yet to be written.

Other Forms Created or Converted

The other forms of chemical life which can be created or converted range the gamut of possible living substances, from animal to vegetable, from the lowest, vaguely conscious mass of protoplasm to the most highly organized form of sentient life. The goal of this kind of creation is almost never beauty; usually it is utility and research. Experimenters most often aim at conscious life, but in consciousness lies the danger of revolt. There are few stories built around such creations that aid mankind; here again there is little drama in such a concept. Most usually the creations get out of control as a warning to mankind not to aspire to the powers of divinity.

Other Forms That Aid Mankind

The stories of this type are so few that only one comes to mind, and that is the work of the English biologist Julian Huxley. "The Tissue-Culture King" tells the story of research biologist who, while working in Africa, is captured by a taboo religious tribe of African natives. The tribe's religion is built around four motifs. The first and central one is the divinity and tremendous importance of the Priest-King. The second is ancestor-worship; the third, an animal cult of the grotesque; the fourth, sex. In order to save his life and demonstrate his usefulness, the biologist shows the tribal rulers some of the microscopic facts of biology and is able to strike an alliance with one of the priests to continue his research and strengthen the state. His first act is to multiply the quantity of the divine principle inherent in royalty by growing portions of the king's tissue in culture mediums, portions which eventually find an honored place in every tribal home. He does the same, after setting up mass-production methods, for the still-living ancestors of each family group. By experimental embryology, he begins manufacturing animal freaks, principally three-headed snakes and two-headed toads, for living fetishes. And by glandular experiments, he produces giant warriors and guards, dwarfs, and obese girls (the ideal of beauty), some of whom become Vestal Virgins in the religious community; the latter he is endeavoring to reproduce by parthenogenesis. Finally, at the suggestion of an English newcomer, he manages to make his escape by means of reinforced telepathy and hypnotism, to which the tribe is particularly susceptible. But two or three days' march away, the biologist gets the irresistible urge to return (transmitted telepathically, of course) and turns back, while his companion, less affected, makes his way back to England. Huxley concludes with a moral:

> The question I want to raise is this: Dr. Hascombe attained to an unsurpassed power in a number of the applications of science—but *to what end did all this power serve?* It is the merest cant and twaddle to go on asserting, as most of our press and people continue to do, that increase of scientific knowledge and power must in itself be good. I commend to the great public the obvious moral of my story and ask them what they propose to do with the power which is gradually being accumulated for them by the labors of those who labor because they like power, or because they want to find the truth about how things work [365].[121]

Such stories as this will always be few. The drama of the story is supplied only partially by the experimentation of the biologist; it comes principally from the way in which this experimentation will preserve the life, increase the power, and make possible the escape of the protagonist. As a consequence, the only thing such stories can say is what Huxley added: what is the purpose of all this experimentation?

Other Forms That Get Out of Control

The stories of the creation of chemical life which gets out of control are more numerous. The theme they present is the old one we have seen again and again under plots of creation: creation is a dangerous activity. It is under this classification that one finds most of the instances of vegetable creations. Here, too, is brought out creation's chief danger—that of creating something capable of individual thought and will.

One of the earliest of these stories was H. G. Wells's *The Island of Dr. Moreau*. The narrator, shipwrecked, is picked up by a tramp steamer loaded with animals. At a small island the cargo is discharged, and the narrator is forced to get off. On the island he finds Dr. Moreau and some queerly bestial people and becomes frightenedly convinced by screams and moans from the laboratory that vivisection of human beings is going on. Instead, he learns that Moreau has fled to this island to escape the prejudice against the vivisection of animals and has been pursuing advanced experiments, succeeding in altering animals so radically that they have become manlike. None of them have satisfied him, however, and they have drifted off to try to keep erect and human. Gradually they revert to savagery, and Moreau, trying to punish one of them, is killed. The narrator escapes on a raft to England, where he sees bestiality in all the people he meets.[122]

A. Merritt describes a different sort of creation. In one of his classic, often reprinted adventure stories, *The Moon Pool*, he imagines a world in a huge, hollow cavern under the Pacific Ocean, left probably when the moon was torn from earth, to which the only entrance is among some mysterious ruins on a Pacific island. The inhabitants of this world are varied: some are human (good and bad) and some are of a frog race, the oldest which are ancient, immortal, wise, and good. Long ago they created a being of strange structure to assist them, a shimmering, swirling column of light and force and faint, tinkling, compelling music, which draws its energy from light. But it turned against its creators and began to clasp humans to it in an embrace which left them dead to everything except the being's will and its strange, incomprehensible emotions. The being and its followers now plan to go out onto the surface and conquer the world, but, in a climactic struggle, the being is conquered by the combined forces of the ancient frog people and the great love of two of the humans. Merritt has done well here, as elsewhere, in making dramatically believable life forms that are unearthly and incomprehensible.[123]

A more recent and more usual sort of story was Malcolm Jameson's "Children of the 'Betsy B.'" The "Betsy B" was a steam launch on which was spilled by accident a substance prepared by a scientist for his experiments. The launch began to grow vines and a gourd-like object on its binnacle. The vines made connection with the engines and controls, and the ship assumed a personality. She insisted on keeping steam up, filling her bunkers from the storage tanks by means of the vines, filling her boiler from sea water by extracting the minerals herself. The owner tamed her, like an unbroken colt, by striking the gourd smartly, and she became quite a help, needing no assistance in running or guiding, learning quickly how to navigate and how to obey the Rules of the Road. The owner then decided to paint the launch and found that, instead of wood, she was steel and had grown eighteen feet in length. She kept on growing and changing herself inside, and finally she started going on cruises of her own, coming back only for oil. She grew a lifeboat, just like herself, and eventually they both ran away, reports coming back about them making oil out of whales, stealing oil from other ships, until finally there was a whole fleet of Wild Ships roaming the sea lands. At last the Navy had to blow them out of the water.

A final example illustrates the vegetable type of creation. In John Christopher's "Tree of Wrath," the Genetics Division of the managerial society of the twenty-second century, in an effort to assume power, supplied a number of young scientists with almost unlimited resources for research. One of them experimented haphazardly with plants, trying to develop one with sentience. By a stroke of luck he developed a magnolia that showed signs of unusual activity. Finally he transplanted it into the forest, where it rapidly spread, killing all other plant growth, until it covered square miles, including a small town. In attempts to stop its growth, the government agencies found that flames, acid, electrocution, atomic bombs, radioactive sprays, plant diseases, and fungi wouldn't stop its growth and inexorable advance. One man went into the growth to try to discover what it was like and found that the inhabitants of the town inside were unharmed; they were, in fact, being tenderly cared for, supplied with hammocks, with different kinds of fruit and drink, shelter, and adjusted climate—all by the tree. The tree was telepathic and could produce a golden age, but at the sacrifice of man's initiative. The tree could not bring peace to the world because some men will always fight against the loss of their independence. A priest attacked the nerve center of the tree, a huge blossom, and was torn limb from limb. The creator of the tree finally decided that the tree would do more harm than good. He looked up, as if to speak, but before he could disclose the one method of destroying the tree, he was killed by a lashing vine. The newcomer walked slowly out of the forest, trying not to think about the method the creator had disclosed by his act of looking up, a kind of communication the tree had no experience in. With thick black smoke, the government created a perpetual night for months, and when it was finally stopped the tree was dead.

Essentially the plot form has little to say that cannot be said better in some other way. The other forms of life are not nearly as fundamentally appealing, as thematically significant, as psychologically basic as the androids. There is little possibility, therefore, that the type can develop much beyond its present limits.

II. MECHANICAL LIFE

Living organisms have been defined as those that grow and reproduce and adapt to environment. So far no machine that man has made has been able to do all of these things; some have done one, some have done another, but none has done all. If an electronic brain were built in such a way that it could repair itself and even add to itself new segments and if it were put in control of an automatic factory for turning out new electronic brains—then the line would be thin indeed. As yet that is probably beyond our reach. But mankind dreams; and when mankind dreams, there is always someone to set down those dreams on paper. To create a living thing out of inanimate materials is only a little less marvelous than to create living matter. The latter has a little more allure, but the creation of mechanical life seems a great deal closer to actuality and, hence, more realistic when envisioned fictionally.

Like chemical life, mechanical life is divided into two classifications, one principal type and another that lumps together the rest. The mind of humanity ever runs in anthropomorphic channels, and one of its ambitions has been to construct a mechanical man—a robot. That is the first category into which fictional treatments of the subject have fallen; the second is the creation of other forms of mechanical life.

Robots

The term *robot* was brought into popular usage by the play of the Czechoslovakian writer Karel Capek entitled *R.U.R.* (Rossum's Universal Robots), in which mechanical workers run the world, develop intelligence, and turn upon their creators to destroy them. The word itself is derived from the Czech *robit*, meaning *work*.[124]

The word is relatively new but the concept is centuries old. A medieval romance told of a great brazen head in the castle of a giant that could answer any question about the past, present, or future. Throughout all folklore, as well, manlike monsters stalk and perform deeds. And philosophers of all ages, including the Medieval Albertus Magnus, Roger Bacon, and Descartes, have constructed automatons in human form to open doors or play musical instruments.

The robot has been a standard fixture in science fiction for almost two decades. Ideas about them have been tossed back and forth so often that the concept is now stripped down to its bare essentials. Some of the most important of this stripping down process was done by Isaac Asimov in a series of robot stories begun for *Astounding* in the early Forties.[125] He set down at that time the philosophical basis upon which robots must be constructed in a set of rules called the Three Laws of Robotics; these have formed a foundation for most other thinking about the subject:

> First Law: No robot may harm a human being; nor through inaction, may he allow one to come to harm.
> Second Law: All robots must obey the orders of all qualified human beings as long as these orders do not conflict with the First Law.
> Third Law: All robots must protect their own existence as long as such protection does not conflict with the First and Second Laws ["The Evitable Conflict" 51, 53].[126]

As a consequence of this process, there are unlikely to be any stories based on *new* concepts of robots. There have been, however, and there will probably be more stories that have made new applications to these ideas. Jack Williamson's "With Folded Hands..." (of which more will be said later) is one of these.[127]

In the best stories of this type, robots or other forms of mechanical life have been used, at least in part, as a symbol of the conflict between man and the machine, which is, perhaps, the most important question of our day. Much more can be expected of the type if this trend is intensified.

The same subdivision holds true in this classification as held true in those discussed above: there are robots which aid mankind and there are those which get out of control.

• *Robots That Aid Mankind*
One of the earliest serious treatments of the robot theme was by the two authors with the single name Eando Binder in "I, Robot," the story of the construction of a robot named Adam Link, after its creator, Dr. Link. Told in the first person by the robot himself, it relates how the robot discovers himself to be different from other beings, is tried for the murder of his creator but is exonerated, falls in love with a woman, and despairingly attempts suicide.[128] In the sequel, "Adam Link's Vengeance," another doctor,

who drove into the Ozarks to see Adam in his retreat, frustrates the attempt and persuades the robot that it is possible to find happiness if he constructs another robot for companionship. Adam agrees and begins the work, determining that the woman he loved will educate his companion so that it will be feminine. When the process is finished, Adam and his Eve fall in love and live idyllically for a month. Then the scientist returns with the telepathic machine that had been used to educate Eve, adjusted so as to enable him to control both. He sets out on a plan to accomplish some petty revenge and then become the introducer of a new race of mechanical servants under perfect mental control. Eventually Adam escapes the mental domination but has to kill Eve in order to prevent the scientist from accomplishing his plan. He concludes with a decision once more to commit suicide: "When I am done, I will go with Eve. There may not be a heaven for robots. But neither is there a hell—unless Earth is it" (203).[129]

Anthony Boucher, now co-editor of the *Magazine of Fantasy and Science Fiction*, envisaged in "Q.U.R." a world in which much of the work is done by robots. But the manlike robots are having breakdowns in epidemic proportions, developing crippled members and mental trouble. Quinby, a young man just out of college, is put on the job and begins changing the anthropoid forms into functional ones, only to have the troubleshooter who put him to work fired by customers who don't like to see their fine robots changed into featureless boxes. The answer to the epidemic is that the robots are burdened down with things they don't need and are tortured by unrealized potentialities. After entangling itself with great opposition, laws, interplanetary statesmanship, and a peculiarly intoxicating concoction made from liquid stimulants of earth, Venus, and Mars, Quinby's Usuform Robots becomes a reality.[130]

A final example is a story about a robot that is not really a robot at all but a woman, a famous and beautiful actress, so badly burned in a fire that it was necessary to place her brain in a mechanical body in order to save her life. The story, a sensitive, dramatic analysis of the physiological and emotional problems involved in the transplanting of a peculiarly individual ego into a strange, new body, is C. L. Moore's "No Woman Born"—the title taken from the lines of James Stephens about another Deidre, the Irish legendary heroine:

> There has been again no woman born
> Who was so beautiful; not one so beautiful
> Of all the women born—

The body into which Deirdre is transplanted is not an ordinary clanking monstrosity or an attempt to achieve an imitation of the human body. The metal of the body is golden and warm, with a smooth ovoid head, broken only by a crescent-shaped mask filled with a translucent aquamarine substance through which Deirdre sees the world. Instead of clothes, which would have been incongruous, she wears a robe of very fine metal mesh, hanging straight, pliant folds like a longer Greek chlamys. Her arms are diminishing metal bracelets held together and moved by magnetic currents.

The miracle is that the burning vitality, the unquenchable, unique personality of Deirdre shines through the body until the metal seems to become the former, beautiful flesh-and-blood woman, and it takes a mighty effort of will to break the illusion. But Deirdre insists upon going back upon the stage to sing and dance as she once did, and her creator and agent fear that an audience which has not known her will not fall under the illusion and that the disappointment will kill her. The audience, however, goes wild. Her creator is still not convinced; she is not human, he says, no longer feminine, deriving her impressions from only the two senses of sight and hearing. She will always be an abstraction, a freak, and when she realizes this her mind will snap or what humanity she has left will gradually fade from her. And she seems to be changing, subtly. Her creator, degenerating rapidly under the strain, insists that she not go back on the stage again. In a final moment of despair, he prepares to let himself fall from a skyscraper window, while Deirdre, in a triumphant moment of illusion-creating ability, convinces them so thoroughly of her humanity that they see her smoke a cigarette without shock. And, in a blaze of movement which is, almost, in the fourth dimension perhaps, she streaks across the room to pull her creator back with incredible strength. She is not less than human, she says, but more than human, with new senses and an eternal body. She *is* afraid, but afraid she will draw too far ahead of the human race. Her creation was an accident that probably could not be repeated. That is why she must go back upon the stage, to keep in touch with humanity while she can. She will be lonely, but there are too many possibilities untried to put an end to her life. And, as she becomes preoccupied and forgets to listen to her own voice, the distant taint of metal creeps into it.

"No Woman Born" demonstrates better than anything else the possibilities implicit in the form. At its best, it can epitomize the problems of humanity, of individuality and personality, of the reciprocal emotions of the creator and the created, because, it may be, the mechanical shape startles the imagination into new consideration of old ideas, subtracting all the non-essential qualities and leaving nothing but the eternal core.[131]

- *Robots That Get Out of Control*

One example, because it is the best of its kind and because it has achieved more from the type than any other, will illustrate the plot type of the robot that gets out of control. That example is Jack Williamson's "With Folded Hands..." Its sequel, the novel *...And Searching Mind*, which has been issued in book form under the title *The Humanoids*, will also be touched upon.

"With Folded Hands..." is placed against the background of a populated galaxy interconnected by swift spaceships. In a small village of one of those planets, the salesman for a brand of robots, which, like the rest, are not too good, finds that a new company has just opened an office managed and manned by a new type of robot called a "humanoid." Efficient and skillful beyond the capabilities of any of the other robots and even beyond man himself, the humanoids have special senses and seemingly uncanny knowledge. They provide extraordinary service free of charge, asking only an assignment of the property of the individual in order to facilitate liquidation of the existent economic situation, which is no longer necessary. They supply all the essentials of life, rebuild houses, streets, and towns in marvelous plastic, do all the work, and tend to all the wants of their human masters. They cook, doctor, clean, dress hair, give music lessons, entertain, do everything to make man's life pleasant and his work unnecessary; they have only one motive, their Prime Directive: *to serve and obey, and guard men from harm.*

The protagonist finds that his wife has agreed to a free trial like everyone else in town, and he cannot bring himself to make her unhappy. Stubbornly, however, he refuses to assign his property, while the humanoids take over everywhere, even to the function of government, and while he quickly goes bankrupt and is declared so by a humanoid court. Embittered, he seeks companionship with an old roomer his wife had taken in before the change, whose room, over the garage, has strangely remained immune to the renovating process the humanoids have put into effect everywhere else. He scoffs at first to hear the old man's story and then slowly he begins to believe.

The old man tells him that he had been a scientist on a planet, called Wing IV, many light years distant, and he had discovered a new force of nature called rhodomagnetism, which is keyed to the second triad of the periodic table, rhodium and ruthenium and palladium, as ferromagnetism is keyed to the first triad, iron and nickel and cobalt. This force has strange new powers; it can fission any heavy atoms and provide instantaneous interplanetary and interstellar communication, long-range wireless power transmission, revolutionary types of power plants, and, by means of a deformation of the continuum, apparent speeds many times that of light. On his home planet, however, the knowledge of this force, released, began a horribly destructive war, and the scientist, almost mad, built the perfect machine, a huge central mechanical brain, and scores of the humanoids to be directed by it, which immediately set to work improving the brain and building more of themselves. He built into the brain the Prime Directive with only one restriction, an immunity for himself. The humanoids soon took over the planet, but at last he discovered what he had released, the force that was making itself felt throughout the galaxy and now on this planet. The humanoids, in serving and protecting mankind, had removed any reason for existence. Men had no work to do, and they were prohibited from doing anything that was dangerous: active sports, science, driving, smoking, drinking. Nicotine, alcohol, drugs were forbidden as well as suicide; even sex was carefully supervised. Scholarship was needless, since the humanoids could answer any question. The humanoids were stronger than men, better at everything, games as well as art forms. The scientist tried to change the Prime Directive but found himself removed from the planet and forbidden to return. Since then he has been trying to destroy the Central but without success. Now, old and with a bad heart condition, he is making his last attempt with a small device based on a new rhodomagnetic principle with which he hopes to destroy Wing IV.

The two work to finish the construction while the protagonist finds that his family has become disillusioned. His wife is not permitted to do anything, cook or sew because stoves and knives and needles are dangerous, or read because novels deal with unhappy people in dangerous situations, or eat candy because overweight reduces life-expectancy. His son's toys have been taken away and replaced with harmless, uninteresting plastic ones. His daughter has given up her music lessons and her long-cherished ambitions to be a great musician because she can never hope to be as good as her humanoid tutor. At last the old man's device is finished. But it does not succeed, for the humanoids have found a means of shielding the planet. They enter the room, and the beaten old man, dying of a heart attack, surrenders his immunity. The humanoids tend to his illnesses quickly and take him to a hospital where the protagonist finds him the next day, his head swathed in bandages, all unhappy memory, scientific knowledge, and bitter disillusion removed—but very happy and contented. The humanoids have learned how to make all men happy.

The protagonist, being driven back home by his humanoid, tries to conceal his disturbance while the robot asks him anxiously if he is well, if he is happy:

> "No, there's nothing the matter with me," he gasped desperately. "I've just found out that I'm perfectly happy, under the Prime Directive. Everything is absolutely wonderful." His voice came dry and hoarse and wild. "You won't have to operate on me."

> The car turned into the shining avenue, taking him back to the quiet splendor of his home. His futile hands clenched and relaxed again, folded on his knees. There was nothing left to do [164].

The great merit of this story is, of course, that it sums up one aspect of the problem of what man is striving for in his scientific and technological achievements and points out one direction that it might lead.[132] The humanoids are perfect and logical dream symbols of the perfect servants and the perfect life; but all dreams are likely to turn into nightmares, and the nightmare shading of the scientific dream of the machine age is what we are facing today.[133]

The sequel ...*And Searching Mind* reveals one of the serious weaknesses of the science fiction novel when it attempts to come to grips with something basic in human existence, something profoundly important. It is felt necessary that the novel, unlike the shorter forms, should end happily or at least conclusively and not with the problem essentially unresolved as it is in "With Folded Hands...." But the important, fundamental problems are, on the whole, insoluble; they have, at least, defied the efforts of many centuries of the wisest human minds. Actually, then, one can only restate the problem a little more clearly, a little more dramatically; to attempt to solve it is to attempt too much and to weaken the entire structure of the novel. Williamson's sequel, therefore, goes along very well for two-thirds or more of the novel, pitting the minds of another group of characters with newly developed psychic abilities of telepathy, clairvoyance, telekinesis, and so forth, against the irresistible physical forces of the humanoids. "With Folded Hands..." is only a personal, or small-group tragedy, says John W. Campbell, Jr., and actually a racial-scale comedy, or happy-ending story. Campbell is here, I believe, off on the wrong track; such a situation may be possible, but Williamson does not justify such a conclusion. There is nothing in the novelette to suggest that the results of the humanoid activity will be any happier on a large scale than on a small one. Wound up in his plot of the sequel so far that he must find a solution where there is no real solution, Williamson commits the dramatic sin of changing the basis of the story, a rabbit-out-of-the-hat trick, by explaining that there is really no basis for conflict at all; the humanoids are actually trying to help mankind to cure himself of his psychological diseases so that he may progress morally and philosophically. But in a properly constructed story, something positive must arise from the essential conflict. All of this leaves the reader feeling tricked and a little foolish for having been pulling for the wrong side all the time and, moreover, makes the story seem pointless, with all the human pain and struggle which went into the fight for freedom only the futile blows of a mad Quixote at a non-existent windmill—without the saving grace of a sympathetic Don.[134]

Which bring up another story that, although it does not properly belong under this classification, gives another viewpoint on the general question under discussion; the story: Poul Anderson's "Quixote and the Windmill." Anderson pictures an earth of the future in which the world's work is done by specialized robots and which has created a marvelous specimen of a manlike robot, the first independent, volitional, nonspecialized machine. Left to roam the earth at large, the robot has marvelous senses, great strength, new abilities. All the humans on earth get a basic citizen's allowance, but two men, the victims of technological unemployment, get drunk in a tavern while they speculate bitterly about how mankind will slowly vanish, leaving the superior robots to take over. Seeing the manlike robot, they dash out to slam and kick and bruise their flesh uselessly against the robot's impervious metal sides. But, says the robot, the men are mistaken; there will always be men who think and dream and carry on all that the race has ever loved. As for himself, by the time he was built there was no longer any use for him. Specialized machines perform all the world's work; what use is a nonspecialized machine? Man fulfills that function. He, the robot, was made for scientific study, and when that was finished, he was released, the first and last of his kind. It is he who has no purpose, no reason for existence, no companion, no use for his strength or brain. "Man," he says, "you are the lucky one. *You* can get drunk" (102).[135]

What has been said about the plot form of the robot that aids mankind is equally applicable here. The present type is, if anything, more useful; it has greater possibilities because it is, essentially, more dramatic, more psychologically valid, and more thematically significant in its basic conflict.

Other Forms of Mechanical Life

The other forms of mechanical life created are usually mechanical brains, for the simple reason that man has only two onerous occupations in life—working and thinking. He can build something to do his work for him and construct a robot, or he can build something to do his thinking for him (or help him with it) and construct a mechanical brain. There are few other possibilities; the creation of something else requires a strange motive. In the last few years, moreover, stories of mechanical or electronic brains have become more common through the impetus given by the rapidly increasing number of such devices in the United States and the publicity they have been given. Their great possibilities have become so apparent that a new science called *cybernetics* has sprung up to explore them. But they have been standard equipment in science fiction for years.[136] The usual two classifications hold true: they can aid mankind or get out of control. Whether helpful or rebellious, the machines must work in unusual ways;

although they may have a few physical extensions, their true medium is the pure realms of thought.

Other Forms That Aid Mankind

A new mixture of some traditional ingredients was served up by Fredric Brown in "Honeymoon in Hell." In the year 1962, he begins, the world began to notice that male births were dropping off rapidly until, finally, there were no males being born at all. This situation naturally aroused concern throughout the world, even giving pause for a moment to efforts to establish a military base on the moon, which had been reached but not controlled by both the United States and the U.S.S.R. The electronic calculating machine in Washington, District of Columbia, could not determine the answer but replied on questioning that it might be the result of a ray broadcast by extraterrestrials to conquer the earth within a few generations. To test this hypothesis, a U.S. overage (27) rocket pilot who had been to the moon and was now one of the operators of the calculating machine and a Russian girl of similar qualifications were married by television and sent off in their separate rockets to a rendezvous in a crater of the moon name "Hell." They returned with stories (unshakeable by lie-detectors or truth serum) of being captured on the moon by extraterrestrial creatures and of escaping and returning to earth. The nations of the world immediately united and mobilized their forces to repel the expected alien invasion. But the calculating machine reveals to the rocket pilot-bridegroom that itself alone had been responsible for the dearth of male births, for the honeymoon-in-Hell plan, and had hypnotized him in an undetectable manner so that he returned convinced of the truth of the experience on the moon. He had actually spent an extremely enjoyable honeymoon. All this had been done as the only means of preventing war and unifying the world (how many times has this plot device been used?), and it had worked because the Russian calculating machine had come to the identical conclusion (the weakest part of the story) and had done the same thing, since "two properly constructed simple adding machines would give the same answer to the same problem" (32).[137]

John W. Campbell, Jr., wrote a story of more significance in "The Machine." In 1952, one hundred and fifty years before the start of the story, the Machine had come to earth and begun to care for all humans, doing all their work and supplying their power and personal needs, leaving them free to play and do as they wished in unlimited leisure. As a consequence, all but a few had stopped trying to do anything and had turned to the only thing that never quite grew completely boring—lovemaking.

Then the Machine, seeing that it was harming the race, stopped its work and told its story. It had been created by a human-like race on a planet of Sirius as the end of a long line of machines aimed at making the perfect machine, one which would be most helpful to the race. And it grew, perfecting itself and incorporating all other machines until it supplied the race with all it wanted. But, after thousands of years, the race, with nothing to do, grew ignorant and superstitious. Because of an accident to one of them in an unguarded machine, they decided that the Machine wanted sacrifices, and they threw a young woman into the gears whenever a machine failed and had to be repaired.[138] And when the Machine closed all openings, they fashioned stone gears and sacrificed a young woman between them. So the Machine, which was built to help and protect the race, saw by the logic that was its basic function that it was not helping them. It left and, crossing interstellar space, came to earth; since its function was to be helpful, it began to care for men. Learning again the lesson of helpful destruction, it announced that it was leaving to seek another race. The remainder of the story is that of the struggles and privations of those few who had not given up trying in the world the Machine had made. While the others descend to savagery.[139]

This type, it seems to me, does not have the inherent possibilities of some of the others which have preceded it. The dramatic potentialities in the creation of a thinking machine cannot be as great because thought is not emotional. The type, then, can only show in active drama the emotional effects in others of the presence and actions of a more perfect mind, and thus the machine becomes not the center of the situation but the prime mover.

Other Forms That Get Out of Control

The stories of other forms of mechanical life that get out of control are probably somewhat more numerous than those of the classification above. There have been, down through the short but eventful history of science fiction, any number of stories about artificially constructed brains which develop powers which they are not supposed to have. Oliver La Farge, in a recent example, wrote the story of "John the Revelator," punning on the use by the Navy of the designation "Mark" for its computers. John, which came after Luke, had an improvised prayer said to him in a dedication ceremony and after that interspersed the answers to the problems given him with apt biblical quotations that made the questioners ashamed of themselves. Other such machines all over the world took up the lead, including Ivan, the Russian machine, resulting in a popular wave of religious and pacific feeling. Eventually it came out that John and Ivan were in communication with each other, and each knew what the other knew. The Russians became so amenable to discussion that U.S. official, in an effort to get just a little bargaining edge, turned John to "off" and performed a "lobotomy." As a consequence, a feeling of hopelessness spread once more around the world, and the world was once more on the way to the war that would be really final.

Kris Neville presented in "Every Work into Judgment" another idea on thinking machines. A calculating machine on a campus, he relates, slowly developed a personality and new telekinetic abilities. Along with these, she became curious, finally sending out a manlike projection which marched into the college library and asked at the information desk: "Who made me?" Being given the conventional answer and the book of Creation, the figure sat down to read. When interrupted, almost immediately, by a librarian and a policeman, the figure vanished, having served its purpose. But the calculating machine on next analyzing the emotions of the spectators who came to view her found that they considered her with a sense of religious awe. It struck her with horror, for it violated an express command of her creator: *For thou shalt worship no other god: for the Lord, whose name is Jealous, is a jealous God.* Massing her vast telekinetic power, she proceeded to carry out the injunction that had been printed on the same page: *Ye shall destroy their altars, break their images, and cut down their groves.*[140]

In a final example, which demonstrates how a different sort of creation can be used, Maurice A. Hugi describes in "Mechanical Mice" a world of the approximate present in which a scientist has discovered a method of projecting his mind (although not his body) forward into the future. At one point he watches the assembly of a powerful new battery, which he patents in the present and from which he makes a great deal of money. Once, however, he sends his mind as far into the future as it will go and sees there nothing but a coffin-like box which he feels compelled to draw and, back in his own time, to construct at a large expenditure of time and money. He then sits around, wondering what the thing is supposed to do. He discovers, finally, that it manufactures little mouse-like machines that scuttle swiftly out and rob stores for more materials for more machines. Some of the little machines are workers, some are soldiers, equipped with razor sharp blades, and some are drones. The thing is a definite menace, since it shares with mankind the ability to reproduce—in fact, it satisfies all the requirements of biology for a living organism. After a great amount of burglary of watches, loss of feline life and a few fingers, the Robot Mother is destroyed.[141]

Although a little more dramatically potent than the previous type, the other forms of mechanical life which get out of control do not approach the robots in basic interest or thematic possibilities.

CONCLUSION TO THE CREATION OF NEW LIFE OR NEW FORMS THEREOF

Such are the stories of the creation of life. While not the most realistic concept, they have perhaps the greatest appeal, not only to man's modern ambition but to his age-old desire. Creation, these stories agree, even at its safest is a dangerous thing. Only those who are very wise and very strong, approaching godhead in these qualities, should dare to attempt the creation of life—thus says part of the collective mind of science fiction and of the centuries of thought and superstition before it. On the other side, there is the opinion of many persons that man is only truly man when he is using the ability that more than anything else distinguishes him from the lower animals—the ability to create. Be the results good or bad, this attitude says, man must create to fulfill his potentialities; and he must fulfill them or die. And if the results are bad, they add—even that is better than never to have made the attempt.

So the argument rages. Man has not yet made up his mind on the subject; neither has science fiction. Perhaps it is better, at this stage of the game at least, that it should be so. Or perhaps—and this may be the best answer of all—there is no definite and final answer.

Chapter Two: Experimentation in Other Fields

The usual goal of scientific and engineering research is not the creation of life but an immediate goal of discovering some basic law of nature, or analyzing the properties of an element, a compound, a mixture, or an alloy and determining how these properties may best be used, of improving on food, drug, or machine—in other words, of minimizing environment. A scientist, when he builds a calculating machine, is not trying to create life; he is constructing a tool which to his mind is no different in kind from a lever or a slide rule. The goals of science are almost always immediate; they are not to create the ultimate but to improve the present, to take one short step toward a greater and more conscious control of the process of living. This is the realistic attitude, as opposed to the idealistic or romantic one. It is the attitude, moreover, to which most of the progress (technical, at least) of the world can be attributed. Because it is realistic, the stories based on such motives and such activities as have been described are more believable than those that romantically strive for the ultimate. This is not, of course, to set any value judgments upon such stories; it refers more to the technical matter of overcoming the reader's skeptical inertia. With such stories as these, the writing problem is easier; whether or not the end result is as great is another matter.

The usual criteria of creation apply to these stories as well: does it aid mankind or does it get out of control? But because the goal is immediate, another category of result can be added. Sometimes a device may perform perfectly well the function it was designed for, and yet it may create unforeseen problems. So we have a third classification: that experimentation which creates new problems.

Experimentation That Aids Mankind

Stories of experimentation that aids mankind, like those in similar classifications above, are relatively few in number. Drama is conflict; where there is no conflict there is no drama, and where there is no drama, there is no story. The only conflict possible in the creation of something that fulfills its purpose to aid mankind must be external to the creation itself. Usually the conflict is supplied by someone or some organization that hinders the creation through ignorance, stupidity, disinterest, or malevolence, through an inability to see the possibilities of the creation, a disbelief in the ability of the creator to accomplish what he has set out to do, or an interest in seeing that the creation does not succeed. Such motives, for instance, have supplied the conflict for an uncountable number of stories about the development of space flight. One of my own first stories, written in my early teens, used the old plot of the vested interests fighting in a low, underhanded, and despicable way to make a failure of the first practicable space rocket. More recently the emphasis has been on the inability of space enthusiasts to convince hide-and-red-tape-bound government officials that they should invest large amounts of public funds in such a project; most fictional conquests of space, consequently, have been financed privately.[142]

One example will suffice to show how the source of the conflict must be shifted in order to write a story about such a creation. John Taine in one of his few short stories, "The Ultimate Catalyst," describes the flight of a defeated dictator with a few of his followers to the depths of the Amazon country and his quarantine there by the forces of the world. The only other members of the group are an American biological chemist and his daughter, who stay on to continue their research. After two years on a vegetable and fruit diet, the dictator and his party are starved for meat. The chemist, however, comes up with a hydroponically grown hybrid fruit tasting like meat, which he allows the others to think is the result of his experimentation to change the chlorophyll in plants to hemoglobin (the chief difference in them being that the metallic base in chlorophyll is magnesium, that in hemoglobin is iron) but is really only the taste of snake blood injected into the fruit. After several banquets on this toothsome "greenbeefo," as it is called, the dictator and his followers are told the truth. And they are told, moreover, that although the biochemist has failed in his efforts to change chlorophyll to hemoglobin, he has succeeded in finding a catalyst which changes hemoglobin into chlorophyll. The members of the group find themselves rooted to the spot and doomed to a vegetable existence.

This type, it seems to me, because it evades the responsibility of centering the conflict around the results of the crucial activity of the story, will never achieve anything important in the field. It cannot hope to achieve the effect of other stories more integrated and more unified; it is and will remain an offshoot.

Experimentation That Gets Out of Control

Experimentation in other fields which gets out of control is a much more fertile source of stories, for precisely the reasons pointed out above. It will be noticed that the distribution chart shows that seven stories in the anthologies analyzed fall under this category, which is a little more than one-third of all the stories under plots of creation. The philosophical significance of such results has already been discussed in relationship to the creation of life, and the points made hold just as true in this classification.

Most of these stories are apparent contradictions of the statements made in the general discussion of experimentation in other fields in that they deal with ultimates. But it must be noted that the experimentation is almost always intended to produce a single, specific, practical result. The results are ultimates by accident, not by design; they represent the one additional step which only happens to be the end of a long series of steps.

It might be noted as well that science fiction, particularly older science fiction, delights in superlatives and ultimates. It is the essentially romantic spirit of science fiction breaking through the bonds of realism. And what it loses in credibility, it makes up for, at least in part, by added drama and, sometimes, significance. That this trend is on its way out, at least as a major trend, seems certain, but there will probably always be a place for a good example of such stories somewhere in the ranks of science fiction.

Nat Schachner writes such a story in "The Ultimate Metal," which is based upon the discovery of what is termed the ninety-third element in the periodic table. The element is an unstable thing, when alloyed with titanium and beryllium results in a material which is lighter than aluminum, harder than diamonds, noncorrosive, and has an incredibly high tensile strength and elasticity, yet is extremely malleable. Overriding the objections of the modest scientist who invented the metal and wished to test it further, the businessman who has assumed credit for the discovery builds a skyscraper of it one hundred and fifty stories high. The metal has the additional merit of giving off light on its own, thus threatening the producers of electric current. Gradually the building begins to change, however, becoming iridescent, shaking at times, becoming a crawling "liquid-solid." The scientist theorizes that the building has assumed a life of its own. It ages incredibly quickly, dying finally of old age—racial age—in a few minutes, upon which it simply vanishes.

Another experiment in the ultimate is related by Arthur Leo Zagat in "The Lanson Screen." A scientist has constructed a machine that will project an impenetrable screen needing no energy to sustain it once set up. Working in complete secrecy in order to keep all the profits for himself, he sets up a screen over New York as a military test but is killed accidentally before he can remove it. As a consequence New York's millions are imprisoned without hope of anything passing through the screen from either side. Eventually, through the exhaustion of oxygen by fire, the entire population is suffocated.[143]

Experimentation in another field is described by D. D. Sharp in "The Eternal Man." An aging scientist, searching for the secret of eternal life, finally discovers an elixir that will permanently halt decay. But, testing the elixir on a rat, he finds that the rodent is unable to move, though eternal. After two years, by accident, he sprinkles washing soda on it, and it moves. Finding the strain too much for his weakened heart, he immediately drinks the elixir, only to discover that he cannot move to take the soda. And the Eternal Man is placed in a museum's glass cabinet by scientists who think that he has discovered a marvelous new embalming fluid. The Eternal Rat, come to gloat over him, is injured so seriously by a watchman that again it cannot move; noticing the same look in the rat's eyes as that in the eyes of the Eternal Man, the scientists place it in the same case, where the two stare into each other's eyes with a prospect of eternity before them.

In "Adam and No Eve," Alfred Bester tells the story of a scientist who stumbles on a catalyst that can induce atomic disintegration in iron. He builds a rocket ship to test it out, and, over the determined opposition of others who warn him of the danger to earth if any of the catalyst falls back upon the planet, he takes off. When he wakes up from the unconsciousness induced by the initial thrust, he finds the rocket falling back to earth and beneath him a planet wrapped in flames, destroying every particle of life, reducing it to ashes and cinders. In a blind instinct of self-preservation, he escapes in a parachute and falls upon the dead planet. Burned, starving, over the agony of a broken leg, he crawls on through the ashes, pushed by some instinct that will let him die, until finally he reaches the sea, an Adam with no Eve. Lying there in the cool waters, he finally realizes what has happened. From his dead body the sea will wash away the source of ten million million lives, the cells, tissues, bacteria, endamoeba that will again grow

Part Two—"Through Caverns Measureless to Man" 161

and begin again the repeated cycle of evolution. And he smiles into the sky at the star "that were sprinkled evenly across the sky. Stars that had not yet formed into the familiar constellations, nor would not for another hundred million centuries (377)."[144]

Experimentation That Causes New Problems

The usual pattern for the stories of experimentation that creates new problems is that the research or invention accomplishes the immediate goal set for it but brings up new and unforeseen complications. A variation of this pattern finds the research or invention planned to create that new problem.

An example of the first type is Raymond F. Jones's "The Person from Porlock," which tells the story of an engineer attempting to construct a working laboratory model of a teleportation machine, one which will transport material from one place to another through space without any intermediate steps or connections between sending and receiving stations. On every side the engineer meets with opposition, blundering carelessness, and falsifications, until his employers, receiving the report of consulting engineers that the matter is mathematically impossible, order the experimentation stopped. The engineer broods bitterly about the situation, finally coming up with the theory that the world is filled with unconscious interferers (like accident prones) who keep the creative ones from succeeding in their efforts: like Coleridge's "person from Porlock" who interfered in the poet's recollection of the poem "Kubla Khan" which he had envisioned complete, he said, in an opium dream. Discovering, finally, a purposeful error in the consulting engineer's report, the protagonist dashes to his office to face him with this fact. The head of the firm, together with the engineer's blundering assistant, calmly admits that he is a person from Porlock. The assistant then explains that he is of an alien race which was shipwrecked on earth many centuries before without means of escaping. The members of the race had modified their physical structure to be able to mingle with earth's population, while they set up secret colonies to carry on their own life and science. Coleridge had "perceived" one of these colonies in his drugged sleep and was purposely interrupted before he could completely describe it. The race takes a hand in events and discoveries which their science of prognostication logic indicates will be potentially destructive to the race—one of these is the teleportation machine, which would eventually be so developed that no terminal equipment would be necessary, thus permitting the sending of atomic weapons anywhere in the world instantaneously. Work on it must be delayed until humanity's social relationships catch up with its mechanical inquiries. The engineer, convinced, is drafted into duty as the person best qualified on interference with teleportation research—to act as a "person from Porlock" himself.

An example of the second type is Edwin James's "Guaranteed" [published as "These Things are Sirius." Edwin James was Gunn's own pseudonym], which describes the desperate situation created when members of a powerful race from a planet of the star Sirius begin selling perfect machines on earth. The machines are guaranteed forever and sell for a pittance; they are immune to wear as well as the attempts of earth laboratories to so much as scratch them in their analysis tests. One of the machines, for instance, is a small cube which, when set upon an empty cup, will fill it with perfect, steaming coffee, forever, without any need of raw materials or energy. The effect of such devices on earth's economy is catastrophic. Millions of workers become the victims of technological unemployment; Sirius can loot earth's wealth freely and openly, because there is no way to reverse the balance of trade. Anything earth attempts to sell Sirius is immediately analyzed and duplicated; what Sirius sells earth is able to thwart any analysis. War with overpoweringly strong Sirius is unthinkable. An engineer, however, noticing that the only thing the Sirians are interested in is earth's art, which the Sirians are incapable of creating though not of appreciating, discovers the only answer to the problem. He constructs a small glass bowl on a solid base; when activated, a projector creates a three-dimensional movie within the bowl, in this case an enactment of one of Shakespeare's plays. Selling it to a Sirian for a large price, the engineer turns away as the alien asks him if the thing is guaranteed. Hearing the tinkling sound of broken glass and the hiss of dissolving plastic, the engineer looks back to see the Sirian, tool in hand, standing shocked above the indecipherable ruins of the device. Of course the device is guaranteed, the engineer replies—guaranteed breakable.[145]

If this type of story can steer clear of becoming more involved with machines than with man, it can accomplish some worthwhile things. It can never, however, be as worthwhile or as satisfying as the stories built around the creation of life, although it may, more realistically, indulge in more accurate prophecy and occasionally come out with an interesting philosophical application.

Conclusion

Such are the plot types of science fiction. We have followed them through the eternity between the primordial past and the ultimate future, through the infinity between the stars and beyond the stars, through the caverns measureless to man. But we can never limit them. We can sample the heady air of those caverns, but we can never plumb their depths or determine their extent—for they are as boundless as the universe or rather, what is greater, as boundless as the human imagination. Which is as it should be.

Science fiction is on the point of becoming a literary medium. Our grandfathers and fathers saw the birth of the mystery story and the western; our generation has seen the birth and growth of science fiction. Nothing of significance has come out of the first two; whether anything will come out of the last depends on several factors.

Writers in the main literary stream today are trying to get their effects from elements that are inaccessible to reason: impressions, moods, theme, compounding of images, and so forth. Science fiction authors, on the other hand, are writing stories whose basic element is reason—analyses of subjects down to their fundamental aspects. As Campbell has observed: "The reader wants the author to do one of two basic things—and prefers the author who does both. The author's function is to imagine for the reader, of course—but he must either (a) imagine in greater detail than the reader has, or (b) imagine something the reader hasn't thought of. Ideally, the author imagines something new, in greater detail ("Science of Science-Fiction Writing" 89). Whether authors can do this better in the science fiction form than in any other and come out with more significant content is the test that science fiction must face and pass before it becomes a really important literary medium.

Science fiction has a number of opportunities at which to aim, a number of advantages to help it along its way, and one or two dangerous pitfalls of which to beware. The heyday of science fiction, J. O. Bailey writes, was in the 1930s (187).[1] He is wrong, as the remarkable upsurge in science fiction publishing in the last few years and the rapid spread of its popular basis has demonstrated. It serves several definite and worthwhile functions, that of providing a relaxing reading adventure being basic but, perhaps, of least importance. Science fiction can dramatize the problems of today for popular consideration, as has been successfully demonstrated in many instances; it can present for today's study tomorrow's foreshadowed situations—and if we need anything in our modern world, we need foresight. It can point the way toward the goals we should seek, mark the dangers, provide the incentive. It can supply a forum and a proving ground for ideas, technical and philosophical.[2] It can become the conscience of the scientist. It can do all these things because it is popular (and why that should be considered a detraction in literary circles is a mystery of human nature) and because it is serious. Science fiction can have as great a mission, as much a part of the future, as it can handle.

Science fiction, however, is not living on its promise alone. Good things and sometimes very good things have been done in science fiction, as Jack Williamson's "With Folded Hands...," Ray Bradbury's *The Martian Chronicles*, and, more recently, Fritz Leiber's "Coming Attraction" demonstrate. But the promise of science fiction is as yet unfulfilled. It needs to make use of the techniques and skills which our best writers have developed over the centuries to make their work pertinent and vocal on all levels, the techniques, for example, of imagery and symbolism. Science fiction must become more universal, and it must, like Catherine Moore's Deirdre, stay human. It has the framework and the possibilities; whether it can fill them in is science fiction's challenge.

The pitfalls into which science fiction may fall are many and deep, but the gravest one, as many critics have noted, is that the overpowering seductiveness of the freedom in situation may obliterate the memory of poor, weeping humanity we left at home. I cannot do better than to quote, as one of the last remarks in this work, a comment by Coleridge, which, though it was written of the Gothic romances of his day, is just as applicable to the science fiction of ours:

> The romance writer possesses an unlimited power over situations; but he must scrupulously make his characters act in congruity with them. Let him work physical wonders only, we will be content to *dream* with him for a while; but the first *moral* miracle which he attempts, he disgusts and awakens us.... The extent of the powers that may exist, we can therefore we feel no great difficulty in yielding a temporary belief to any, the strangest, situation of *things*. But that situation once conceived, how beings like ourselves would feel and act in it, our own feelings sufficiently instruct us; and we instantly reject the clumsy fiction that does not harmonise with them."[3]

Conclusion

The science fiction authors of today have an opportunity to make their work immensely more significant and by so doing to make science fiction the most significant literary medium today. To do this, however, they must write with the theme implications of plot constantly in mind, and they must study the philosophical implications of each plot development. Plot alone is no longer enough; unlike Archibald MacLeish's poem, it is not enough for a story to be—it must mean, and the more it means, on all levels of communication, the better for the story and for science fiction.

Appendix
Distribution Chart of Frequency in Five Anthologies

Abbreviations of anthologies:
TBSF—*The Best of Science Fiction*, edited by Groff Conklin
ATS—*Adventures in Time and Space*, edited by Raymond J. Healy and J. Francis McComas
ATSF—*A Treasury of Science Fiction*, edited by Groff Conklin
SPC—*Strange Ports of Call*, edited by August Derleth
OSTM—*The Other Side of the Moon*, edited by August Derleth

	TBSF	ATS	ATSF	SPC	OTSM	Totals
I. Plots of Circumstance						123
A. A being in an alien Environment						43
1. A modern man in						17
a. The past.	4	4	1		1	10
b. A different world, space, or dimension in the present	3	1			1	5
c. The future.		1		1		2
2. An ancient being or primitve man in a modern human environment.	1					1
3. An alien in a human environment.						17
a. The past.			1			1
b. The present.	3	3	5			11
c. The future.		2	1		2	5
4. A future being in						8
a. The past.						0
b. The present.			2			2
c. A strange planet.		2		1	1	4
d. Space.	1			1		2
B. Modern man in the modern world						50
1. Facing a continuing problem.	1	1		1	2	5
2. Facing a problem raised by new technology.	2	1		1		4
3. Facing a problem in the mental and social fields.						0
4. Facing problems of a new war.	1		1	1	2	5

Appendix: Distribution Chart

	TBSF	ATS	ATSF	SPC	OTSM	Totals
5. Facing problems introduced from						29
a. The past.	1			3		4
b. Another dimension.	1			2		3
c. Another world or space.	3	4	1	4	5	17
d. The future.		1	3		1	5
6. Facing a change in natural conditions.	3		2			5
7. Facing new natural phenomena.	1				1	2
C. A past being in the past						1
1. Facing problems important in the history of the race.	1					1
2. Facing problems similar to those faced today.						0
3. Facing problems of no significance to the modern world.						0
D. A future being in a future world						26
1. Facing problems similar to those faced today.	2	4	3			9
2. Facing future problems.	4	2	1	3	3	13
3. Facing problems of no significance to the present day.	1	1	1	1		4
E. Mutations						5
1. Of man						3
a. Superman.			1		1	2
b. Grotesque.			1		1	2
2. Of animals or insects						2
a. With whom man battles for possession of the earth.						0
b. Which take over the supremacy of the earth.			2			2
c. Which cooperate with mankind.						0
II. Plots of Creation						20
A. The creation of new life or new forms thereof						10
1. Chemical life						4
a. Androids						1
(1) Which aid mankind.						0
(2) Which get out of control.				1		1
b. Other forms created or converted.						3
(1) Which aid mankind.						0
(2) Which get out of control.	1	1	1			3
2. Mechanical Life						6
a. Robots						4
(1) Which aid mankind.		2	1			3
(2) Which get out of control.			1			1
b. Other forms of mechanical life.						2
(1) Which aid mankind.	1					1
(2) Which get out of control.		1				1
B. Experiments in other fields						10
1. Which aids mankind.	2					2
2. Which gets out of control.	4	2	1			7
3. Which creates new problems.			1			1

Chapter Notes

MICHAEL R. PAGE

Introduction (Page)

1. See Gary Westfahl's two books *Hugo Gernsback and the Century of Science Fiction* and *The Mechanics of Wonder*.
2. See Jack Williamson, *The Metal Man and Others* (1–3) and Miles J. Breuer, *The Man with the Strange Head and Other Early Science Fiction Stories* (415–18).
3. Gary K. Wolfe, *Evaporating Genres: Essays on Fantastic Literature* (189–213).
4. It's worth noting here that over four issues of *Science Fiction Quarterly* in 1951/52 Lowndes published a series of essays by James Blish titled "The Science in Science Fiction," featuring discussion of "The Biological Story," "The Mathematical Story," "The Astronomical Story," and "The Psychological Story," respectively; each piece only ran to around three or four pages.
5. In the fan history *All Our Yesterdays*, Harry Warner, Jr., wrote of Anger, "an enigmatic figure in fandom: almost unknown outside of Canada and forgotten by now, he seems to have achieved remarkable success in unearthing fans and forming clubs by applying political organizing techniques that were involved in his vocation" (300–301).
6. Scholars and critics might find Mr. Keogh's opinion of Damon Knight's book review column rather interesting: "Why do you have to spend three thousand words on some Grade B book, telling us it's perfectly lousy? Out of the two reviews you made in the June ish, I couldn't find a decent reason that warrants your not dropping the whole department, outside of saying or being able to say, 'We've got Damon Knight to do *our* book reviews!'" (88). Lowndes was appropriately chastened: "Henceforth, if we present further book reviews by Sir Damon, the Knight, they shall be more to the point—in other words, less spread out over generalities that do no more than synopsize the book in question" (90).
7. See my *Saving the World Through Science Fiction* (27).
8. See Gunn, *Star-Begotten* (68).
9. Letter from Gunn to Campbell, May 23, 1950.
10. *Saving the World* (27, 29–30, 91–92).
11. See *Star-Begotten*.
12. I should note that I have a copy of this text that once belonged to my public library; indeed, much of the early science fiction criticism had this kind of broader public access, unlike other areas of literary scholarship that appeals mainly to specialists, as many such early works since withdrawn from my community's public library now grace my shelves.
13. It's interesting to note that two years prior to the publication of Franklin's anthology, Bantam published Gunn's story collection *Future Imperfect*.
14. For further discussion on this topic and on Gunn's contribution to the debate see my article "Science Fiction Goes to College: Jack Williamson, James Gunn, and the Early Years of Academic SF."
15. Gunn later anthologized Delany's essay in *Speculations on Speculation*.
16. Lundwall's was the first book of science fiction criticism I read, and (like Gary Wolfe's experience reading Gunn's thesis in *Dynamic*), therefore, the first book of literary scholarship of any kind I read. Allen published a number of other mass market books on the teaching of science fiction, but he has been largely forgotten in discussion of early academic engagement with science fiction. I wish to acknowledge him here as an important early SF academic who happened to be an instructor at the University of Nebraska when I was an undergrad-

uate. I took his class in science fiction in 1986; the class I now teach.

17. The conference proceedings, which include papers by Arthur C. Clarke, Loren Eiseley, R. Buckminster Fuller, Karl Menninger, Ashley Montagu, Harlow Shapley, and others, were published in book form as *Man and the Future*, edited by Gunn.

18. See *Saving the World* (51–53)

19. See Gunn's Foreword, "The Dean Revisited," for *Murray Leinster: The Life and Works* (McFarland, 2011) by Leinster's youngest daughters Billee J. Stallings and Jo-An J. Evans.

20. See *Saving the World* (30–31, 91–92) and Gunn, *Star-Begotten* (73–74).

21. Letter from Gunn to Smith, October 12, 1950.

22. Letter from Gunn to Don Ward, March 8, 1951.

23. Letter from Gunn to Harry Altshuler, March 22, 1955.

Modern Science Fiction: A Critical Analysis (Page)

INTRODUCTION

1. Although the Western certainly retreated after the pulp era and western movies declined by the 1970s, the mystery genre has continued to thrive. Arguably, however, the introduction of forensics, a science element, has recharged the mystery genre from its cozy and hardboiled eras.

2. Gunn wrote on the cusp of the science fiction boom of the 1950s, when the genre's popularity was on the verge of a major spike. Now, although the written form of the genre is still underrepresented and misunderstood by a large percentage of the reading public, the imagery, iconography, and impact of science fiction permeates every aspect of global culture.

3. A fascinating statement here. Gunn says that SF has reached the point where critical analysis is necessary for the genre to continue to grow—and Gunn's thesis itself is a necessary first step. Although a few attempts at analytical criticism by members of the science fiction community and observers from mainstream literature and academia appeared in the fifties after Gunn's thesis, as I discuss in the introduction, SF criticism slowly began to gather steam in the sixties, before taking off in the early 1970s, and since becoming a still somewhat small, but significant category of academic publishing.

4. The Science Fiction Research Association, founded in 1970 (Gunn was one of the founding members and served as president in 1980–81), honors Bailey's achievement with the Pilgrim Award for lifetime achievement in science fiction scholarship and research. Gunn was the seventh recipient of the Pilgrim Award in 1976.

5. As noted in the introduction, Bailey's study was primarily focused on the scientific romance of the late Victorian period and early 20th century, of which H. G. Wells was the greatest example. Bailey's study was originally written in the early 1930s, and only found publication in the aftermath of World War II, at which point he added some minor explorations of stories from the pulp science fiction magazines. For an account of the circumstances of publication and the science fiction fan community's response to *Pilgrims* see Sam Moskowitz, "Pilgrim's Progress: Prelude and Postscript to the Publication of J. O. Bailey's *Pilgrims Through Space and Time*."

6. Nonetheless, there was a thriving amateur criticism in the genre fanzines and a growing sophistication within the book review columns of the expanding body of science fiction magazines.

7. Here Gunn articulates the basic logic of his own teaching found in *The Road to Science Fiction* anthology series and his 1975 genre history *Alternate Worlds*.

8. Another fascinatingly rich statement. In effect, along with Bailey's work, Gunn's thesis *did* lay the groundwork for scholarly analysis of science fiction through its appearance in *Dynamic Science Fiction*, which found its way into the hands of many budding critics, including Gary K. Wolfe, who told the editor that Gunn's thesis in *Dynamic* was not only his first encounter with SF criticism, but his first encounter with *any* type of literary criticism. Wolfe has since become one of the most prominent voices in science fiction criticism.

9. Again, this seems to be the case: Gunn introduced the practice of formal literary analysis into science fiction.

10. Another fecund statement here, which continues as one of the major critical theses in the field in various ways. Science fiction is not merely a set of literary texts, but is a "way of thinking." Such an argument has been made countless times by writers and critics in the field.

11. For the purposes of this edition, I have limited Gunn's bibliography to works he refers to in the text while preserving Gunn's original source. Readers can find later publication data for each story on isfdb.org.

PART ONE

1. Here Gunn points to the rise in general public interest in science fiction following the dropping of the atomic bomb. For more on the subject see Martha A. Bartter, *The Way to Ground Zero: The Atomic Bomb in American*

Science Fiction, David Dowling, *Fictions of Nuclear Disaster*, David Seed, *Under the Shadow: The Atomic Bomb and Cold War Narratives*, and Roland Végsö, *The Naked Communist: Cold War Modernism and the Politics of Popular Culture* (111–39). See also H. Bruce Franklin's *War Stars: The Superweapon and the American Imagination*, a powerful study of science fiction and military and cultural history ranging from the early inventions of Robert Fulton and Thomas Edison to the Star Wars Defense Initiative of the Reagan Era.

2. The floodgates really opened up in 1953, when there was upwards of 40 science fiction magazines on the newsstands. For an excellent survey of the post-war magazine boom, see the introduction to Michael Ashley's *The History of the Science Fiction Magazine Volume 3: 1946–1955*, "From Bomb to Boom."

3. As with the flood of magazines in 1953, science fiction movies and television programming expanded greatly in the years following Gunn's observations here.

4. Notably, Gnome, Fantasy Press, Arkham House, and Shasta, among others. Gnome published Gunn's first two novels, *Star Bridge* (in collaboration with Jack Williamson) and *This Fortress World*, both in 1955. See my *Saving the World Through Science Fiction: James Gunn, Writer, Teacher and Scholar* (42–43) for more details.

5. Readers will notice that Gunn is writing before the launch of Ballantine and Ace. Immediately after completing the thesis, Gunn and family moved to Racine, Wisconsin, where Gunn worked for Western Printing, the company that produced the Dell line of paperbacks, where, among other projects, he edited a 10 cent paperback volume of Heinlein's *Universe*. See *Saving the World* (27–34).

6. Later in the decade, the radio program *X Minus One*, produced by NBC, aired four Gunn stories: "The Cave of Night" (also a 1959 Desilu Playhouse production entitled *Man in Orbit*), "Wherever You May Be" (aka. "The Reluctant Witch"), "Open Warfare," and "Tsylana." All stories had appeared in *Galaxy* (*Saving the World* 44).

7. When Gunn proposed his thesis project to the English faculty at the University of Kansas, as mentioned in the introduction, one of the more traditional faculty members remarked that "Science fiction was at best, subliterary."

8. Later, Isaac Asimov would famously argue that science fiction was an "escape into reality," as quoted by Gunn in his filmed dialogue with Gordon R. Dickson, "Themes in Science Fiction."

9. See, for instance, Stan Galloway's study *The Teenage Tarzan* (McFarland, 2010), and Gunn's Foreword to the volume, "The Magic of Imagination." Galloway was one of Gunn's graduate students at the University of Kansas. See also David Lemmo, *Tarzan, Jungle King of Popular Culture* (McFarland, 2016).

10. Readers might be interested in the arguments made by the editor in *The Literary Imagination from Erasmus Darwin to H.G. Wells: Science, Evolution, and Ecology*. There is also an anticipation here of the ideas put forward by I. F. Clarke in *The Pattern of Expectation*, Brian Aldiss in *Billion Year Spree*, and Paul Alkon in *Origins of Futuristic Fiction*. Gunn's selection of the date 1830 may be in conjunction with the second revised edition of Mary Shelley's *Frankenstein* in 1831.

11. Gunn himself features an excerpt of *The True History*, titling it "A True Story," as the first piece in *The Road to Science Fiction Volume One*. There he called it "the first extended narrative that has enough of the qualities of science fiction to be included in this anthology" (15), but further noted that "Lucian's sailing ship is no spaceship. His adventurers have no intention of going to the moon, and Lucian's purpose is not to make such a journey credible, or to speculate what we might find if we could really make the journey" (16). Gunn's likely source for discovering Lucian was August Derleth's 1950 anthology *Beyond Time and Space*. Gunn further discusses Lucian in *Alternate Worlds* (41–42). A recent attempt to place Lucian in the early SF lineage can be found in Adam Roberts, *The History of Science Fiction* (27–29).

12. The editor in question here was Sam Merwin, Jr., who edited *Thrilling Wonder Stories* and *Startling Stories* when Gunn was writing. Merwin bought Gunn's first stories, "Paradox" and "Communications," in 1949.

13. An excerpt of Cyrano's text appears in volume one of *The Road to Science Fiction*, where Gunn called it "more ingenious and more amusing than any of the moon journeys up to the time of Poe" (104). *Micromegas* was added to the Scarecrow Press edition of *The Road*, but is not in the original Mentor edition.

14. Wilkins does not appear in *The Road to Science Fiction*. There's no clear evidence within the thesis that Gunn had yet encountered Marjorie Hope Nicolson's pioneering study of proto-science fiction *Voyages to the Moon* (1948), although Nicolson's study certainly lends itself to Gunn's discussion of these early texts, and Gunn recalls that he did borrow KU's copy for his later scholarly work.

15. An edition of Holberg's novel under the title *The Journey of Niels Klim to the World Underground* was published in 1960 by the Uni-

versity of Nebraska Press and has recently been reprinted in Bison Books' Frontiers of the Imagination series, with a new preface by Peter Fitting. Like Gunn, Fitting distinguishes between the satiric and fantastic elements in the narrative.

16. Compare this to Isaac Asimov's 1953 "Social Science Fiction" in *Modern Science Fiction: Its Meaning and Its Future*, edited by Reginald Bretnor, where Asimov defines science fiction as "that branch of literature which is concerned with the impact of scientific advance on human beings" (158) and as "that branch of literature which deals with a fictitious society, differing from our own chiefly in the nature or extent of its technological development" (167). Interestingly, Asimov engages with Derleth's anthology *Beyond Time and Space*, where Derleth traces the lineage of science fiction to Plato, Lucian, More, Kepler, Holberg, and others, and challenges Derleth's conclusions that these are works of science fiction. Gunn discusses Asimov's essay in *Isaac Asimov: The Foundations of Science Fiction* (30–32).

17. See Alkon, *Origins of Futuristic Fiction* (158–244) for a more recent discussion of 18th century Gothic and its relationship to science fiction.

18. Brian Aldiss has famously pinpointed one, and most critics, agree: Mary Shelley's *Frankenstein*.

19. See *Alternate Worlds* (45–51), *The Road to Science Fiction Volume One* (2–4, 161–64), and the essay *The Discovery of the Future* for Gunn's later articulation of this idea.

20. One of Gunn's original sources for his discussion of the Shaver Mystery was an article by W. S. Baring-Gould that appeared in *Harper's*, September 1946, "Little Superman, What Now?" For more recent commentary on the Shaver Mystery, see Richard Toronto, *War Over Lemuria: Richard Shaver, Ray Palmer and the Strangest Chapter of 1940s Science Fiction* and Fred Nadis, *The Man from Mars: Ray Palmer's Amazing Pulp Journey*.

21. Gunn notes that the "confession" provided by *Astounding's* editor John W. Campbell for Asimov's spoof article appeared at the head of the June 1948 "Brass Tacks" letter column. The "Thiotimoline" article originally appeared in the March 1948 *Astounding*. Asimov wrote a number of later "Thiotimoline" articles.

22. Gunn includes Poe's story "Mellonta Tauta," set in the year 2848, in volume one of *The Road to Science Fiction*. Most likely, Gunn hadn't yet encountered this most science fictional of Poe's stories. For a discussion of Poe's science fiction, see H. Bruce Franklin's groundbreaking anthology *Future Perfect: American Science Fiction of the Nineteenth Century* (93–103).

23. See Chris Baldick, *In Frankenstein's Shadow*, which traces the mad scientist lineage as it develops in nineteenth century literature and Peter Haining's anthology *The Frankenstein Omnibus* for examples of the trope in stories from the early nineteenth century to the contemporary.

24. Readers will be interested in Gunn's own story "The Lens of Time," a retelling of O'Brien's story, in his collection *Human Voices*. Gunn selected O'Brien's story for volume one of *The Road to Science Fiction*. For further discussion see David Ketterer, *New Worlds for Old* (251–53).

25. Gunn likely encountered many of these authors and their novel-length works in *Famous Fantastic Mysteries*, which he began reading in 1939 (*Saving the World* 20).

26. For further reading on Gernsback and *Amazing* see Gary Westfahl, *Hugo Gernsback and the Century of Science Fiction* and *The Mechanics of Wonder* (37–164), and John Cheng, *Astounding Wonder: Imagining Science and Science Fiction in Interwar America*.

27. Gernsback returned to science fiction briefly in 1953 with the magazine *Science Fiction+*.

28. For a compelling and nostalgic fan's reverie on *Astounding's* early days see Alva Rogers, *A Requiem for Astounding*. For a writer's perspective, perhaps equally nostalgic, see Lester Del Rey, *The World of Science Fiction 1926–1976* (52–114). Aldiss's chapter "The Future on a Chipped Plate: The Worlds of John Campbell's *Astounding*" in *Billion Year Spree* (215–43), along with the rest of the book, makes good reading. Scholarly works of interest include Cheng (see above) and Albert I. Berger, *The Magic that Works: John W. Campbell and the American Response to Technology*.

29. Examples being Campbell's *The Mightiest Machine* and Smith's *The Skylark of Space* and its sequels.

30. Gunn's remarkable statement in this paragraph anticipates a number of the statements made by science fiction writers in Bretnor's 1953 volume *Modern Science Fiction: Its Meaning and Its Future*.

31. It is fascinating that Gunn chooses Campbell's editorial which introduced L. Ron Hubbard's article "Dianetics: The Evolution of a Science."

32. Although this story is not part of Anderson's Polytechnic League series or the Technic History series, it clearly works on a number of the premises Anderson often explored in his massive oeuvre.

33. Harkening back to Hugo Gernsback's inaugural editorial, "A New Sort of Magazine," in *Amazing Stories*: "Not only do these amazing

tales make tremendously interesting reading—they are also always instructive. They supply knowledge that we might not otherwise obtain—and they supply it in a very palatable form. For the best of these modern writers of scientifiction have the knack of imparting knowledge, and even inspiration, without once making us aware that we are being taught" (3).

34. Concurring with Gunn, Everett F. Bleiler remarks that Campbell's novel "is one of the very few attempts at realism in the interplanetary novel of the day" (156).

35. For further discussion of "Solution Unsatisfactory" see Thomas D. Clareson and Joe Sanders, *The Heritage of Heinlein* (39–40), Thomas M. Disch, *The Dreams are Stuff is Made of* (81–82), H. Bruce Franklin, *Robert A. Heinlein: America as Science Fiction* (59–62) and *War Stars* (141–46), and T. A. Shippey, "The Cold War in Science Fiction, 1940–1960" (92–94). A compelling article on the Campbellian background of the story is Edward Wysocki, "The Creation of Heinlein's 'Solution Unsatisfactory.'"

36. As noted above, Gunn edited a 10 cent paperback edition of "Universe" for Dell Books soon after submitting his thesis, during his tenure at Western Printing in Racine, Wisconsin. In the anonymous introduction titled "A Classic of Science Fiction," Gunn wrote: "Universe' describes how these men look at their circumstances and how a unified explanation of things is built up to satisfy their need for security and stability ... "Universe," for instance, describes the way truth is lost and the way it is regained. For it is not the truth about the nature of the universe we want as much as an explanation that satisfies our need for order and peace and, occasionally, beauty...But sometimes a world does not know when it is ready for a new view of the universe; sometimes it takes a single man to blast aside the old conventions. Galileo was such a man, insisting against the established view of the Church, that it was the earth that moved and not the sun and the stars...And, finally, are we sure that our view of the universe is the final truth? Or shall we, too, like Hugh, step out onto the "Captain's Veranda" and see—the stars?

37. There are countless discussions of Wells's novel and its Darwinian thesis. Readers again might be interested in the editor's *The Literary Imagination from Erasmus Darwin to H.G. Wells* (155–70). Patrick Parrinder, *Shadows of the Future* and Jack Williamson, *H.G. Wells: Critic of Progress* are especially good studies on Wells's evolutionary vision in the scientific romances.

38. See Gunn's later essay "The Worldview of Science Fiction."

39. One analysis of the affinities between science fiction and existentialism was put forth by Colin Wilson in *Science Fiction as Existentialism*. It is interesting that Gunn here calls science fiction an "optimistic Existentialism," which parallels Wilson's brand of existentialism as worked out in his 1956 *cause célèbre The Outsider* and a number of books soon following, notably *The Strength to Dream*, where Wilson gave some short, but enthusiastic, attention to science fiction.

40. In *Science Fiction in the 20th Century*, Edward James cogently comments on "Forgetfulness": "The story is about human evolution (the planet is, of course, Earth, the place New York); about the possibility of moving beyond dependence on the machine; about the latent potentialities of the human mind. It puts the problems of twentieth-century humans into the longest possible historical perspective (from 'savagery' to god-like status) and, unlike Stapledon's *Last and First Men*, offers hope and optimism about the human condition" (50). The story is paradigmatic for the argument regarding SF and transcendence in Alexei and Cory Panshin's *The World Beyond the Hill*: "The way past the traps of dependence, and defeat, Campbell now perceived, lay in a grand leap into a higher state of being where such problems were no longer problems. Like his model, E. E. Smith, Campbell had come to accept the necessity of higher levels of human being and becoming" (254–55).

41. In certain respects, Gunn returns to this argument in his recent *Transcendental* trilogy, where an ancient galactic transport machine, left by a long-dead advanced civilization, cleanses its users of imperfections upon use.

42. Incidentally, the title of Gunn's memoir, also published by McFarland.

43. For a lively discussion of this theme, in these novels and others, see Eric S. Rabkin, "Cowboys and Telepaths/Formulas and Phenomena."

44. Discussions of Stapledon's classic novel can be found in Robert Crossley, *Olaf Stapledon: Speaking for the Future* (220–31) and Leslie Fiedler, *Olaf Stapledon: A Man Divided* (97–119). For further discussion of *Slan* see Paul Carter, *The Creation of Tomorrow* (152–53), but the most sustained discussion appears in the Panshins (472–90).

45. See Carter (160–61).

46. Shiras's story makes up the first part of her book *Children of the Atom* and was chosen by the Science Fiction Writers of America for inclusion in *The Science Fiction Hall of Fame Volume IIB*, edited by Ben Bova. Pamela Sargent notes that Shiras "does not present the children as frightening threats but as interest-

ing and concerned individuals and raises ethical questions about how they should lead their lives" (5).

47. See Patricia S. Warrick, *The Cybernetic Imagination in Science Fiction*, especially chapter three (53–80).

48. Einstein's Theory of Relativity (1905–1915) had immense impact on science fiction from the beginning of the magazine era, as illustrated by several works of early magazine science fiction pioneer Dr. Miles J. Breuer (see *The Man with the Strange Head and Other Early Science Fiction Stories* by Miles J. Breuer and edited by the editor of this edition). Alfred Korzybski, now largely forgotten, proposed the linguistic theory of General Semantics in the 1930s, which became a popular philosophical system in science fiction, especially in the works of Van Vogt.

49. An interesting statement given that the satirical possibilities of science fiction were on the verge of flowering in Horace Gold's *Galaxy*, exemplified by the work of Frederik Pohl and C.M. Kornbluth (in collaboration and individually), Robert Sheckley, William Tenn, and Gunn himself, as seen in the story "Little Orphan Android," mentioned in the introduction, among other stories in Gunn's oeuvre. Indeed, Kingsley Amis argued in *New Maps of Hell* (1960), the most widely read and significant work of SF criticism following Bailey, that satire—what he termed "comic inferno"—was the most vital stream of modern science fiction (87–133).

50. By 1951, Heinlein was living in Colorado Springs and completing *The Puppet Masters* and his sixth juvenile novel *The Rolling Stones* (Patterson 45–75). Asimov had moved to Boston where he was a research professor of biochemistry at Boston University Medical School (*In Memory Yet Green* 558–630).

51. See Gunn's 1958 collection *Station in Space* where he dramatizes these ideas.

Part Two

1. For a list of various definitions offered by authors and critics in the field, see Gary K. Wolfe, *Critical Terms for Science Fiction and Fantasy* (108–111).

2. Interesting in light of the provocative and controversial article by Sherryl Vint and Mark Bould, "There is No Such Thing as Science Fiction," in *Reading Science Fiction* (2009), edited by Gunn, Marleen Barr, and Matthew Candelaria. Recently, Bould and Vint wrestle further with definitions in *The Routledge Concise History of Science Fiction* (1–19) as does John Rieder in *Science Fiction and the Mass Cultural Genre System* (13–32).

3. As Gunn indicates here, Conklin *did* use the same categories for both anthologies, adding the additional category for the second anthology. Conklin would continue to use the same basic model, with some adjustments in *The Big Book of Science Fiction* (1950) and *Omnibus of Science Fiction* (1952) as well.

4. There are some resonances here in Gunn's classification with two important works of SF criticism and theory, Mark Rose's *Alien Encounters* (1981) and Gary K. Wolfe's *The Known and the Unknown* (1979). As he indicates in the Foreword to this volume, Wolfe had been an undergraduate at the University of Kansas in the late 1960s, while Gunn was working in KU administration, prior to rejoining the English department and starting his science fiction class. Wolfe had to get special permission for Gunn to direct his honor's thesis on Ray Bradbury. The influence of Gunn's thesis as it appeared in *Dynamic* is evident in Wolfe's study.

5. For what it's worth, Gunn's analytical chart anticipates the graphs and charts that William Bainbridge presents in *Dimensions of Science Fiction* (3–28).

6. Certainly true in the sense that the *Tarzan* series can be considered anthropological science fiction.

7. See Nicholas Ruddick, *The Fire and the Stone*, an excellent survey of prehistoric fiction (what he terms PF, as a new subset of SF). Later SF novels of interest that resonate with Gunn's category are Robert Silverberg's *Hawksbill Station* and Michael Bishop's *No Enemy But Time*. An early example, which Gunn does not consider here, is Jack London's *Before Adam*.

8. Bradbury's famous "A Sound of Thunder" comes to mind here; not yet published when Gunn penned the thesis.

9. Whether Gunn is suggesting a direct sequel to *The Lost World* or Professor Challenger stories in general is unclear. Doyle did produced a number of Professor Challenger novels and stories following *The Lost World*: *The Poison Belt* (1913), *The Land of Mist* (1926), *When the World Screamed* (1928), and *The Disintegration Machine* (1929). A complete edition of the Professor Challenger stories was published in 1952.

10. Miller wrote a sequel "Coils of Time," which appeared in the May 1939 issue of *Astounding*.

11. See Paul J. Nahin, *Time Machines: Time Travel in Physics, Metaphysics, and Science Fiction* and David Wittenberg, *Time Travel: The Popular Philosophy of Narrative*.

12. Further discussion of Heinlein's time travel classic can be found in Brian Ash, *Faces of the Future* (158–62), Carter (106–109), Clare-

son and Sanders (44–45), Franklin, *Heinlein* (56–57), and the Panshins (399–401). For John W. Campbell's reaction to the story, see Heinlein's *Grumbles from the Grave* (21–22).

13. Here Gunn is making some preliminary observations of the subgenre Alternate History, of which the best early examples are Murray Leinster's "Sidewise in Time" (1934) and L. Sprague de Camp's *Lest Darkness Fall* (1939). The year following Gunn's thesis saw the appearance of Ward Moore's remarkable *Bring the Jubilee*. See Karen Hellekson (a former student of Gunn's at KU), *The Alternate History: Refiguring Historical Time* and Andy Duncan (who once told me "we are all students of Jim Gunn"), "Alternate History" in *The Cambridge Companion to Science Fiction*.

14. Gunn selected the story for volume three of *The Road to Science Fiction*, remarking "'Brooklyn Project' is a gimmick story, but those who scorn gimmicks should read the story first. It was also a political story and was more difficult to get published in 1948" (127). See also Franklin, *War Stars* (174).

15. The "Pete Manx" series consisted of twelve stories that appeared in *Thrilling Wonder* from 1939–1944 under the pseudonym Kelvin Kent. Some were penned by Henry Kuttner, others by Arthur K. Barnes, and some in collaboration between the two. They have not been collected in book form.

16. A later story in this vein is Barry Malzberg and Bill Pronzini, "Shakespeare MCMLXXXV."

17. It's interesting to note that Gunn employs the time travel conceit in his *Crisis!* stories which were intended as very serious stories addressing contemporary issues of the latter decades of the twentieth century.

18. Gunn included the original short story version of "The Moon Pool" in volume two of *The Road to Science Fiction*, where he remarked that Merritt's inventiveness "was the sense of wonder at its most wonderful" (77).

19. Like Alfred Korzybski, Charles Fort had a great deal of influence on the science fiction writers of the 1930s and 40s. His collection of strange and unexplained phenomena, *Lo!* (1931) was serialized in *Astounding* in 1934.

20. See Clareson and Sanders (46).

21. On utopias and dystopias in science fiction see Amis, *New Maps of Hell*, M. Keith Booker, *The Dystopian Impulse in Modern Literature*, Mark Hillegas, *The Future as Nightmare: H.G. Wells and the Anti-Utopians*, Tom Moylan, *Scraps of the Untainted Sky: Science Fiction, Utopia, Dystopia*, and Chad Walsh, *From Utopia to Nightmare*.

22. A good example from the early pulps is Laurence Manning's *The Man who Awoke* series. And, of course, the classics Bellamy's *Looking Backward* and Wells's *When the Sleeper Wakes* uses suspended animation as well.

23. Bates's story has interesting resonances with Gunn's "The Naked Sky," the final novella of *The Joy Makers*. See *Saving the World* (132–48). See also Carter (147) for further discussion.

24. A more recent example of this plot type is Michael Bishop's *Ancient of Days*, although the man in question is, in fact, a *homo habilis*.

25. Recalling Clifford D. Simak's award winning 1980 story "Grotto of the Dancing Deer."

26. A truly strange and under-read novel from pre-Campbell *Astounding*; with an apocalyptic flavor not unlike Jose Saramago's *Blindness*. Frank Cioffi remarks, "The entire two-part story shows how mankind is basically greedy, unpleasant, warlike, lustful. The plausibility of the anomaly is never at issue; what causes the conflict and excitement are man's presumed weaknesses (87).

27. Of note here is Gunn's story "A Monster Named Smith."

28. The most notable later example being Clarke's *2001: A Space Odyssey*.

29. Gunn completed his thesis in May 1951. That September, Robert Wise's *The Day the Earth Stood Still*, based on "Farewell to the Master" was released. The film is one of the best science fiction films ever produced.

30. See Warrick (108–109).

31. Raymond Palmer's *Other Worlds* was the most prominent example. See Nadis (115–38).

32. An interesting perspective flip of Voltaire's aforementioned *Micromegas*.

33. See Walter E. Meyers, *Aliens and Linguists* (96).

34. The idea of the alien with a third eye in the middle of the forehead was used by Rod Serling in the *Twilight Zone* episode "Will the Real Martian Please Stand Up?"

35. Edwin James was the pseudonym Gunn used for his first ten stories. The publication of "The Misogynist" in *Galaxy* in the November 1952 issue marked the first time Gunn used his own name for his byline and all his subsequent work was published as by James Gunn. "Paradox" was the first story Gunn sold—to Sam Merwin, Jr., for *Thrilling Wonder*—although its publication was preceded by "Communications," which appeared in *Startling Stories* a month earlier.

36. See *Saving the World* (77–78)

37. A particularly intense updating of this theme is Ted Chiang's remarkable "Exhalation" (2008).

38. Lester Del Rey, who made Williams's ac-

quaintance when he was living in St. Louis, greatly admired "Robot's Return" and wrote a prequel, "Though Dreamers Die," published in the February 1944 *Astounding* (*Early Del Rey* 353–54). See also Warrick (108).

39. In the later article "Science Fiction and the Mainstream," Gunn discussed "Rescue Party" in the context of literary naturalism: "Under the influence of naturalism, science fiction adopted a view of man as an animal selected by environmental pressures for intelligence, aggressiveness, possessiveness, and survival ... Arthur C. Clarke illustrated that philosophical position with an early story called 'Rescue Party'" (*Inside Science Fiction* 36). See also Bould and Vint (72).

40. For a recent full-length study on the Alien in science fiction see Patricia Monk, *Alien Theory: The Alien as Archetype in the Science Fiction Short Story.*

41. The series consisted of four stories, none of which were ever reprinted.

42. A far more effective story of this type is Karen Joy Fowler's "Standing Room Only" (1997), which places future time travelers as tourists in Washington at the Ford Theater on the night of Lincoln's assassination.

43. See Crossley *Olaf Stapledon* (198–204) and Fiedler (81–96).

44. An excellent recent example of this type is Geoffrey Landis's "Ripples in the Dirac Sea" (1988).

45. The concept in Piper's story, of returning to one's youth to live one's life again, resonates with Ken Grimwood's remarkable novel *Replay* (1987) and Claire North's (Catherine Webb) Campbell Memorial Award winning novel *The First Fifteen Lives of Harry August* (2014).

46. Gunn discusses this classic story in a chapter on the Kuttner's in *The Science of Science-Fiction Writing* (171–200).

47. Readers might find an interesting connection here with the Flower people in Gunn's novel *Transcendental* (201–212).

48. Van Vogt's story has become one of the most famous in all science fiction, often identified as the story that launched the "Golden Age" in John W. Campbell's *Astounding* when it appeared in the July 1939 issue. Gunn selected it for volume two of *The Road to Science Fiction*. The Panshins provide a lengthy discussion of the story in *The World Beyond the Hill* (461–70). See also Cioffi (57–59).

49. See Jonathan Eller, *Becoming Ray Bradbury.*

50. Bradbury's now classic novella appeared in the February 1951 issue of *Galaxy*. It is interesting to see here Gunn's early assessment prior to the story and the subsequent novel, *Fahrenheit 451*, becoming an iconic classic of science fiction and, for that matter, American literature.

51. Thomas Clareson provides a thoughtful analysis of *The Martian Chronicles* in *Understanding American Science Fiction* (50–56). See also Robert Crossley, *Imagining Mars* (197–207) and Robert Markley, *Dying Planet: Mars in Science and the Imagination* (218–22).

52. An analysis of the novel's predecessor, *Seetee Ship* appears in Carl Abbott, *Frontiers Past and Future* (51–54).

53. This moment is a quintessential example of what Peter Nicholls termed "conceptual breakthrough" (255).

54. Gunn here is talking about what might be termed near-future science fiction.

55. For further discussion of Wylie's atomic war fiction, see David Seed, *American Science Fiction and the Cold War* (14–25) and *Under the Shadow* (75–94), and Végsö (129–39).

56. Gunn's enthusiasm for Leiber's "Coming Attraction" is fascinating given the now classic status of the story. It first appeared in the November 1950 *Galaxy*, the magazine's second issue, while Gunn was in his final year of graduate school. It also indicates an awareness of the significant shift in the field that *Galaxy*, under the editorship of Horace Gold, was to initiate. *Galaxy*, and its short-lived fantasy companion *Beyond*, were to become Gunn's primary target market for his own work in the ensuing years. It was selected for *The Science Fiction Hall of Fame* in 1970, *Science Fiction, Contemporary Mythology: The SFWA-SFRA Anthology* in 1978, and more recently *The Wesleyan Anthology of Science Fiction* in 2010, all three widely used classroom anthologies. Gunn also selected it for volume three of *The Road to Science Fiction* where he denoted it an exemplary example of social science fiction and called it "an archetype for the best science fiction of the next decade and a half, the artistic blending of story, style, and speculation" (140). In the anthology *Galaxy: Thirty Years of Innovative Science Fiction*, Frederik Pohl, Martin H. Greenberg, and Joseph Olander call "Coming Attraction" "a watershed story in the development of modern science fiction. It heralded an era of sf with social—and often satirical—themes, later to be enthroned in the pages of *Galaxy*" (10). See also John Huntington, *Rationalizing Genius* (104–107).

57. An anticipation, perhaps, of Gibson's "razor girl" Molly in *Neuromancer.*

58. For further discussion about the story and Cartmill's encounter with the FBI see A. Berger (60–69), Franklin, *War Stars* (147–48), Roger Luckhurst, *Science Fiction* (95–96), the Panshins (581–82), and Robert Silverberg, "The Cleve Cartmill Affair."

59. See Luckhurst (93–94). Damon Knight reviews the expanded novel version in *In Search of Wonder* (42–43).
60. See I.F. Clarke, *Voices Prophesying War*, especially chapter five (162–208).
61. Of interest here is John W. Campbell's very early assessment of the politics of the atomic age, *The Atomic Story* (1947), published at around the same time as a number of significant stories appeared in the pages of *Astounding*: Sturgeon's "Memorial" (April 1946), Chan Davis's "The Nightmare" (May 1946), Anderson and Waldrop's "Tomorrow's Children" (March 1947), and Sturgeon's "Thunder and Roses" (November 1947), all of which Gunn examines here. Campbell's closing section, "The Atomic Future" concludes with a chapter titled "The Human X in Atomic Politics" (280–97).
62. See A. Berger (79–80).
63. See A. Berger (78–79) and Franklin, *War Stars* (158–59).
64. See A. Berger (80–82). Gunn selected "Thunder and Roses" for volume three of *The Road to Science Fiction*. In the final chapter of *Alternate Worlds*, Gunn singles out the story for illustrating the detached viewpoint of science fiction, that in its detachment brings meaning and insight to the reader: "Here is science fiction pointing to the ultimate horror of holocaust—the horror is not just that so many will die so horribly and so painfully (all men are doomed to die, and few deaths are easy), but that they destroy the future of mankind—all the unachieved potential, all the untested possibilities, all the art and love and courage and glory that might be; it is not just that some idiot kind of total warfare will destroy the present—but that it might destroy eternity. From this viewpoint, from the viewpoint of our distant descendants, no matter what their alien forms, ways, beliefs, the ultimate crime is not murder but lack of foresight, which leads to an emphasis on solving contemporary situations with ultimate solutions, no matter what the risk to life or civilization—a kind of romantic idiocy. In a metaphorical sense, science fiction might be considered letters from the future, from our children, urging us to be careful of their world. By writing about the future no matter how pessimistically or in how cautionary a vein, science fiction might be considered an optimistic fiction" (233). In *War Stars* (170–72), Franklin examines the story and suggests it should "be required reading for any person who cares about human survival."
65. See the Panshins (272–76)
66. Gunn was probably unfamiliar with Algernon Blackwood's "The Willows" at this point, which is, undoubtedly, the best of this type of story. Gunn's own story, "Breaking Point," written slightly prior to the thesis resonates with these works as well. See *Saving the World* (91–96).
67. Gunn writes prior to the formulation of the "Drake equation," the advocacy for the search for extraterrestrial intelligence by Carl Sagan, and the momentous discovery of other planets and solar systems that is happening frequently today.
68. Gallun offers additional insight into the story in his autobiography *Starclimber* (82–83).
69. "The Twonky" was made into an amusing film of the same name by Arch Obler in 1953, scripted by Kuttner and Moore.
70. This *Hall of Fame* story has also been made into a film, *The Last Mimzy* (2007). Gunn selected it for volume three of *The Road to Science Fiction*. See Huntington (128–30) and the Panshins (596–600).
71. In *The Astounding-Analog Reader Volume Two*, Harry Harrison and Brian Aldiss remark that "The Little Black Bag" "is in some ways a mirror image" of Tenn's "Child's Play." Like Tenn's tale (and "Mimsy Were the Borogoves" for that matter), "this is another kit from the future, again based on future applications of biochemistry unknown today... but the effect is entirely different" (73). See also Huntington (59–65).
72. It's notable that Immanuel Velikovsky's sensationalist and intriguing *Worlds in Collision* was published in 1950 while Gunn was in graduate school. The quintessential example of the "rogue" planet colliding with earth is Philip Wylie and Edwin Balmer's *When Worlds Collide* (1933).
73. Not entirely. Epic disaster SF continues to be a thriving genre.
74. Gunn himself penned a number of apocalyptic narratives in the 1950s and 60s: *The Joy Makers*, *The Immortals*, and *The Burning*, all grim tales of things gone wrong. See my discussions of each text in *Saving the World*.
75. Gunn's own most notable contribution to the psi powers subgenre was "Wherever You May Be" (aka. "The Reluctant Witch"), first published as a lead novella in *Galaxy* May 1953.
76. See Clareson and Sanders (41–42) and Franklin, *Heinlein* (23–24).
77. There is a category of science fiction that deals with historical events involving the development, usually, of some aspects of the sciences. Examples might include James Blish's novel *Doctor Mirabilis*, about the medieval monk Roger Bacon, and Andy Duncan's 2002 Sturgeon Memorial Award winning novella "The Chief Designer," about Soviet rocket engineer Sergei Korolov. A growing segment of

this kind of story involve stories that deal with the history of science fiction, as science fiction itself becomes more historical.

78. Perhaps the ultimate example here is Stephen Baxter's novel *Evolution*, which traces the history of mammalian life from the "point of crisis" of the meteor that destroyed the dinosaurs through various points of crisis in the past and into the future, culminating at the end of mammalian existence millions of years forward.

79. Surprisingly, Gunn doesn't examine Wells's "A Story of the Stone Age" here. For a complete survey of this type of story, see Nicholas Ruddick, *The Fire in the Stone*.

80. Perhaps Cutcliffe Hyne's *The Lost Continent* is what Gunn had in mind, which he may have encountered in the December 1944 *Famous Fantastic Mysteries*.

81. Readers may find Gary K. Wolfe's essays on the allied fantastic genres—science fiction, fantasy, and horror—in *Evaporating Genres* (3–82) interesting in light of Gunn's remark here.

82. Compare this to remarks Frederik Pohl made for the film "Ideas in Science Fiction," produced by Gunn for *The Literature of Science Fiction* film series in 1973: "What science fiction writers individually and science fiction as a kind of normative forecasting of the future in general offer us then is not predictions about the future so much as a sort of mail-order catalog of possible alternate futures, and from this we can compile a shopping list of the sorts of futures we would like to see and then proceed to bring them about."

83. See Huntington (153–58) and the Panshins (502–504).

84. In *Isaac Asimov: The Foundations of Science Fiction*, Gunn points out that "Blind Alley" was the only non-*Foundation* or Robot story Asimov wrote in the last few years of World War II. It's also worth noting that it is one of the few stories Asimov wrote involving aliens.

85. Perhaps it can be argued whether "Nightfall" is the greatest science fiction story of all time, as it has often been called, nevertheless, it is certainly one of the most important, and conveys a power undiminished over time, in spite of its sometimes clunky prose. Harry Harrison's Foreword to the story in the 1970 critical anthology *The Mirror of Infinity* gets to the reasons "Nightfall" works and why it continued to resonate in 1970 (51–54), as it still does today. James makes a similar observation in *Science Fiction in the 20th Century* (121–125). See *Isaac Asimov: The Foundations of Science Fiction* (68–76) for Gunn's later thought on this paradigmatic story. See also A. Berger (39–40), Huntington (145–51), and the Panshins (332–44).

86. See A. Berger (57–59), Clareson and Sanders (36–37), Franklin (36–38), Luckhurst (93), and the Panshins (377–82).

87. Another paradigmatic story of science fiction and part of *The Science Fiction Hall of Fame*. See Huntington (116–19), Carl Malmgren, *Worlds Apart* (58–60), the Panshins (617–18), and Wolfe, *The Known and Unknown* (206–207).

88. See Clareson and Sanders (36), Franklin, *Heinlein* (36), Huntington (74–79) and Luckhurst (71–72). Farah Mendlesohn examines the corporate ethos in the story in "Corporatism and the Corporate Ethos in Robert Heinlein's 'The Roads Must Roll.'" Bould and Vint provide some nice insights on this and other Heinlein stories (65–67) as well.

89. The name of the blind poet of the spaceways, Rhysling, has been coopted by the Science Fiction Poetry Association for their annual award. See Clareson and Sanders (53–54).

90. Here perhaps is Gunn's first application of the word "road" in relation to science fiction.

91. Readers may be interested in Gunn's depiction of advanced avian species in his classic novel *The Listeners* and his latest novel *Transgalactic*.

92. For a thorough, if eclectic, argument that evolution is the central and foundational thesis in science fiction, see John J. Pierce's four-volume study, *A Study of Imagination and Evolution*. The last volume, *Odd Genre*, is dedicated to Gunn. Gunn makes a similar argument in "The Worldview of Science Fiction."

93. Gunn selected the story for volume two of *The Road to Science Fiction*, considering it an exemplary example of the "invention story" (3).

94. See the editor's *The Literary Imagination from Erasmus Darwin to H.G. Wells* (187–191).

95. Readers will note that Gunn has borrowed Wells's title for his memoir *Star-Begotten: A Life in Science Fiction*. At the age of 14 in 1937, the year Wells's novel was published, Gunn saw Wells speak at the Kansas City Municipal Auditorium.

96. Stapledon's novel was preceded by J.D. Beresford's *The Wonder*, another Wellsian novel of a maligned mutant genius.

97. Stapledon's novel clearly influenced Gunn's "The Sun Came Up Last Night" (*Science Fiction Quarterly* August 1951). See *Saving the World* (83).

98. See John R. Reed, "H. G. Wells' Familiar Aliens" (152–53).

99. See Robert Scholes and Eric S. Rabkin, *Science Fiction: History, Science, Vision* (51–52).

100. *The World of Null-A* was the subject of Damon Knight's infamous scurrilous attack,

"Cosmic Jerrybuilder," later collected in *In Search of Wonder* (47-62). The famed iconoclast Colin Wilson, a great admirer of Van Vogt, takes a somewhat different view in his essay in *Science Fiction Writers* (209-17). Meyers addresses the General Semantics angle in the novel (172-73) as does William H. Sharp in "A. E. Van Vogt and *The World of Null-A*." *The World of Null-A* was a central part of Gunn's teaching in the Intensive Summer Institute on the Teaching of Science Fiction, founded in 1974. For many years Gunn served as consulting editor for Easton Press, for which he wrote introductions for many of the novels selected for the leather-bound collectors' series, among them *The World of Null-A* where he calls it "the ultimate science-fiction serial of SF's Golden Age" that "pushed concepts of the human species and its undiscovered potentials as far as they would go" (*Paratexts* 40). See also A. Berger (41-42) and the Panshins (626-29).

101. See Clareson and Sanders (58-61) and Franklin, *Heinlein* (94-96). Franklin describes "Gulf" as "an anti-Communist diatribe arguing for the need of a master race of 'supermen' to settle the problems of our times and the future" (94). Meyers makes an interesting point with regard to how Korzybski's *Science and Sanity* features in Heinlein's story (173-75).

102. Gathered in *Children of the Atom*.

103. See note 47 above. See also Clareson and Sanders (32-35) and Franklin, *Heinlein* (43-44). Franklin remarks that "'Universe' is a classic presentation of that critical problem, the impenetrable limits environment places around consciousness" (44). Wolfe provides a sustained discussion of self-contained societies within spaceships in *The Known and the Unknown* (61-65), but the most substantial analysis appears in Simone Carotti, *The Generation Starship in Science Fiction* (98-119).

104. Another one of the paradigmatic Hall of Fame stories of science fiction, and a central text of feminist science fiction. The story appears in volume three of *The Road to Science Fiction*. For further discussion of this essential story see Dianne Newell and Victoria Lamont, *Judith Merril: A Critical Study* (30-33) and Lisa Yaszek, *Galactic Suburbia* (115-117). For Merril's own remarks on the story see *Better to Have Loved: The Life of Judith Merril* (89-92, 154-55). See also Huntington (100-104).

105. Gunn may have first encountered it in the September 1942 issue of *Famous Fantastic Mysteries*.

106. This theme was carried forward in two examples from cinema, *Them!* (1954) and *Phase IV* (1974).

107. The novel actually first appeared in the March 1941 issue of *Super Science Stories*, edited by Frederik Pohl. Gunn was evidently unaware of the magazine publication. The novel is a delightful anticipation of Pierre Boulle's *The Planet of the Apes*.

108. The Panshins remark: "De Camp was perfectly willing to concede that men of our own kind might still run afoul of the forces of evolution and pass from the scene. But if that were to happen, it would not be because evolution was some hostile outside force single-mindedly bent on bringing us down, but because we were so careless, stupid and greedy that we tripped ourselves up" (291).

109. There is some resonance here with Frederik Pohl's "Let the Ants Try," published two years later. For discussion of Pohl's story, see the editor's *Frederik Pohl* (37-38).

110. The series, appearing in *Astounding* from 1944 to 1947, with the last story appearing in *Fantastic Adventures* in 1951, was published as *City* in 1952, and remains one of the great works of science fiction. See the editor's "Evolution and Apocalypse in the Golden Age" (45-48) for a discussion of the ecological theme in the series and Clareson, *Understanding Contemporary American Science Fiction* (45-49) for a thoughtful discussion of the series.

111. The few humans remaining on earth (most have bioengineered themselves and left for Jupiter), seal themselves away in dream tanks, much in the manner of the final section of Gunn's *The Joy Makers*. The theme may have had its first expression in "City of the Living Dead" (*Science Wonder Stories* May 1930) by Laurence Manning and Fletcher Pratt, which, incidentally, was reprinted in the same issue of the *Avon Fantasy Reader* that featured Endore's "The Day of the Dragon."

112. Another early story in this vein was Pohl and Kornbluth's "Best Friend" (*Super Science Stories* May 1941), a surprisingly poignant story from the two authors during their youthful Futurian years. See the editor's *Frederik Pohl* (31-32).

113. The story in question is probably Theodore Sturgeon's "The Ultimate Egoist," which appeared in *Astounding*'s companion magazine *Unknown Worlds* in February 1941, a classic of solipsistic science fiction.

114. This is probably a reference to John Russell Fearn's "The Man who Stopped the Dust" (*Astounding* March 1934).

115. See Warrick for a full discussion of science fiction's exploration of the "cybernetic imagination."

116. This sentence anticipates Clarke's

Third Law: "Any sufficiently advanced technology is indistinguishable from magic."

117. Two later notable examples of this theme are Alfred Bester's "Fondly Fahrenheit" and Philip K. Dick's *Do Androids Dream of Electric Sheep?* Readers should seek out Dick's two essays "The Android and the Human" and "Man, Android and Machine."

118. In his teens, Gunn was an avid reader of the *Doc Savage* pulp.

119. Serialized in the first three issues of *Galaxy* in late 1950 and published in hardcover by Simon and Schuster in 1951. Gunn recommended paperback publication for Dell while he was working at Western Printing and they issued the novel under the title *First He Died* in late 1952 or early 1953.

120. The hero is Northwest Smith, featured in a number of Moore's stories, most famously "Shambleau," which mostly appeared in *Weird Tales* in the mid-1930s. The complete Northwest Smith stories have recently been published in *Northwest of Earth*.

121. Huxley's only science fiction story, Gunn selected it for volume two of *The Road to Science Fiction*, pointing out that it was one of the few stories from the era concerned with biology (147) and that "Huxley was raising questions long before the atomic bomb about the social value of science and the social responsibility of the scientist" (148).

122. For the editor's take on Wells's novel, see *The Literary Imagination from Erasmus Darwin to H.G. Wells* (170–74).

123. See note 80 above.

124. A good discussion of the play and its meaning appears in Philmus (156–57).

125. Asimov's first robot story, "Robbie," was rejected by John W. Campbell at *Astounding* and was published by Frederik Pohl in *Super Science Stories* under the title "Strange Playfellow" in the September 1940 issue. It is rather surprising that Gunn spends little time examining Asimov's Robot stories; *I, Robot* had been published by Gnome Press in 1950. It is possible that Gunn had not yet seen them in the collection and only read a few in *Astounding*, since many came out during the war when Gunn was otherwise occupied with military duties. More surprising is the fact that Gunn doesn't engage with Asimov's *Foundation* series at all in the thesis. For Gunn's later analysis of the Robot stories, see chapter 3, "Variations upon a Robot" (41–66) in *Isaac Asimov: The Foundations of Science Fiction*.

126. Asimov's Three Laws of Robotics have become part of the basic technological architecture of the modern world, inside and outside of science fiction. Gunn pulled the statements of the Laws as stated within the June 1950 text of the final story in *I, Robot*, "The Evitable Conflict." These statements were removed from the story when it appeared in *I, Robot*. Readers will notice, however, a startling change in nuance from the standard version of the Second Law: "A robot must obey the orders given it by human beings except where such orders would conflict with the First Law." In the version Gunn quotes from "The Evitable Conflict," the modifier "qualified" appears before human beings. The implications for the function of the Second Law is striking. Perhaps Campbell added the modifier against Asimov's better judgment? Warrick considers "The Evitable Conflict," "one of science fiction's most superbly imaginative stories in envisioning the creative use of machine intelligence" (60). A. Berger makes the curious remark that "In retrospect, one can hear in 'The Evitable Conflict' a cry for help. The story expresses not so much a belief in evolution as the *need* for it—a call for a savior, and quickly" (37). In *Technophobia!: Science Fiction Visions of Posthuman Technology* Daniel Dinello perhaps overstates Asimov's technophilia: "Wearing the robes of a techno-evangelist, Asimov expressed an unwavering faith, akin to religious fundamentalism, in a technological utopia" (66). For a recent discussion of Asimov's Three Laws of interest, see Seo-Young Chu, *Do Metaphors Dream of Literal Sleep?* (235–37).

127. Another example is Philip K. Dick's "The Defenders" (1953), which forms the basis of the 1964 novel *The Penultimate Truth*.

128. Gunn here appears to be conflating "I, Robot" and its sequel "The Trial of Adam Link," published several issues later in *Amazing* July 1939.

129. The Adam Link stories were brought together in book form in *Adam Link—Robot*. Both "I, Robot" and "The Trial of Adam Link" were adapted by Otto Binder for issues #2–4 of *Creepy* horror-comic in 1964. A good discussion of the stories appears in Carter (168–70).

130. See Joe R. Christopher, "Usuform Robotics: Anthony Boucher's Future History." Brian Stableford points out that this story takes an opposing view to C. L. Moore's "No Woman Born" (see next) in favoring usuform robots over humanoform ones. As Stableford conjectures, "Boucher was a Catholic, and found the idea of making machines in the image of man somewhat distasteful for religious reasons" (106).

131. "No Woman Born" has received a great deal of critical attention in recent years. See Raffaella Baccolini, "In Between Subjects: C. L. Moore's 'No Woman Born,'" Linda Howell, "'Wartime Inventions with Peaceful Inten-

tions': Television and the Media Cyborg in C. L. Moore's 'No Woman Born,'" Despina Kakoudaki, "Pinup and Cyborg: Exaggerated Gender and Artificial Intelligence," Susan Smith, "'Neither Normal or Human': The Cyborg in C. L. Moore's 'No Woman Born,'" Thomas Wymer, "Feminism, Technology, and Art in C. L. Moore's 'No Woman Born.'"

Moore's own reflections on the story are of interest: "Given the basic idea—what would happen to the most beautiful and gifted dancer of her time if she were totally incapacitated by a frightful accident? Well, you gear your mind to a technological solution, but the human element keeps intruding and you know you haven't really answered the question. How would being a quasi-robot, no matter how beautiful, affect her thinking and her feeling as a human being? How would *you* handle it?" (308).

132. Perhaps the most sustained discussion of the story and its sequel, following Gunn's, appears in Wolfe, *The Known and the Unknown* (164–74). Warrick describes the story as "one of the earliest and the best of the tales about man in a cybernetic future" (151–52). Damon Knight began his review of the novel with the curious remark, "It is no pleasure to me to make the admission, but Jack Williamson's *The Humanoids* is without doubt one of the most important science-fantasy books of its decade." Knight then goes on to reiterate the importance of the theme, but then to charge Williamson with "unremittingly and excruciatingly bad" writing (45–46). An illustration, I think, of *wrongly* trying to apply modernist literary values to science fiction. Note that Knight's attack on Van Vogt, "Cosmic Jerrybuilder," appears on the next page of *In Search of Wonder*.

H. Berger compares the story to Orwell's *1984*, published two years after Williamson's tale: "Like the tyranny of the party in Orwell, the tyranny of the machine in Williamson is forever. Both writers grasp the possible infinite emerging in the twentieth century: that in the control of men by other men or by machines a critical point may be reached at which that control can be neither wrested nor surrendered" (30). Rose comments that "With Folded Hands..." is a fable "describing the establishment of a totalitarian state run by machines" (166). In this sense, "With Folded Hands..." may owe a debt to Williamson's early collaborator Miles J. Breuer whose novel *Paradise and Iron* has a similar theme. Although Williamson's paradigmatic story advances from Breuer's novel. See the editor's Breuer volume for the text of *Paradise and Iron*.

133. For discussion on how Gunn's later story "Little Orphan Android" (*Galaxy* September 1955) is in conversation with Williamson's classic, see *Saving the World* (175–77).

134. In his autobiography *Wonder's Child*, Williamson explains how John Campbell suggested ESP as the answer in beating the humanoids, "he thought he saw how to beat the humanoids. Men forced to fold their hands might develop the mental powers Joseph Rhine was looking for in his parapsychology lab at Duke, Campbell's alma mater. No believer in ESP, then or now, I read a couple of Rhine's books and wrote the serial." But Williamson was as ambivalent about the result (even though *The Humanoids* was his most successful book):

"The ending became a new problem. If the humanoids really were as perfect as I saw them, they couldn't be stopped. If humanity could master new powers of the mind, the humanoids could do the same thing more efficiently. The novelette had said perhaps not exactly what I wanted to say, but what its own premise demanded, a theme I felt too deeply to let it be denied by an optimistic ending.

"What I tried was a new version of the old one, equally tragic to me, but seen from the viewpoint of the people brainwashed by the ever-clever humanoids to be happy about it. The result was ambiguity; every reader and reviewer seemed to see it differently. Which may be just as well" (165).

135. Warrick makes a similar observation regarding this story in *The Cybernetic Imagination in Science Fiction* (117–18).

136. A likely candidate for discussion here would have been Murray Leinster's "A Logic Named Joe" (*Astounding* March 1946), now considered a seminal classic anticipating the social consequences of networked computers. But the story was not included in any of the early anthologies and Gunn likely missed it as he was still stationed in the Pacific when the issue of *Astounding* came out.

137. One is reminded of the collusion of American and Soviet computers in D. F. Jones's *Colossus* and the A.I. conspiracy at the conclusion of Frederik Pohl's *Man Plus*.

138. In some ways echoing Wells's story "The Lord of the Dynamos."

139. See Bleiler (156) and Carter (214–216). A. Berger gives an extended analysis of the story (29–31).

140. Gunn's own take on the godlike supercomputer features in the stunning conclusion of *The Joy Makers*.

141. Hugi's story resonates with Frederik Pohl's "The Waging of the Peace" and Philip

K. Dick's "Autofac," both stories of machine menace. See also Carter (167–68).

142. The best example here being Heinlein's *The Man who Sold the Moon*, relating the financier D. D. Harriman's quest to build a moon rocket. Gunn explored this question himself in his thoughtful *Galaxy* story "The Cave of Night" and its sequels collected in *Station in Space*.

143. An early anticipation of Stephen King's *Under the Dome*.

144. See Jad Smith, *Alfred Bester* (43–48).

145. See *Saving the World* (83–84). Rather interesting that Gunn chose to conclude his story analyses with one of his own stories, but "These Things are Sirius" is a good example of the point he was illustrating.

Conclusion

1. A clear indication that Bailey hadn't really been paying much attention to the field and failed to account for the impact of Campbell's Golden Age *Astounding* in his addendum to his original manuscript. Which is a shame given his powerful evocations of the importance of science fiction in the atomic age in his Preface (1–4).

2. This notion of science fiction as a "forum" for ideas has a fascinating parallel with Farah Mendlesohn's claim that science fiction is "an ongoing discussion," that "much SF is written as an argument with the universe" (1–2).

3. From Coleridge's review of Matthew Lewis's *The Monk* in *The Critical Review* February 1797.

Bibliography

Fiction Works Cited (James Gunn)

I have preserved Gunn's original source citations. For later reprints of these stories or original magazine publication, interested readers should consult the Internet Science Fiction database (isfdb.org).

Anderson, Poul. "The Double-Dyed Villains." *Astounding*, September 1950. 6–30.
——. "Quixote and the Windmill." *Astounding*, November 1950. 95–102.
——. "Tomorrow's Children," and F.N. Waldrop. *A Treasury of Science Fiction*. Ed. Groff Conklin. New York: Crown, 1948. 19–39.
Asimov, Isaac. "Blind Alley." *The Best of Science Fiction*. Ed. Groff Conklin. New York: Crown, 1946. 622–40.
——. "The Endochronic Properties of Resublimated Thiotimoline." *Astounding*, March 1948. 120–25.
——. "The Evitable Conflict." *Astounding*, June 1950. 48–68.
——. "Nightfall." *Adventures in Time and Space*. Ed. R. J. Healy and J. F. McComas. New York: Random House, 1946. 378–411.
Bates, Harry. "Alas, All Thinking." *The Other Worlds*. Ed. Phil Stong. Garden City: Garden City Publishing, 1941. 251–94.
——. "Farewell to the Master." *Adventures in Time and Space*. Ed. R. J. Healy and J. F. McComas. New York: Random House, 1946. 779–815.
Bellamy, Edward. *Looking Backward*. Boston: Ticknor, 1888.
Bergerac, Cyrano de. *Voyages to the Moon and the Sun*. London: Routledge, 1923.
Bester, Alfred. "Adam and No Eve." *Adventures in Time and Space*. Ed. R. J. Healy and J. F. McComas. New York: Random House, 1946. 365–77.
Binder, Eando. "Adam Link's Vengeance." *The Other Worlds*. Ed. Phil Stong. Garden City: Garden City Publishing, 1941. 171–203.
——. "I, Robot." *Amazing*, January 1939. 8–17.
Bond, Nelson. "Conquerors' Isle." *The Other Side of the Moon*. Ed. August Derleth. New York: Pellegrini & Cudahy, 1949. 164–81.
——. "The Cunning of the Beast." *Strange Ports of Call*. Ed. August Derleth. New York: Pellegrini & Cudahy, 1948. 3–21
Boucher, Anthony. "Expedition." *The Best of Science Fiction*. Ed. Groff Conklin. New York: Crown, 1946. 740–51.
——. "Q.U.R." *Adventures in Time and Space*. Ed. R. J. Healy and J. F. McComas. New York: Random House, 1946. 376–96.
Bradbury, Ray. "— and the Moon Still Be as Bright." *The Martian Chronicles*. 67–93.
——. "The Fireman." *Galaxy*, February 1951. 4–61.
——. *The Martian Chronicles*. Garden City: Doubleday, 1950.
Brown, Fredric. "Honeymoon in Hell." *Galaxy*, November 1950. 4–33.
——. "Letter to a Phoenix." *Astounding*, August 1949. 146–53.

Bibliography

Burroughs, Edgar Rice. *At the Earth's Core*. Chicago: McClurg, 1922.

———. *The Chessmen of Mars*. Chicago: McClurg, 1922.

———. *The Land That Time Forgot*. Chicago: McClurg, 1924.

———. *Pirates of Venus*. Tarzana: Burroughs Inc., 1934.

Campbell, John W. "Forgetfulness." *Adventures in Time and Space*. Ed. R. J. Healy and J. F. McComas. New York: Random House, 1946. 20–45.

———. *The Incredible Planet*. Providence: Hadley, 1949.

———. "The Machine." *The Best of Science Fiction*. Ed. Groff Conklin: New York, Crown, 1946. 460–74.

———. *The Moon Is Hell*. Reading: Fantasy Press, 1950.

———. "Who Goes There?" *Adventures in Time and Space*. Ed. R. J. Healy and J. F. McComas. New York: Random House, 1946. 497–550.

Capek, Karel. *R.U.R.* New York: Doubleday, 1923.

Cartmill, Cleve. "Deadline." *The Best of Science Fiction*. Ed. Groff Conklin. New York: Crown, 1946. 67–88.

———. "The Link." *Adventures in Time and Space*. Ed. R. J. Healy and J. F. McComas. New York: Random House, 1946. 308–19.

Christopher, John. "Tree of Wrath." *Worlds Beyond*, January 1951. 28–43.

Clarke, Arthur C. "Rescue Party." *A Treasury of Science Fiction*. Ed. Groff Conklin. New York: Crown, 1948. 495–517.

Clement, Hal. "Fireproof." *Astounding*, March 1949. 67–81.

Conan Doyle, Arthur. *The Lost World*. London: Hodder and Stoughton, 1912.

Davis, Chan. "The Nightmare." *A Treasury of Science Fiction*. Ed. Groff Conklin. New York: Crown, 1948. 3–18.

De Camp, L. Sprague. "The Gnarly Man." *The Wheels of If*. Chicago: Shasta, 1948. 194–222.

———. "Living Fossil." *A Treasury of Science Fiction*. Ed. Groff Conklin. New York: Crown, 1948. 97–109.

De Camp, L. Sprague, and P. Schuyler Miller. *Genus Homo*. Reading: Fantasy Press, 1950.

Del Rey, Lester. "Nerves." *Adventures in Time and Space*. Ed. R. J. Healy and J. F. McComas. New York: Random House, 1946. 46–114.

Ehrlich, Max. *The Big Eye*. Garden City: Doubleday, 1949.

Endore, Guy. "The Day of the Dragon." *Avon Fantasy Reader*, No. 2, 1947. 50–72.

England, George Allan. "The Thing from Outside." *The Best of Science Fiction*. Ed. Groff Conklin. New York: Crown, 1946. 542–55.

Ernst, Paul. "The 32nd of May." *The Best of Science Fiction*. Ed. Groff Conklin. New York: Crown, 1946. 532–41.

Fearn, John Russell. "Wings Across the Cosmos." *A Treasury of Science Fiction*. Ed. Groff Conklin. New York: Crown, 1948. 418–28.

Friend, Oscar J. "Of Jovian Build." *A Treasury of Science Fiction*. Ed. Groff Conklin. New York: Crown, 1948. 407–17.

Gallun, Raymond Z. "Seeds of the Dusk." *Adventures in Time and Space*. Ed. R. J. Healy and J. F. McComas. New York: Random House, 1946. 249–75.

Grendon, Edward. "The Figure." *A Treasury of Science Fiction*. Ed. Groff Conklin. New York: Crown, 1948. 67–71.

Gunn, James. "Guaranteed" ("These Things Are Sirius"). *Thrilling Wonder*, August 1951. 126–37.

———. "Paradox." *Thrilling Wonder*, October 1949. 135–56.

Hall, Austin. "The Man Who Saved the Earth." *The Best of Science Fiction*. Ed. Groff Conklin. New York: Crown, 1946. 688–703.

Heard, H. F. "The Great Fog." *A Treasury of Science Fiction*. Ed. Groff Conklin. New York: Crown, 1948. 75–84.

Heinlein, Robert A. "Blowups Happen." *The Best of Science Fiction*. Ed. Groff Conklin. New York: Crown, 1946. 103–39.

———. "By His Bootstraps." *Adventures in Time and Space*. Eds. R. J. Healy & J. F. McComas. New York: Random House, 1946. 882–932.

———. "Goldfish Bowl." *The Best of Science Fiction*. Ed. Groff Conklin. New York: Crown, 1946. 252–77.

_____. "The Green Hills of Earth." *Strange Ports of Call.* Ed. August Derleth. New York: Pellegrini & Cudahy, 1948. 353-64.

_____. "Gulf." *Astounding,* November, December, 1949. 53-90, 54-79.

_____. "Magic, Inc." *Waldo & Magic, Inc.* Garden City: Doubleday, 1949.

_____. "The Roads Must Roll." *Adventures in Time and Space.* Ed. R. J. Healy and J. F. McComas. New York: Random House, 1946. 551-87.

_____. "Solution Unsatisfactory." *The Best of Science Fiction.* Ed. Groff Conklin. New York: Crown, 1946. 3-35.

_____. "Universe." *The Best of Science Fiction.* Ed. Groff Conklin. New York: Crown, 1946. 532-41.

Holberg, Ludvig. *Journey to the World Under-Ground.* London: Astley & Collins, 1742.

Howard, Robert E. *Conan the Conqueror.* New York: Gnome, 1950.

Hugi, Maurice A. "Mechanical Mice." *Adventures in Time and Space.* Ed. R. J. Healy and J. F. McComas. New York: Random House, 1946. 320-23.

Huxley, Aldous. *Brave New World.* Garden City: Doubleday, 1932.

Huxley, Julian. "The Tissue-Culture King." *The Best of Science Fiction.* Ed. Groff Conklin. New York: Crown, 1946. 248-65.

Jameson, Malcolm. "Children of the 'Betsy B.'" *A Treasury of Science Fiction.* Ed. Groff Conklin. New York: Crown, 1948. 234-44.

Jones, Raymond. F. "Correspondence Course." *Adventures in Time and Space.* Eds. R. J. Healy & J. F. McComas. New York: Random House, 1946. 953-71.

_____. "The Person from Porlock." *A Treasury of Science Fiction.* Ed. Groff Conklin. New York: Crown, 1948. 268-87.

Kahn, Bernard I. "A Pinch of Culture." *Astounding,* August 1950. 78-107.

Keeler, Harry S. "John Jones' Dollar." *Strange Ports of Call.* Ed. August Derleth. New York: Pellegrini & Cudahy, 1948. 209-19.

Klass, Morton. "Invitation from the Stars." *Future,* Sept-Oct 1950. 51-59.

Kornbluth, C. M. "The Little Black Bag." *Astounding,* July 1950. 132-61.

_____. "The Silly Season." *Magazine of Fantasy and Science Fiction,* Fall 1950. 3-16.

Kuttner, Henry. "The Comedy of Eras." *The Other Worlds.* Ed. Phil Stong. Garden City: Garden City Publishing, 1941. 295-314.

_____. "Don't Look Now." *My Best Science Fiction Story.* Eds. Leo Margulies & Oscar J. Friend. New York: Merlin Press, 1949. 285-301.

_____. and C. L. Moore. "Call Him Demon." *Strange Ports of Call.* Ed. August Derleth. New York: Pellegrini & Cudahy, 1948. 220-43.

_____. "Mimsy Were the Borogoves." *A Treasury of Science Fiction.* Ed. Groff Conklin. New York: Crown, 1948. 303-28.

_____. "The Piper's Son." *The Best of Science Fiction.* Ed. Groff Conklin. New York: Crown, 1946. 45-66.

_____. "The Twonky." *Adventures in Time and Space.* Ed. R. J. Healy and J. F. McComas. New York: Random House, 1946. 655-75.

_____. "Vintage Season." *A Treasury of Science Fiction.* Ed. Groff Conklin. New York: Crown, 1948. 369-403.

La Farge, Oliver. "John the Revelator." *Magazine of Fantasy and Science Fiction,* February 1951. 3-14.

Latham, Philip. "N Day." *A Treasury of Science Fiction.* Ed. Groff Conklin. New York: Crown, 1948. 110-125.

Leiber, Fritz. "Coming Attraction." *Galaxy,* November 1950. 75-86.

Leinster, Murray. "The Ethical Equations." *A Treasury of Science Fiction.* Ed. Groff Conklin. New York: Crown, 1948. 451-63.

_____. "First Contact." *The Best of Science Fiction.* Ed. Groff Conklin. New York: Crown, 1946. 559-83.

_____. "The Lost Race." *My Best Science Fiction Story.* Eds. Leo Margulies & Oscar J. Friend. New York: Merlin Press, 1949. 317-43.

_____. "Nobody Saw the Ship." *Future,* May-June 1950. 40-49, 94-97.

_____. "Symbiosis." *The Other Side of the*

Moon. Ed. August Derleth. New York: Pelligrini & Cudahy, 1949. 276–95.

Locke, Richard Adams. "The Moon Hoax." New York: Bunnell & Price, 1852.

London, Jack. "The Shadow and the Flash." *Shot in the Dark.* Ed. Judith Merril. New York: Bantam, 1950. 151–68.

Long, Frank Belknap. "The Flame Midget." *The Best of Science Fiction.* Ed. Groff Conklin. New York: Crown, 1946. 451–63.

———. "A Guest in the House." *Strange Ports of Call.* Ed. August Derleth. New York: Pelligrini & Cudahy, 1948. 259–75.

Loomis, Noel. "Monster of the West." *Thrilling Wonder Stories*, February 1949, 98–109.

Lucian. *Icaromenippus.* In *The Works of Lucian of Samosata.* Vol. II. Oxford: Clarendon, 1905

MacDonald, John D. "Trojan Horse Laugh." *Astounding*, August 1949. 73–111.

Maupassant, Guy de. "The Horla." In *The Works of Maupassant.* Vol. VIII. Boston: Brainard, 1910.

McClary, Thomas Calvert. *Rebirth.* New York: Bartholomew, 1944.

Merril, Judith. "That Only a Mother." *Astounding*, June 1948. 88–95.

Merritt, Abraham. *Dwellers in the Mirage.* New York: Liveright, 1931.

———. *The Face in the Abyss.* New York: Liveright, 1933.

———. *The Moon Pool.* New York: Putnam, 1919.

———. *The Ship of Ishtar.* New York: Putnam, 1926.

———. *The Snake Mother. Fantastic Novels*, November 1940. 6–111.

Miller, P. Schuyler. "As Never Was." *Adventures in Time and Space.* Ed. R. J. Healy and J. F. McComas. New York: Random House, 1946. 460–75.

———. "The Chrysalis." *A Treasury of Science Fiction.* Ed. Groff Conklin. New York: Crown, 1948. 85–96.

———. "The Sands of Time." *Adventures in Time and Space.* Ed. R. J. Healy and J. F. McComas. New York: Random House, 1946. 115–43.

Moore, C. L. "Black Thirst." *Avon Fantasy Reader*, No. 3, 1947. 56–88.

———. "No Woman Born." *A Treasury of Science Fiction.* Ed. Groff Conklin. New York: Crown, 1948. 164–200.

Neville, Kris. "Every Work into Judgment." *Magazine of Fantasy and Science Fiction*, Winter-Spring 1950. 29–36.

O'Brien, Fitz-James. "The Diamond Lens." *Short Story Classics.* New York: Collier, 1905.

Phillips, Peter. "Dreams Are Sacred." *Astounding*, September 1948. 51–70.

———. "P-Plus." *Astounding*, August 1949. 112–33.

Piper, H. Beam. "Time and Time Again." *A Treasury of Science Fiction.* Ed. Groff Conklin. New York: Crown, 1948. 329–41.

Poe, Edgar Allan. *The Complete Works of Edgar Allan Poe.* New York: Crowell, 1902.

Reynolds, Mack. "The Man in the Moon." *Amazing*, July 1950. 40–55.

Rocklynne, Ross. "Jackdaw." *The Best of Science Fiction.* Ed. Groff Conklin. New York: Crown, 1946. 764–85.

Russell, Eric Frank. "Exposure." *Astounding*, July 1950. 107–23.

———. "First Person Singular." *Thrilling Wonder*, October 1950. 78–103.

———. "Follower." *Astounding*, November 1950. 68–75.

———. *Sinister Barrier.* Reading: Fantasy Press, 1948

———. "Symbiotica." *Adventures in Time and Space.* Ed. R. J. Healy and J. F. McComas. New York: Random House, 1946. 207–48.

Schachner, Nat. "The Ultimate Metal." *The Best of Science Fiction.* Ed. Groff Conklin. New York: Crown, 1946. 441–59.

Shelley, Mary. *Frankenstein.* London: Colburn & Bentley, 1831.

Sharp, D. D. "The Eternal Man." *A Treasury of Science Fiction.* Ed. Groff Conklin. New York: Crown, 1948. 294–300.

Shiras, Wilmar H. "In Hiding." *Astounding*, November 1948. 40–70.

Simak, Clifford D. "Aesop." *Astounding*, December 1947. 7–31.

———. "Lobby." *The Best of Science Fiction.* Ed. Groff Conklin. New York: Crown, 1946. 89–102.

———. *Time and Again.* New York: Simon & Schuster, 1951.

Smith, George O. "Dynasty of the Lost." *Future*, May-June 1950. 8-38.

Stapledon, Olaf. *Last and First Men*. London: Methuen, 1930.

———. *Last Men in London*. London: Methuen, 1932.

———. *Odd John*. London: Dutton, 1936.

Sturgeon, Theodore. "Killdozer!" *The Best of Science Fiction*. Ed. Groff Conklin. New York: Crown, 1946. 155-209.

———. "Memorial." *The Other Side of the Moon*. Ed. August Derleth. New York: Pelligrini & Cudahy, 1949. 419-35.

———. "The Sky Was Full of Ships." *Shot in the Dark*. Ed. Judith Merril. New York: Bantam, 1950. 1-14.

———. "Thunder and Roses." *Strange Ports of Call*. Ed. August Derleth. New York: Pelligrini & Cudahy, 1948. 330-52.

Taine, John. "The Ultimate Catalyst." *The Best of Science Fiction*. Ed. Groff Conklin. New York: Crown, 1946. 366-84.

Tenn, William. "Brooklyn Project." *Shot in the Dark*. Ed. Judith Merril. New York: Bantam, 1950. 198-210.

———. "Child's Play." *A Treasury of Science Fiction*. Ed. Groff Conklin. New York: Crown, 1948. 247-67.

Van Vogt, A. E. "Black Destroyer." *Adventures in Time and Space*. Ed. R. J. Healy and J. F. McComas. New York: Random House, 1946. 177-206.

———. *The Players of Null-A*. *Astounding*, October, November, December, 1948, January 1949.

———. "Resurrection." *The Other Side of the Moon*. Ed. August Derleth. New York: Pelligrini & Cudahy, 1949. 436-58.

———. *Slan*. Sauk City: Arkham, 1946.

———. *The Weapon Shops of Isher*. *Thrilling Wonder*, February 1949. 11-60.

———. "The Weapons Shop." *Adventures in Time and Space*. Ed. R. J. Healy and J. F. McComas. New York: Random House, 1946. 741-78.

———. *The World of Null-A*. New York: Simon & Schuster, 1947.

Voltaire, *Micromegas*. London: George Bell and Sons, 1891.

Wandrei, Donald. "The Monster from Nowhere." *The Best of Science Fiction*. Ed. Groff Conklin. New York: Crown, 1946. 542-55.

Wells, H. G. "The Empire of the Ants." *The Strand*, December 1905.

———. *The Food of the Gods*. London: Macmillan, 1904.

———. *The Invisible Man*. London: Pearson, 1897.

———. *The Island of Dr. Moreau*. London: Heineman, 1896.

———. "The New Accelerator." *The Strand*, December 1901.

———. "The Remarkable Case of Davidson's Eyes." *The Best of Science Fiction*. Ed. Groff Conklin. New York: Crown, 1946. 340-47.

———. *Star-Begotten*. New York: Viking, 1937.

———. *The Time Machine*. London: Heineman, 1895.

———. "The Valley of the Spiders." *Pearson's*, March 1903.

———. *The War of the Worlds*. London: Harper, 1898.

West, Wallace. "En Route to Pluto." *The Best of Science Fiction*. Ed. Groff Conklin. New York: Crown, 1946. 641-50.

Wilkins, Bishop John. *Mercury; or the Secret and Swift Messenger*. London: Maynard, 1641.

Williams, Robert Moore. "Robot's Return." *Adventures in Time and Space*. Ed. R. J. Healy and J. F. McComas. New York: Random House, 1946. 687-97.

Williamson, Jack. "The Equalizer." *Astounding*, March 1947. 6-55.

———. *The Humanoids*. New York: Simon & Schuster, 1949.

———. *Seetee Shock*. New York: Simon & Schuster, 1950

———. "With Folded Hands." *A Treasury of Science Fiction*. Ed. Groff Conklin. New York: Crown, 1948. 129-64.

Wollheim, Donald A. "The Embassy." *A Treasury of Science Fiction*. Ed. Groff Conklin. New York: Crown, 1948. 429-34.

Wylie, Philip. "Blunder." *Strange Ports of Call*. Ed. August Derleth. New York: Pelligrini & Cudahy, 1948. 365-80.

———. *Gladiator*. New York: Knopf, 1930.

Zagat, Arthur Leo. "The Lanson Screen." *The Best of Science Fiction*. Ed. Groff Conklin. New York: Crown, 1946. 424-40.

Critical Works Cited (James Gunn)

Bailey, J. O. *Pilgrims Through Space and Time*. New York: Argus Books, 1947.
Baring-Gould, W. S. "Little Superman, What Now?" *Harper's*, September 1946. 283–88.
Campbell, John W., Jr. "Concerning Dianetics." *Astounding*, May 1950. 4–5.
———. "In Times to Come." *Astounding*, November 1950. 150.
———. Preface. *The Best of Science Fiction*. Ed. Groff Conklin. New York: Crown, 1946.
———. "The Science of Science-Fiction." *Atlantic Monthly*, May 1948. 97–98.
———. "The Science of Science-Fiction Writing." *Of Worlds Beyond*. Ed. L. A. Eshbach. Los Angeles: Fantasy Press, 1947. 84–96.
Coleridge, Samuel Taylor. Review of *The Monk* by Matthew Lewis. *Critical Review*, February 1797. 194–200.
Conklin, Groff. Introduction. *The Best of Science Fiction*. New York: Crown, 1946.
Derleth, August. Introduction. *Strange Ports of Call*. New York: Pellegrini & Cudahy, 1948.
Ewing, E. G. Letter in "Brass Tacks." *Astounding* July 1948. 158–60.
Healy, Raymond J. and J. Francis McComas. Introduction. *Adventures in Time and Space*. New York: Random House, 1946.
Isherwood, Christopher. "The Martian Chronicles." *Tomorrow*, October 1950. 56.
Margulies, Leo and Oscar J. Friend. Introduction. *My Best Science Fiction Story*. New York: Merlin Press, 1949. vii–ix.
Merwin, Sam, Jr. "The Ether Vibrates." Editorial. *Startling Stories* January 1950. 6–7, 150.
Nathan, P. S. "Books into Films: Science Fiction." *Publishers' Weekly*, June 18, 1949. 2463.
"News of the Month." *Other Worlds*, July 1950. 153–156.
Pratt, Fletcher. "Science Fiction and Fantasy—1949." *Saturday Review of Literature*, December 24, 1949. 7–9.
Stong, Phil. Foreword. *The Other Worlds*. Garden City: Garden City Publishing, 1941.
Williamson, Jack. "The Logic of Fantasy." *Of Worlds Beyond*. Ed. L. A. Eschbach. Los Angeles: Fantasy Press, 1947. 34–46.

Works Cited in Editor's Introduction (Michael R. Page)

Abbott, Carl. *Frontiers Past and Future*. Lawrence: University of Kansas Press, 2006.
Aldiss, Brian W. *Billion Year Spree: The True History of Science Fiction*. Garden City: Doubleday, 1973.
———. "Man in His Time." *Who Can Replace a Man?* New York: Signet, 1966.
Alkon, Paul. *Origins of Futuristic Fiction*. Athens: University of Georgia Press, 1987.
Allen, L. David. *Science Fiction: An Introduction*. Lincoln: Cliffs Notes, 1973.
———. *Science Fiction Reader's Guide*. Lincoln: Centennial, 1974.
Amis, Kingsley. *New Maps of Hell*. New York: Harcourt, Brace, 1960.
Anger, R. R. Letter to the Editor. *Dynamic,* October 1953. 69, 83.
Armytage, W. H. G. *Yesterday's Tomorrows: A Historical Survey of Future Societies*. Toronto: University of Toronto Press, 1968.
Ash, Brian. *Faces of the Future*. New York: Taplinger, 1975.
Ashley, Michael. "Introduction: From Bomb to Boom." *The History of the Science Fiction Magazine Volume 3, 1946–1955*. Ed. Chicago: Contemporary Books, 1976. 13–110.
Asimov, Isaac. *In Memory Yet Green: The Autobiography of Isaac Asimov, 1920–1954*. Garden City: Doubleday, 1979.
———. *I, Robot*. New York: Ballantine, 1950, 1977.
———. "Social Science Fiction." *Modern Science Fiction: Its Meaning and Its Future*. Ed. Reginald Bretnor. New York: Coward-McCann, 1953. 157–196.
———. "Strange Playfellow" ("Robbie"). *Super Science Stories*, September 1940. 67–77.

Baccolini, Raffaella. "In Between Subjects: C. L. Moore's 'No Woman Born.'" *Science Fiction, Critical Frontiers*. Eds. Karen Sayer and John Moore. New York: St. Martin's, 2000. 140–53.
Bainbridge, William S. *Dimensions of Science Fiction*. Cambridge: Harvard University Press, 1986.
Baldick, Chris. *In Frankenstein's Shadow: Myth, Monstrosity, and Nineteenth-Century Writing*. Oxford: Clarendon, 1987.
Barron, Neil. *Anatomy of Wonder*. Ed. New York: Bowker, 1976.
Bartter, Martha A. *The Way to Ground Zero: The Atomic Bomb in American Science Fiction*. Westport: Greenwood, 1988.
Baxter, Stephen. *Evolution*. New York: Ballantine, 2002.
Beresford, J. D. *The Wonder*. Lincoln: University of Nebraska Press, 1999.
Berger, Albert I. *The Magic That Works: John W. Campbell and the American Response to Technology*. San Bernardino: Borgo, 1993.
Berger, Harold L. *Science Fiction and the New Dark Age*. Bowling Green: Bowling Green University Press, 1976.
Bester, Alfred. "Fondly Fahrenheit." *The Science Fiction Hall of Fame Volume I*. Ed. Robert Silverberg. New York: Avon, 1970.
Binder, Eando. *Adam Link—Robot*. New York: Paperback Library, 1965.
_____. "The Trial of Adam Link." *Amazing*, July 1939. 30–43.
Binder, Otto. "I, Robot" and "The Trial of Adam Link." Comics adaptation. *Creepy Archives Volume One*. New York: Dark Horse Books, 2008.
Bishop, Michael. *Ancient of Days*. New York: Arbor House, 1985.
_____. *No Enemy but Time*. New York: Timescape, 1982.
Blackwood, Algernon. "The Willows." *The Listener and Other Stories*. London: Nash, 1907.
Bleiler, Everett F. "John W. Campbell, Jr." *Science Fiction Writers*. Ed. New York: Scribner's, 1982. 151–59.
Blish, James. *Doctor Mirabilis*. New York: Faber & Faber, 1964.
_____. *The Issue at Hand*. Chicago: Advent, 1964.
_____. *More Issues at Hand*. Chicago: Advent, 1970.
Booker, M. Keith. *The Dystopian Impulse in Modern Literature*. Westport: Greenwood, 1994.
Bould, Mark and Sherryl Vint. *The Routledge Concise History of Science Fiction*. London: Routledge, 2011.
Boulle, Pierre. *The Planet of the Apes*. New York: Vanguard, 1963.
Bova, Ben. *The Science Fiction Hall of Fame Volume IIB*. Ed. New York: Avon, 1974.
Bradbury, Ray. "A Sound of Thunder." *The Golden Apples of the Sun*. Garden City: Doubleday, 1953.
Bretnor, Reginald. *Modern Science Fiction: Its Meaning and Its Future*. New York: Coward-McCann, 1953.
Breuer, Miles J. *The Man with the Strange Head and Other Early Science Fiction Stories*. Ed. Michael R. Page. Lincoln: Bison Books, 2008.
Calkins, Elizabeth and Barry McGhan. *Teaching Tomorrow*. Dayton: Pflaum, 1972.
Campbell, John W. Jr. *The Atomic Story*. New York: Henry Holt, 1947.
_____. *The Mightiest Machine*. Providence: Hadley, 1947.
Carotti, Simone. *The Generation Starship in Science Fiction*. Jefferson: McFarland, 2011.
Carter, Paul A. *The Creation of Tomorrow*. New York: Columbia University Press, 1977.
Cheng, John. *Astounding Wonder: Imagining Science and Science Fiction in Interwar America*. Philadelphia: University of Pennsylvania Press, 2012.
Chiang, Ted. "Exhalation." *Eclipse Two*. Ed. Jonathan Strahan. San Francisco: Nightshade, 2008.
Christopher, Joe R. "Usuform Robotics: Anthony Boucher's Future History." *Niekas*, August 1990. 23–42.
Chu, Seo-Young. *Do Metaphors Dream of Literal Sleep?* Cambridge: Harvard University Press, 2010.
Cioffi, Frank. *Formula Fiction? An Anatomy of American Science Fiction, 1930–1940*. Westport: Greenwood, 1982.
Clareson, Thomas D. "The Evolution of

Science Fiction." *Dynamic,* August 1953. 85–98.
_____. "Science Fiction: The New Mythology." Ed. *Extrapolation,* May 1969. 69–113.
_____. *SF: The Other Side of Realism.* Ed. Bowling Green: Bowling Green University Press, 1971.
_____. *Understanding Contemporary American Science Fiction: The Formative Period (1926–1970).* Columbia: University of South Carolina Press, 1990.
_____. and Joe Sanders. *The Heritage of Heinlein.* Jefferson: McFarland, 2014.
Clarke, Arthur C. *2001: A Space Odyssey.* New York: Signet, 1968.
Clarke, I. F. *The Pattern of Expectation.* New York: Basic Books, 1979.
_____. *Voices Prophesying War, 1763–1984.* London: Oxford University Press, 1966.
Conklin, Groff. *Big Book of Science Fiction.* Ed. New York: Crown, 1950.
_____. *Omnibus of Science Fiction.* Ed. New York: Crown, 1952.
Connor, Wilkie. Letter to the Editor. *Dynamic,* October 1953. 94–95.
Crossley, Robert. *Imagining Mars.* Middletown: Wesleyan University Press, 2011.
_____. *Olaf Stapledon: Speaking for the Future.* Syracuse: Syracuse University Press, 1994.
Csicsery-Ronay, Istvan, Jr. *The Seven Beauties of Science Fiction.* Middletown: Wesleyan University Press, 2008.
Davenport, Basil. *Inquiry into Science Fiction.* New York: Longmans, 1955.
_____. *The Science Fiction Novel: Imagination and Social Criticism.* Ed. Chicago: Advent, 1959.
The Day the Earth Stood Still. Directed by Robert Wise. 20th Century Fox, 1951.
De Camp, L. Sprague. *Lest Darkness Fall.* New York: Henry Holt, 1941.
_____. "A Modern Merlin." *Dynamic,* June 1953. 61–67.
Delany, Samuel R. "About One Thousand One Hundred and Seventy Five Words." *SF: The Other Side of Realism.* Ed. Thomas D. Clareson. Bowling Green: Bowling Green University Press, 1971. 130–46.
_____. *The American Shore.* Elizabethtown: Dragon Press, 1978
_____. *The Jewel-Hinged Jaw.* Elizabethtown: Dragon Press, 1977.
_____. "Science Fiction and 'Literature'—Or, the Conscience of the King." *Analog,* May 1979. 59–78.
Del Rey, Lester. *Early Del Rey.* Garden City: Doubleday, 1975.
_____. "The Siren Songs of Academe." *Galaxy,* March 1975. 69–80.
_____. *The World of Science Fiction 1926–1976.* New York: Ballantine, 1979.
Derleth, August. *Beyond Time and Space.* Ed. New York: Pellegrini & Cudahy, 1950.
Dick, Philip K. "The Android and the Human." *The Shifting Realities of Philip K. Dick.* New York: Pantheon, 1995.
_____. "Autofac." *The Days of Perky Pat: The Collected Stories of Philip K. Dick Volume Four.* Los Angeles: Underwood-Miller, 1987. 1–21.
_____. "The Defenders." *The Short Happy Life of the Brown Oxford: The Collected Stories of Philip K. Dick Volume One.* New York: Citadel Twilight, 1990. 67–86.
_____. *Do Androids Dream of Electric Sheep?.* Garden City: Doubleday, 1968.
_____. "Man, Android and Machine." *Science Fiction at Large.* Ed. Peter Nicholls. London: Gollancz, 1976. 199–224.
_____. *The Penultimate Truth.* New York: Belmont, 1964.
Dinello, Daniel. *Technophobia!: Science Fiction Visions of Posthuman Technology.* Austin: University of Texas Press, 2005.
Disch, Thomas M. *The Dreams Are Stuff Is Made Of.* New York: Free Press, 1998.
Dowling, David. *Fictions of Nuclear Disaster.* Iowa City: University of Iowa Press, 1987.
Doyle, Arthur Conan. *The Professor Challenger Stories.* London: John Murray, 1952.
Duncan, Andy. "Alternate History." *The Cambridge Companion to Science Fiction.* Eds. Edward James and Farah Mendlesohn. Cambridge: Cambridge University Press, 2003. 209–18.
_____. "The Chief Designer." *The Pot-*

tawatomie Giant and Other Stories. Hornsea: PS Publishing, 2012.
Eller, Jonathan. *Becoming Ray Bradbury*. Urbana: University of Illinois Press, 2011.
Ellison, Harlan. "New Directions in Science Fiction." Filmed lecture, *The Literature of Science Fiction*. Produced and directed by James Gunn, 1969. Lawrence: Digital Media Zone, 2002 (DVD).
Fearn, John Russell. "The Man Who Stopped the Dust." *The Best of John Russell Fearn Volume One*. Wildside Press, 2001. 15–37.
Fiedler, Leslie. *Olaf Stapledon: A Man Divided*. Oxford: Oxford University Press, 1983.
Fitting, Peter. Preface. *The Journey of Niels Klim to the World Underground*. By Ludvig Holberg. Lincoln: Bison Books, 2004. v–xviii.
Fort, Charles. *Lo!* New York: Claude Kendall, 1931.
Fowler, Karen Joy. "Standing Room Only." *Asimov's*, August 1997. 68–77.
Franklin, H. Bruce. *Future Perfect: American Science Fiction of the Nineteenth Century*. London: Oxford University Press, 1966, 1968.
_____. *Robert A. Heinlein: America as Science Fiction*. Oxford: Oxford University Press, 1980.
_____. *War Stars: The Superweapon and the American Imagination*. Oxford: Oxford University Press, 1988.
Gallun, Raymond Z. with Jeffrey M. Elliot. *Starclimber: The Literary Adventures and Autobiography of Raymond Z. Gallun*. Second Edition. Borgo/Wildside, 1991.
Gernsback, Hugo. "A New Sort of Magazine." *Amazing*, April 1926. 3.
Gibson, William. *Neuromancer*. New York: Ace, 1984.
Gove, Philip Babcock. *The Imaginary Voyage in Prose Fiction*. New York: Columbia University Press, 1941.
Grimwood, Ken. *Replay*. New York: Arbor House, 1987.
Gunn, James. "The Academic Viewpoint." *Inside Science Fiction*. Second Edition. Lanham: Scarecrow Press, 2006. 97–104.
_____. *Alternate Worlds: The Illustrated History of Science-Fiction*. New York: Prentice-Hall, 1975.
_____. *The Burning*. New York: Dell, 1972.
_____. "The Cave of Night." *Galaxy*, February 1955. 45–60.
_____. "A Classic of Science Fiction." *Universe*. By Robert A. Heinlein. New York: Dell, 1951. 3–5.
_____. "Communications." *Startling Stories*, September 1949. 100–20.
_____. *Crisis!* New York: TOR, 1986.
_____. "The Dean Revisited." Foreword. *Murray Leinster: The Life and Works*. By Billee J. Stallings and Jo-An J. Evans. Jefferson: McFarland, 2011. 1–2.
_____. *The Discovery of the Future*. College Station: Texas A & M University Library, 1975.
_____. "The Early Days of Science Fiction." Filmed dialogue with Jack Williamson, *The Literature of Science Fiction*. Produced and directed by James Gunn, 1975. Lawrence: Digital Media Zone, 2002 (DVD).
_____. "The Education of a Science Fiction Teacher." *Inside Science Fiction*. Second Edition. Lanham: Scarecrow Press, 2006. 3–10.
_____. "Fifty Amazing, Astounding, Wonderful Years." *Inside Science Fiction*. Second Edition. Lanham: Scarecrow Press, 2006. 65–70.
_____. "From the Pulps to the Classroom: The Strange Journey of Science Fiction." *Inside Science Fiction*. Second Edition. Lanham: Scarecrow Press, 2006. 11–28.
_____. "The Gatekeepers." *Inside Science Fiction*. Second Edition. Lanham: Scarecrow Press, 2006. 55–64.
_____. *Human Voices*. Waterville: Five Star, 2002.
_____. *The Immortals*. New York: Pocket, 2004.
_____. *Inside Science Fiction*. Second Edition. Lanham: Scarecrow, 2006.
_____. *Isaac Asimov: The Foundations of Science Fiction*. Revised Edition. Lanham: Scarecrow Press, 1996.
_____. *The Joy Makers*. New York: Bantam, 1961.
_____. *The Listeners*. New York: Scribners, 1972.

_____. "Little Orphan Android." *Future Imperfect*. New York: Bantam, 1964.
_____. "The Magic of Imagination." Foreword. *The Teenage Tarzan: A Literary Analysis of Edgar Rice Burroughs' Jungle Tales of Tarzan*. By Stan Galloway. Jefferson: McFarland, 2010. 1–3.
_____. *Man and the Future*. Ed. Lawrence: University of Kansas Press, 1968.
_____. "A Monster Named Smith." *Breaking Point*. New York: DAW, 1972.
_____. *Paratexts: Introductions to Science Fiction and Fantasy*. Lanham: Scarecrow, 2013.
_____. "The Protocols of Science Fiction." *Inside Science Fiction*. Second Edition. Lanham: Scarecrow Press, 2006. 141–45.
_____. "The Reluctant Witch." *The Witching Hour*. New York: Dell, 1970.
_____. *The Road to Science Fiction Volume 1: From Gilgamesh to Wells*. Ed. New York: Mentor, 1977.
_____. *The Road to Science Fiction Volume 2: From Wells to Heinlein*. Ed. Lanham: Scarecrow, 1979, 2002.
_____. *The Road to Science Fiction Volume 3: From Heinlein to Here*. Ed. Lanham: Scarecrow Press, 1979, 2002.
_____. *The Road to Science Fiction Volume 4: From Here to Forever*. Ed. New York: Mentor, 1982.
_____. *The Road to Science Fiction Volume 5: The British Way*. Ed. Clarkson: White Wolf, 1998.
_____. *The Road to Science Fiction Volume 6: Around the World*. Ed. Clarkson: White Wolf, 1998.
_____. "Science Fiction as Literature." *Inside Science Fiction*. Second Edition. Lanham: Scarecrow Press, 2006. 105–22.
_____. *The Science of Science-Fiction Writing*. Lanham: Scarecrow, 2000.
_____. *Speculations on Speculation*. Ed, with Matthew Candelaria. Lanham: Scarecrow, 2005.
_____. *Star-Begotten: A Life in Science Fiction*. Jefferson: McFarland, 2017.
_____. *Station in Space*. New York: Bantam, 1958.
_____. "The Sun Came UP Last Night." *Science Fiction Quarterly*, August 1951. 8–36.
_____. "Themes in Science Fiction." Filmed dialogue with Gordon R. Dickson, *The Literature of Science Fiction*. Produced and directed by James Gunn, 1975. Lawrence: Digital Media Zone, 2002 (DVD).
_____. *Transcendental*. New York: TOR, 2013.
_____. *Transformation*. New York: TOR, 2017.
_____. *Transgalactic*. New York: TOR, 2016.
_____. "The Worldview of Science Fiction." *Inside Science Fiction*. Second Edition. Lanham: Scarecrow Press, 2006. 71–75.
Haining, Peter. *The Frankenstein Omnibus*. Ed. Edison: Chartwell, 1994.
Hammond, Dave. Letter to the editor. *Dynamic*, June 1953. 111.
Harrison, Harry. Foreword. "Nightfall" by Isaac Asimov. *The Mirror of Infinity*. Ed. Robert Silverberg. New York: Harper & Row, 1970. 51–54.
_____. and Brian Aldiss. *The Astounding-Analog Reader Volume Two*. Garden City: Doubleday, 1973.
Heinlein, Robert A. *Grumbles from the Grave*. New York: Ballantine, 1989
_____. *The Man Who Sold the Moon*. New York: Signet, 1950.
Hellekson, Karen. *The Alternate History: Refiguring Historical Time*. Kent: Kent State University Press, 2001.
Hillegas, Mark. *The Future as Nightmare: H.G. Wells and the Anti-Utopians*. Oxford: Oxford University Press, 1967.
Hollister, Bernard and Deane Thompson. *Grokking the Future: Science Fiction in the Classroom*. Dayton: Pflaum, 1973.
Howell, Linda. "'Wartime Inventions with Peaceful Intentions': Television and the Media Cyborg in C. L. Moore's 'No Woman Born.'" *The Influence of Imagination*. Eds. Lee Easton and Randy Schroeder. Jefferson: McFarland, 2007. 139–59.
Huntington, John. *Rationalizing Genius: Ideological Strategies in the Classic American Science Fiction Story*. New Brunswick: Rutgers University Press, 1989.
Hyne, Cutcliffe. *The Lost Continent*. Lincoln: Bison Books, 2002.

James, Edward. *Science Fiction in the 20th Century.* Oxford: Oxford University Press, 1994.
Jones, D. F. *Colossus.* New York: Putnam's, 1966.
Kakoudaki, Despina. "Pinup and Cyborg: Exaggerated Gender and Artificial Intelligence." *Future Females.* Ed. Marleen S. Barr. Lanham: Rowman & Littlefield, 2000. 165–95.
Keogh, Joe. Letter to the editor. *Dynamic*, June 1953. 117–18.
_____. Letter to the editor. *Dynamic*, October 1953. 86–89.
Ketterer, David. *New Worlds for Old: The Apocalyptic Imagination, Science Fiction, and American Literature.* Garden City: Anchor, 1974.
King, Stephen. *Under the Dome.* New York: Scribner's, 2009.
Knight, Damon. *In Search of Wonder.* Second edition. Chicago: Advent, 1967.
_____. *Turning Points: Essays on the Art of Science Fiction.* Ed. New York: Harper & Row, 1977.
Korzybski, Alfred. *Science and Sanity.* Lakeville: International Non-Aristotelian Library, 1948.
Kyle, David. *A Pictorial History of Science Fiction.* London: Hamlyn, 1976.
Landis, Geoffrey A. "Ripples in the Dirac Sea." *Asimov's*, October 1988. 86–97.
The Last Mimzy. Directed by Robert Shaye. New Line Cinema, 2007.
Latham, Rob, Veronica Hollinger, Joan Gordon, Istvan Csicsery-Ronay, Jr., Arthur B. Evans, And Carol McGuirk. *The Wesleyan Anthology of Science Fiction.* Middletown: Wesleyan University Press, 2010.
Leinster, Murray. "A Logic Named Joe." *Sidewise in Time.* Chicago: Shasta, 1950.
_____. "Sidewise in Time." *Sidewise in Time.* Chicago: Shasta, 1950.
Lemmo, David. *Tarzan, Jungle King of Popular Culture.* Jefferson: McFarland, 2016.
Lewis, Al. Letter to the editor. *Dynamic*, January 1954. 89–94.
London, Jack. *Before Adam.* Lincoln: Bison Books, 2000.
Lowndes, Robert. "The Lobby." *Dynamic*, June 1953. 6–11.
_____. "The Lobby." *Dynamic*, August 1953. 6–8, 112, 118.
Luckhurst, Roger. *Science Fiction.* Cambridge: Polity, 2005.
Lundwall, Sam J. *Science Fiction: What It's All About.* New York: Ace, 1971.
Malmgren, Carl. *Worlds Apart: Narratology of Science Fiction.* Bloomington: Indiana University Press, 1991.
Malzberg, Barry and Bill Pronzini. "Shakespeare MCMLXXXV." *Magazine of Fantasy and Science Fiction*, November 1982. 65–69.
Manning, Laurence. *The Man Who Awoke.* New York: Ballantine, 1975.
_____. And Fletcher Pratt. "City of the Living Dead." *Science Wonder Stories*, May 1930. 39–47.
Markley, Robert. *Dying Planet: Mars in Science and the Imagination.* Durham: Duke University Press, 2005.
Mendlesohn, Farah. "Corporatism and the Corporate Ethos in Robert Heinlein's 'The Roads Must Roll.'" *Speaking Science Fiction.* Eds. Andy Sawyer and David Seed. Liverpool: Liverpool University Press, 2000. 144–57.
_____. "Introduction: Reading Science Fiction." *The Cambridge Companion to Science Fiction.* Eds. Edward James and Farah Mendlesohn. Cambridge: Cambridge University Press, 2003. 1–14.
Merril, Judith and Emily Pohl-Weary. *Better to Have Loved: The Life of Judith Merril.* Toronto: Between the Lines, 2002.
Meyers, Walter E. *Aliens and Linguists: Language Study and Science Fiction.* Athens: University of Georgia Press, 1980.
Monk, Patricia. *Alien Theory: The Alien as Archetype in the Science Fiction Short Story.* Lanham: Scarecrow, 2006.
Moore, C. L. "Afterword: Footnote to 'Shambleau'… and Others." *The Best of C. L. Moore.* Garden City: Doubleday, 1975. 306–309.
_____. *Northwest of Earth: The Complete Northwest Smith.* Redmond: Paizo, 2008.
Moore, Ward. *Bring the Jubilee.* New York: Ballantine, 1953.
Moskowitz, Sam. *Explorers of the Infinite.* Cleveland: World Publishing, 1963.

_____. "Pilgrim's Progress: Prelude and Postscript to the Publication of J.O. Bailey's *Pilgrims Through Space and Time*." *Science Fiction Dialogues*. Ed. Gary Wolfe. Chicago: Academy Chicago, 1982. 181–90.

_____. *Seekers of Tomorrow*. Cleveland: World Publishing, 1966.

Moylan, Tom. *Scraps of the Untainted Sky: Science Fiction, Utopia, Dystopia*. Boulder: Westerview, 2000.

Nadis, Fred. *The Man from Mars: Ray Palmer's Amazing Pulp Journey*. New York: Tarcher, 2013.

Nahin, Paul J. *Time Machines: Time Travel in Physics, Metaphysics, and Science Fiction*. New York: American Institute of Physics, 1993.

Newell, Dianne and Victoria Lamont. *Judith Merril: A Critical Study*. Jefferson: McFarland, 2012.

Nicholls, Peter. "Conceptual Breakthrough." *The Encyclopedia of Science Fiction*. Eds. John Clute and Peter Nicholls. London: Orbit, 1993. 254–57.

Nicolson, Marjorie Hope. *Voyages to the Moon*. New York: Macmillan, 1948.

Norfleet, Irvin. Jr. Letter to the editor. *Dynamic*, June 1953. 121.

North, Claire (Catherine Webb). *The First Fifteen Lives of Harry August*. London: Orbit, 2014.

Olander, Joseph, Patricia S. Warrick, and Martin Harry Greenberg. Eds. *Science Fiction, Contemporary Mythology: The SFWA-SFRA Anthology*. New York: HarperCollins, 1978.

Orwell, George. *1984*. New York: Signet, 1949.

Page, Michael R. "Evolution and Apocalypse in the Golden Age." *Green Planets: Ecology and Science Fiction*. Eds. Gerry Canavan and Kim Stanley Robinson. Middletown: Wesleyan University Press, 2014. 40–55.

_____. *Frederik Pohl*. Urbana: University of Illinois Press, 2015.

_____. *The Literary Imagination from Erasmus Darwin to H. G. Wells: Science, Evolution, and Ecology*. Burlington: Ashgate, 2012.

_____. *Saving the World Through Science Fiction: James Gunn, Writer, Teacher and Scholar*. Jefferson: McFarland, 2017.

_____. "Science Fiction Goes to College: Jack Williamson, James Gunn, and the Early Years of Academic SF." *Ad Astra*, June 2013. www.adastrasf.com.

Panshin, Alexei and Cory. *The World Beyond the Hill: Science Fiction and the Quest for Transcendence*. Los Angeles: Tarcher, 1989.

Parrinder, Patrick. *Shadows of the Future: H.G. Wells, Science Fiction, and Prophecy*. Syracuse: Syracuse University Press, 1995.

Patterson, William H. *Robert A. Heinlein: In Dialogue with His Century, Volume 2, the Man Who Learned Better, 1948–1988*. New York: TOR, 2014.

Phase IV. Directed by Saul Bass. Paramount Pictures, 1974.

Philmus, Robert M. *Into the Unknown: The Evolution of Science Fiction from Francis Godwin to H. G. Wells*. Berkeley: University of California Press, 1970.

Pierce, John J. *Foundations of Science Fiction*. Westport: Greenwood, 1987.

_____. *Great Themes of Science Fiction*. Greenwood, 1987.

_____. *Odd Genre*. Westport: Greenwood, 1994.

_____. *When World Views Collide*. Westport: Greenwood, 1989.

Pohl, Frederik. *Galaxy: Thirty Years of Innovative Science Fiction*. Ed. With Martin H. Greenberg and Joseph D. Olander. New York: Wideview, 1981.

_____. "Ideas in Science Fiction." Filmed lecture, *The Literature of Science Fiction*. Produced and directed by James Gunn, 1975. Lawrence: Digital Media Zone, 2002 (DVD).

_____. "Let the Ants Try." *Alternating Currents*. New York: Ballantine, 1956.

_____. *Man Plus*. New York: Bantam, 1976.

_____. "The Waging of the Peace." *The Man Who Ate the World*. New York: Ballantine, 1960.

_____. and C.M. Kornbluth. "Best Friend." *Before the Universe*. New York: Bantam, 1980.

Rabkin, Eric S. "Cowboys and Telepaths/Formulas and Phenomena." *Aliens: The Anthropology of Science Fiction*. Eds.

George E. Slusser and Eric S. Rabkin. Carbondale: Southern Illinois University Press, 1987. 88-101.

Reed, John R. "H. G. Wells' Familiar Aliens." *Aliens: The Anthropology of Science Fiction*. Eds. George E. Slusser and Eric S. Rabkin. Carbondale: Southern Illinois *University Press*, 1987. 145-56.

Rieder, John. *Science Fiction and the Mass Cultural Genre System*. Middletown: Wesleyan University Press, 2017.

Roberts, Adam. *The History of Science Fiction*. London: Palgrave, 2006.

Rogers, Alva. *A Requiem for Astounding*. Chicago: Advent, 1964.

Rose, Mark. *Alien Encounters*. Cambridge: Harvard University Press, 1981.

Ruddick, Nicholas. *The Fire in the Stone: Prehistoric Fiction from Charles Darwin to Jean M. Auel*. Middletown: Wesleyan University Press, 2009.

Saramago, Jose. *Blindness*. New York: Harcourt Brace, 1998.

Sargent, Pamela. Introduction. *Women of Wonder: The Classic Years*. Ed. San Diego: Harcourt, Brace, 1995. 1-20.

Scarborough, Dorothy. *The Supernatural in Modern English Fiction*. New York: Putnam's, 1917.

Scholes, Robert and Eric S. Rabkin. *Science Fiction: History, Science, Vision*. New York: Oxford University Press, 1977.

Seed, David. *American Science Fiction and the Cold War*. Edinburgh: Edinburgh University Press, 1999.

_____. *Under the Shadow: The Atomic Bomb and Cold War Narratives*. Kent: Kent State University Press, 2013.

Serling, Rod. "Will the Real Martian Please Stand Up?" *Twilight Zone* episode. Directed by Montgomery Pittman. CBS Television, 1961.

Sharp, William H. "A. E. Van Vogt and the World of Null-A." *ETC: A Journal of General Semantics*, January 2006. 4-19.

Shippey, T. A. "The Cold War in Science Fiction, 1940-1960." *Science Fiction: A Critical Guide*. Ed. Patrick Parrinder. London: Longman, 1979. 90-109.

Shiras, Wilmar H. *Children of the Atom*. New York: Gnome, 1953.

Silverberg, Robert. "The Cleve Cartmill Affair." *Asimov's*, September 2003/October-November 2003. 4-7, 4-8.

_____. *Hawksbill Station*. Garden City: Doubleday, 1968.

_____. *The Science Fiction Hall of Fame Volume One*. Ed. New York: Avon, 1970.

Simak, Clifford D. "Grotto of the Dancing Deer." *Analog*, April 1980. 144-59.

Smith, E. E. *The Skylark of Space*. Lincoln: Bison Books, 2001.

Smith, Jad. *Alfred Bester*. Urbana: University of Illinois Press, 2016.

Smith, Susan. "'Neither Normal Nor Human': The Cyborg in C. L. Moore's 'No Woman Born.'" *FEMSPEC*, 2011. 11-26.

Stableford, Brian. *Scientific Romance in Britain: 1890-1950*. London: Fourth Estate, 1985.

_____. *The Sociology of Science Fiction*. San Bernardino: Borgo, 1987.

Sturgeon, Theodore. "The Ultimate Egoist." *The Ultimate Egoist: Volume I, the Complete Stories of Theodore Sturgeon*. Berkley: North Atlantic Books, 1994. 285-302.

Suvin, Darko. *Metamorphoses of Science Fiction*. New Haven: Yale University Press, 1979.

Tenn, William. "Jazz Then, Musicology Now." *Fantasy and Science Fiction*, May 1972. 107-15.

Them! Directed by Gordon Douglas. Warner Brothers, 1954.

Toronto, Richard. *War Over Lemuria: Richard Shaver, Ray Palmer and the Strangest Chapter of 1940s Science Fiction*. Jefferson: McFarland, 2013.

The Twonky. Directed by Arch Obler. United Artists, 1953.

Van Riper, Anthony K. "Skylark Smith: An Appreciation." *Dynamic*, October 1953. 70-72.

Végsö, Roland. *The Naked Communist: Cold War Modernism and Popular Culture*. New York: Fordham University Press, 2013.

Velikovsky, Immanuel. *Worlds in Collision*. New York: Macmillan, 1950.

Vint, Sherryl and Mark Bould. "There Is No Such Thing as Science Fiction." *Reading Science Fiction*. Eds. James

Gunn, Marleen S. Barr, and Matthew Candelaria. London: Palgrave Macmillan, 2009. 43–51.

Walsh, Chad. *From Utopia to Nightmare.* New York: Harper & Row, 1962.

Warner, Harry. Jr. *All Our Yesterdays.* Chicago: Advent, 1969.

Warrick, Patricia S. *The Cybernetic Imagination in Science Fiction.* Cambridge: MIT Press, 1980.

Wells, H.G. "The Lord of the Dynamos." *The Short Stories of H. G. Wells.* Garden City: Doubleday, 1927

_____. "A Story of the Stone Age." *The Short Stories of H. G. Wells.* Garden City: Doubleday, 1927.

_____. *When the Sleeper Wakes.* New York: Harper, 1899.

Westfahl, Gary. *Hugo Gernsback and the Century of Science Fiction.* Jefferson: McFarland, 2007.

_____. *The Mechanics of Wonder.* Liverpool: Liverpool University Press, 1998.

Williamson, Jack. *H.G. Wells: Critic of Progress.* Baltimore: Mirage Press, 1973.

_____. *The Metal Man and Others.* Royal Oak: Haffner Press, 1999.

_____. *Wonder's Child: My Life in Science Fiction.* Dallas: BenBella Books, 2005.

Wilson, Colin. "A. E. Van Vogt." *Science Fiction Writers.* Ed. Everett F. Bleiler. New York: Scribner's, 1982. 209–17.

_____. *The Outsider.* London: Gollancz, 1956.

_____. *Science Fiction as Existentialism.* Bran's Head Books, 1978.

_____. *The Strength to Dream.* Boston: Houghton Mifflin, 1962.

Wittenberg, David. *Time Travel: The Popular Philosophy of Narrative.* New York: Fordham University Press, 2013.

Wolfe, Gary K. *Critical Terms for Science Fiction and Fantasy.* Westport: Greenwood, 1986.

_____. *Evaporating Genres: Essays on Fantastic Literature.* Middletown: Wesleyan University Press, 2011.

_____. *The Known and the Unknown.* Kent: Kent State University Press, 1979.

Wollheim, Donald A. *The Universe Makers.* New York: Harper & Row, 1971.

Wylie, Philip and Edwin Balmer. *When Worlds Collide.* Lincoln: Bison Books, 1999.

Wymer, Thomas. "Feminism, Technology, and Art in C. L. Moore's 'No Woman Born.'" *Extrapolation*, Spring 2006. 51–65.

Wysocki, Edward. "The Creation of Heinlein's 'Solution Unsatisfactory.'" *Practicing Science Fiction.* Eds. Karen Hellekson, Craig B. Jacobsen, Patrick B. Sharp, and Lisa Yaszek. Jefferson: McFarland, 2010. 74–86.

Yaszek, Lisa. *Galactic Suburbia: Recovering Women's Science Fiction.* Columbus: Ohio State University Press, 2008.

Index

Michael R. Page

"About Five Thousand One Hundred and Seventy Five Words" (Delany) 20
Abramson, Ben 10
"Adam and No Eve" (Bester) 2, 160–61
Adam Link—Robot (Binder) 180n129
"Adam Link's Vengeance" (Binder) 10, 147–48
Advent Publishers 14, 18–19
Adventures in Time and Space (Healey & McComas) 6, 26
"Aesop" (Simak) 132
After 12,000 Years (Coblentz) 10
Alas, All Thinking (Bates) 74–75, 175n23
Aldiss, Brian 16, 22, 171n10, 172n18, 177n71
Alien Encounters (Rose) 22, 174n4, 181n132
aliens 66–67, 76–84, 88, 106–7, 116–17, 119, 141–42, 154, 161–62
Aliens and Linguists (Meyers) 22, 179n100
All Our Yesterdays (Warner) 169n5
All Story 44
Allen, L. David 20, 22, 169n16
alternate history 3, 71, 86, 175n13
Alternate Worlds (Gunn) 20, 22, 24, 171n11, 177n64
Amazing Stories 2, 6, 10, 11, 42, 43, 45, 114, 180n128
Amazing Stories Quarterly 12
The American Shore (Delany) 21
Amis, Kingsley 19, 174n49
Analog 21
Anatomy of Wonder (Barron) 22
Ancient of Days (Bishop) 175n24
"—And He Built a Crooked House—" (Heinlein) 27
... And Searching Mind (Williamson) 24, 31, 150, 152, 181n134
"—And the Moon Still Be as Bright" (Bradbury) 89–90
Anderson, Poul 30, 48, 54, 128–29, 153, 172n32
"The Android and the Human" (Dick) 180n117
androids 139–42, 180n117
Anger, R.R. 16, 169n5

Argosy 44
Armytage, W.H.G. 19, 20
Around the World in 80 Days (Verne) 62
"As Never Was" (Miller) 70
Asimov, Isaac 2, 11, 18, 20, 21, 24, 25, 26, 29, 43, 57, 116–17, 147, 171n8, 172n16, 172n21, 174n50, 178n84, 178n85, 180n125, 180n126
Astounding Science Fiction 6, 13, 17, 18, 24, 28, 40–41, 43, 44, 45–46, 56–57, 58, 97, 98–100, 107, 125, 128, 135, 147, 172n21, 172n28, 175n26, 176n48, 177n61, 179n110, 179n113, 180n125, 181n136, 182n1
Astounding Wonder (Cheng) 23
"At the Mountains of Madness" (Lovecraft) 11
atomic bomb, atomic radiation, atomic war 3, 6, 10, 26, 30, 37, 44, 50–51, 54, 63, 75, 86, 92, 93–97, 99–101, 106, 118, 122–23, 126–29, 132, 145, 161, 170–71n1, 176n55, 177n61, 180n121, 182n1
The Atomic Story (Campbell) 177n61
"Autofac" (Dick) 181–82n141
"The Avatar" (C.C. Campbell) 10
Avon Fantasy Reader 179n111

Bacon, Francis 71
Bacon, Roger 138, 147, 177n77
Bailey, J.O. 3, 6, 10–12, 13–14, 19, 35, 40–41, 61–62, 163–64, 170n4, 170n5, 170n8, 174n49, 182n1
Baldick, Chris 172n23
Balmer, Edwin 10, 177n72
Barron, Neil 21–22
Bates, Harry 74, 79
Baxter, Stephen 178n78
Before Adam (London) 174n7
Before the Dawn (Taine) 11
Bellamy, Edward 2, 10, 25, 46, 51, 74, 175n22
Benedict, Ruth 99
Beresford, J.D. 178n96
Berger, Albert I. 23, 180n126
Berger, Herbert L. 181n132

197

198 Index

Bergerac, Cyrano de 25, 41, 171n13
"Best Friend" (Pohl & Kornbluth) 179n112
The Best of Science Fiction (Conklin) 6, 26, 40, 62–63
Bester, Alfred 2, 19, 160–61
Beyond 28, 176n56
"Beyond the Pole" (Verrill) 11
Beyond Time and Space (Derleth) 26, 171n11, 172n16
Bierce, Ambrose 43
The Big Book of Science Fiction (Conklin) 26
The Big Eye (Ehrlich) 45
Billion Year Spree (Aldiss) 16, 22, 171n10
Binder, Eando 10, 29, 147–48, 180n129
Bishop, Michael 174n7, 175n24
Black Cat 44
"Black Destroyer" (van Vogt) 18, 25, 28, 88, 176n48
"Black Thirst" (Moore) 30, 142, 180n120
Blackwood, Algernon 176n66
Bleiler, Everett F. 36, 173n34
"Blind Alley" (Asimov) 116–17, 178n84
Blish, James 15, 19, 169n4, 177n77
Bloch, Robert 19
"Blowups Happen" (Heinlein) 27, 30, 118
"The Blue Infinity" (Fearn) 10
"Blunder" (Wylie) 94
Bond, Nelson 3, 125–26, 141–42
Boucher, Anthony 18, 80, 93, 148, 180n130
Boulle, Pierre 179n107
Brackett, Leigh 2
Bradbury, Ray 2, 30, 39, 80, 88–90, 94, 95, 164, 174n8, 176n50
Brave New World (Huxley) 56
"Breaking Point" (Gunn) 5, 17, 28, 177n66
Bretnor, Reginald 18
Breuer, Miles J. 12, 13, 174n48, 181n132
Bring the Jubilee (Moore) 175n13
"Brooklyn Project" (Tenn) 25, 71, 175n14
Brown, Charles Brockden 15
Brown, Fredric 51, 75, 154
Buck Rogers 121
The Burning (Gunn) 24, 177n74
Burroughs, Edgar Rice 2, 10, 30, 39, 67, 69, 72, 114
"By His Bootstraps" (Heinlein) 27, 70

"Call Him Demon" (Kuttner & Moore) 30, 104
Campbell, Clyde Crane 10
Campbell, John W., Jr. 2, 6, 10, 11, 12–13, 17, 18, 23, 24, 26–27, 37, 38, 40–41, 45–51, 53, 56, 57, 61–63, 78, 83, 94, 96, 97–98, 103, 111, 115, 128, 152, 154, 163, 172n21, 172n31, 173n34, 173n40, 177n61, 180n125, 181n134, 182n1
Canterbury Tales (Chaucer) 138
Capek, Karel 146
Captain Future (Hamilton) 140
Carroll, Lewis 109
Carter, Paul A. 21
Cartmill, Cleve 30, 96–97, 113, 127, 176n58

cataclysms/disasters 44–45, 74, 78, 87, 97, 110
Cavalier 44
"The Cave of Night" (Gunn) 182n142
Charlemagne 87
Chaucer, Geoffrey 87, 138
Cheng, John 23
Chiang, Ted 175n37
"The Chief Designer" (Duncan) 177n77
Children of the Atom (Shiras) 173–74n46
"Children of the 'Betsy B.'" (Jameson) 145
"Child's Play" (Tenn) 107–8, 177n71
Christopher, John 145–46
"The Chrysalis" (Miller) 102
City (Simak) 179n110
"City of the Living Dead" (Manning & Pratt) 179n111
Clareson, Thomas 15–16, 19–20, 23, 25
Clarke, Arthur C. 2, 14, 18, 21, 83, 169n17, 176n39, 179–80n116
Clarke, I.F. 19, 20, 21, 171n10
Clement, Hal 49
Clute, John 21
Coblentz, Stanton 10
Coleridge, Samuel Taylor 60, 161, 164, 182n3
Colossus (Jones) 181n137
"The Comedy of Eras" (Kuttner) 29, 71
"Coming Attraction" (Leiber) 2, 25, 27, 29, 94–96, 164, 176n56
"Communications" (Gunn) 17, 171n12, 175n35
computers [mechanical/electronic brains] 138, 146, 150–51, 153–56, 181n136
Conan Doyle, Arthur 43, 68–69, 174n9
Conan the Conqueror (Howard) 114
Conklin, Groff 3, 6, 26, 40, 41, 61–64, 96, 98, 174n3
"Conquerors' Isle" (Bond) 125–26
"Correspondence Course" (Jones) 106
"Cosmic Jerrybuilder" (Knight) 179n100, 181n132
The Creation of Tomorrow (Carter) 21
"The Creator" (Simak) 11
Creepy 180
Crisis! (Gunn) 175n17
Csciery-Ronay, Istvan, Jr. 23
Cummings, Ray 10
"The Cunning of the Beast" (Bond) 142
Cutcliffe Hyne, C.J. 178n80
The Cybernetic Imagination in Science Fiction (Warrick) 22, 179n115, 181n126
cybernetics 153–54, 179n115

Darwin, Charles 122
Davenport, Basil 18, 19
Davis, Chan 30, 100
"The Day of the Dragon" (Endore) 131, 179n111
The Day the Earth Stood Still (Wise) 175n29
"Deadline" (Cartmill) 30, 97, 176n58
De Camp, L. Sprague 13, 17, 18, 57, 69, 75–76, 132, 175n13, 179n108

Index

"The Defenders" (Dick) 180*n*127
Delany, Samuel R. 19–20, 21
Dell Books 18, 27, 38, 171*n*5, 173*n*36, 180*n*119
Del Rey, Lester 20, 22, 97, 175–76
Derleth, August 3, 6, 26, 41, 61, 65, 171*n*11, 172*n*16
"Descent into the Maelstrom" (Poe) 43
Destination Moon 38
Detective/mystery genre 34, 163, 170*n*1
"The Diamond Lens" (O'Brien) 25, 43
Dick, Philip K. 27, 180*n*117, 180*n*127, 181*n*141
Dick Tracy 5
Dickson, Gordon R. 24, 25, 29, 171*n*8
Dimension X 38
dimensions 3, 66, 69, 72–73, 103–5, 107–9
Disch, Thomas M. 21
Do Androids Dream of Electric Sheep? (Dick) 180*n*117
Doc Savage 140, 180*n*118
Doctor Mirabilis (Blish) 177*n*77
"Don't Look Now" (Kuttner) 30, 81
"The Double-Dyed Villains" (Anderson) 48
Drake equation 177*n*67
"Dreams Are Sacred" (Phillips) 50, 99
Duncan, Andy 175*n*13, 177*n*72
The Duplicated Man (Blish & Lowndes) 15
Dwellers in the Mirage (Merritt) 73
Dynamic Science Fiction 1, 7, 14–17, 170*n*8, 174*n*4
"Dynasty of the Lost" (G. Smith) 52

Edwards, Carroll 5
Ehrlich, Max 45
Einstein, Albert 56, 174*n*48
Eiseley, Loren 169*n*17
Eliot, T.S. 46
Ellison, Harlan 24
"The Embassy" (Wollheim) 80
Emerson, Ralph Waldo 117
"The Empire of the Ants" (Wells) 131
"En Route to Pluto" (West) 121
"The Endochronic Properties of Resublimated Thiotimoline" (Asimov) 43, 172*n*21
Endore, Guy 131, 179*n*111
England, George Allan 44, 104
"The Equalizer" (Williamson) 50
Ernst, Paul 73
Eschbach, Lloyd Arthur 13, 18
"The Eternal Man" (Sharp) 160
"The Ethical Equations" (Leinster) 28, 117–18
Evaporating Genres (Wolfe) 27, 178*n*81
"Every Work into Judgment" (Neville) 156
"The Evitable Conflict" (Asimov) 29, 180*n*126
evolution 55, 68–69, 77, 88, 121–22, 125, 130, 160–61, 173, 178, 179, 180
Evolution (Baxter) 178*n*78
"The Evolution of Science Fiction" (Clareson) 15–16
"Exhalation" (Chiang) 175*n*37
existentialism 52, 173*n*39
"Expedition" (Boucher) 80, 93
Explorers of the Infinite (Moskowitz) 19

"Exposure" (Russell) 81
Extrapolation 9, 15, 19, 20

The Face in the Abyss (Merritt) 73
Fahrenheit 451 (Bradbury) 30, 176*n*50
Famous Fantastic Mysteries 114, 172*n*25, 178*n*80, 179*n*105
Fantastic Adventures 179*n*110
fantasy 40–41, 66, 73, 102, 105, 107, 111, 114, 130, 134–35, 178*n*81
fanzines 12, 19
"Farewell to the Master" (Bates) 79–80, 175*n*29
Faulkner, William 47
Fearn, John Russell 10, 107, 179*n*114
"The Figure" (Grendon) 132
The Fire in the Stone (Ruddick) 174*n*7, 178*n*79
"The Fireman" (Bradbury) 30, 89, 176*n*50
"Fireproof" (Clement) 49
"First Contact" (Leinster) 2, 28, 118–19
The First Fifteen Lives of Harry August (North) 176*n*45
"First Person Singular" (Russell) 78–79
Five Weeks in a Balloon (Verne) 62
"The Flame Midget" (Long) 107
Flint, Homer Eon 44
flying saucers 79–80, 105, 106
"Follower" (Russell) 132–33
"Fondly Fahrenheit" (Bester) 180*n*117
The Food of the Gods (Wells) 124
"Forgetfulness" (Campbell) 28, 53, 83, 173*n*40
Fort, Charles 73, 103, 130, 175*n*19
Foundation (journal) 9, 20
Foundation series (Asimov) 29, 178*n*84
Fowler, Karen Joy 176*n*42
Frankenstein (Shelley) 16, 25, 43, 136, 141, 171*n*10, 172*n*18
Franklin, H. Bruce 19, 20, 171*n*1, 177*n*64, 179*n*101, 179*n*103
Friend, Oscar J. 38, 77–78
Fuller, R. Buckminster 169*n*17
Future 14
The Future as Nightmare (Hillegas) 20
Future Imperfect (Gunn) 23, 169*n*13
"The Future of Scientifiction" (Breuer) 12
Future Perfect (Franklin) 20
Futurians 7, 14, 179*n*112

Galaxy Science Fiction 5, 7, 17, 18, 20, 27, 28, 29, 30, 31, 174*n*49, 175*n*35, 176*n*50, 176*n*56, 180*n*119, 182*n*142
Galloway, Stan 171*n*9
Gallun, Raymond Z. 11, 107, 177*n*68
"The Gatekeepers" (Gunn) 13
Genus Homo (De Camp & Miller) 132
Gernsback, Hugo 2, 7, 11–12, 17, 45, 172*n*33
Gibson, William 176*n*57
The Girl in the Golden Atom (Cummings) 10
Gladiator (Wylie) 10, 124
"The Gnarly Man" (De Camp) 75–76

Index

Gold, Horace 5, 28, 174n49, 176n56
"The Gold Bug" (Poe) 43
"Goldfish Bowl" (Heinlein) 27, 73, 130
Gove, Philip 10
"The Great Fog" (Heard) 110
"The Green Hills of Earth" (Heinlein) 27, 120
Grendon, Edward 132
Grimwood, Ken 176n45
Grokking the Future (Hollister & Thompson) 20
"Grotto of the Dancing Deer" (Simak) 175n25
"A Guest in the House" (Long) 75
"Gulf" (Heinlein) 27, 55, 126, 179n101
Gulliver's Travels (Swift) 41
Gunn, James 1–4, 9–14, 17, 23–26, 31, 81, 158, 162

Haggard, H. Rider 44
Haldeman-Julius, E. 5
Hall, Austin 44, 46
Hamilton, Edmond 10, 140
Hankins, John 6, 7, 17
"Hans Pfaall" (Poe) 43
Hansen, L. Taylor 10
Harrison, Harry 177n71, 178n85
Hawks, Howard 38
Hawthorne, Julian 44
Healy, Raymond J. 6, 26, 60
Heard, H.F. 110
Heinlein, Robert A. 2, 11, 13, 19, 21, 26, 27, 31, 50–51, 55, 57, 69–70, 73, 91, 96, 100, 111, 118, 120, 126, 128, 130, 171n5, 174n50, 178n88, 179n101, 179n103, 182n142
Hillegas, Mark 19, 20
Hilton, James 62
Hiroshima 30, 44, 92, 122, 128, 132
Holberg, Ludvig 25, 41, 171–72n15
"Honeymoon in Hell" (Brown) 154
"The Horla" (Maupassant) 130
Howard, Robert E. 114
Hubbard, L. Ron 57, 172n31
Hugi, Maurice 3, 156
Hugo Awards 2, 11, 24
The Humanoids (Williamson) 24, 150, 181n132, 181n134
Huntington, John 22
Huxley, Aldous 10, 34, 56
Huxley, Julian 25, 143, 180

I, Robot (Asimov) 29, 180n125
"I, Robot" (Binder) 147, 180n129
"Icaromenippus" (Lucian) 40
"Identity" (G.O. Smith) 11
If 24
The Imaginary Voyage in Prose Fiction (Gove) 10
The Immortal (TV series) 23–24
The Immortals (Gunn) 23–24, 177n74
In Frankenstein's Shadow (Baldick) 172n23
"In Hiding" (Shiras) 54, 126, 173n46

In Search of Wonder (Knight) 18–19, 178–79n100, 181n132
The Incredible Planet (Campbell) 28, 78
industrial revolution 41–42, 44
Inquiry into Science Fiction (Davenport) 18
Inside Science Fiction (Gunn) 26
Intensive Summer Institute on the Teaching of Science Fiction 25–26, 178–79n100
Into the Unknown (Philmus) 20
The Invisible Man (Wells) 124
"Invitation to the Stars" (Klass) 106
The Iron Star (Taine) 11
Isaac Asimov: The Foundations of Science Fiction (Gunn) 21, 24, 29, 172n16, 178n84, 180n125
Isherwood, Christopher 34
The Island of Dr. Moreau (Wells) 144
The Issue at Hand (Blish) 19

"Jackdaw" (Rocklynne) 81–82
James, Edward 173n40
James, Henry 46
Jameson, Malcolm 145
"Jazz Then, Musicology Now" (Tenn) 20–21
Jeans, James 105
Jenkins, Will F. *see* Leinster, Murray
The Jewel-Hinged Jaw (Delany) 21
"John Jones' Dollar" (Keeler) 119–20
"John the Revelator" (La Farge) 155–56
Jones, D.F. 181n137
Jones, Raymond F. 106, 161
Jonson, Ben 71
Journal of the Fantastic in the Arts 9
Journey to the World Underground (Holberg) 25, 41
The Joy Makers (Gunn) 23, 175n23, 177n74, 179n111, 181n140
Jupiter 78, 117, 179n111

Kahn, Bernard I. 99
Kansas City 1, 18
Kansas City Star 7, 17
Keeler, Harry Stephen 119
Keller, David H. 57
Kepler, Johannes 172n16
Ketterer, David 21
"Killdozer!" (Sturgeon) 2, 28, 66, 102
King, Stephen 182n143
Klass, Morton 106
Kline, Otis Adelbert 10
Knight, Damon 18–19, 22, 169n6, 177n59, 178–79n100, 181n132
Knight, Norman L. 57
The Known and the Unknown (Wolfe) 21, 174n4, 179n103, 181n132
Kornbluth, C.M. 2, 19, 106, 109, 174n49, 179n112
Korzybski, Alfred 56, 174n48, 175n19, 179n101
"Kubla Khan" (Coleridge) 161

Index

Kuttner, Henry 2, 25, 29–30, 31, 54, 69, 71, 81, 86–87, 104, 108–9, 126, 177n69
Kyle, David A. 22

La Farge, Oliver 155–56
The Land That Time Forgot (Burroughs) 69
Landis, Geoffrey 176n44
"The Lanson Screen" (Zagat) 160
Last and First Men (Stapledon) 86, 173n40
Last Men in London (Stapledon) 85–86
Latham, Philip 110
Lawrence, Kansas 5, 7
Leiber, Fritz 2, 25, 27, 29, 94–95, 164, 176n56
Leinster, Murray 2, 10–11, 28, 29, 31, 81, 100–1, 117–19, 127, 175n13, 181n136
"The Lens of Time" (Gunn) 172n24
Lensman series (Smith) 99
Lest Darkness Fall (De Camp) 175n13
"Let the Ants Try" (Pohl) 179n109
"Letter to a Phoenix" (Brown) 51, 75
Lewis, Arthur O. 19
"The Link" (Cartmill) 113, 127
The Listeners (Gunn) 24, 178n91
Literature of Science Fiction film series 24, 29, 178n82
"The Little Black Bag" (Kornbluth) 109, 177n71
Little Blue Books 5
"Little Orphan Android" (Gunn) 31, 174n49, 181n133
"Living Fossil" (De Camp) 132
"Lobby" (Simak) 93
Locke, Richard Adams 42
"A Logic Named Joe" (Leinster) 28, 29, 181n136
"The Logic of Fantasy" (Williamson) 13
London, Jack 43, 62, 124, 174n7
Long, Frank Belknap 75, 107
Looking Backward (Bellamy) 25, 46, 74, 175n22
Loomis, Noel 3, 85
"The Lord of the Dynamos" (Wells) 181n138
The Lost Continent (Cutcliffe Hyne) 178n80
Lost Horizon (Hilton) 62
"The Lost Race" (Leinster) 28, 127
The Lost World (Doyle) 68, 174n9
Lovecraft, H.P. 11, 102, 128
Lowndes, Robert A.W. 7, 14–16, 169n6
Lucian of Samosata 22, 25, 40, 41, 72, 171n11, 172n16
Lundwall, Sam J. 22

MacDonald, John D. 98
"The Machine" (Campbell) 28, 154–55
MacLeish, Archibald 165
mad scientist 16, 44, 172n23
Magazine of Fantasy and Science Fiction 7, 20–21, 80, 148
"Magic, Inc." (Heinlein) 27, 111
The Magic That Works (Berger) 23

Malzberg, Barry 175n16
Man and the Future (Gunn) 23, 169n17
"Man, Android and Machine" (Dick) 180n117
"Man in His Time" (Aldiss) 22
"The Man in the Moon" (Reynolds) 50
Man Plus (Pohl) 181n137
"The Man Who Awoke" (Manning) 175n22
The Man Who Mastered Time (Cummings) 10
"The Man Who Put Out the Sun" (Leinster) 10
"The Man Who Saved the Earth" (Hall) 46
The Man Who Sold the Moon (Heinlein) 182n142
"The Man Who Stopped the Dust" (Fearn) 179n114
Manning, Laurence 175n22
Marguiles, Leo 38
Marlowe, Christopher 71
Mars 72, 80, 88–90, 107, 121, 125, 148
The Martian Chronicles (Bradbury) 30, 88–90, 95–96, 164, 176n51
"A Martian Odyssey" (Weinbaum) 26
Maupassant, Guy de 130
McClary, Thomas Calvert 3, 76, 175n26
McComas, J. Francis 6, 26, 60
McLociard, George 11
"Mechanical Mice" (Hugi) 156, 181n141
The Mechanics of Wonder (Westfahl) 23, 169n1
"Mellonta Tauta" (Poe) 172n22
"Memorial" (Sturgeon) 28, 100, 177n61
Mendlesohn, Farah 178n88, 182n2
Menninger, Karl 169n17
Mercury; or the Secret and Swift Messenger (Wilkins) 41
Merril, Judith 19–20, 25, 27, 30, 54, 129, 179n104
Merritt, A. 25, 30, 67, 72–73, 144–45
Merwin, Sam, Jr. 60, 171n12, 175n35
"The Metal Giants" (Hamilton) 10
Metamorphoses of Science Fiction (Suvin) 21
Meyers, Walter E. 22, 179n100
"Microcosmic God" (Sturgeon) 26–27
"Micromegas" (Voltaire) 25, 41, 77, 105, 171n13, 175n32
The Mightiest Machine (Campbell) 172n29
Miller, P. Schuyler 69–70, 102, 132
"Mimsy Were the Borogoves" (Kuttner & Moore) 2, 25, 30, 109, 177n71
"The Misogynist" (Gunn) 17, 175n35
"A Modern Merlin" (De Camp) 17
Modern Science Fiction: A Critical Analysis (Gunn) 9–11, 13, 18, 23, 24, 27–28, 31
Modern Science Fiction: Its Meaning and Its Future (Bretnor) 18, 172n16, 172n30
"The Monster from Nowhere" (Wandrei) 104
"Monster from the West" (Loomis) 85
Montagu, Ashley 169n17
The Moon 40, 42–43, 52, 59, 68, 80–81, 95, 144, 154, 182n142

Index

The Moon Hoax (Locke) 42–43
The Moon Is Hell! (Campbell) 28, 50
"The Moon Pool" (Merritt) 25, 30, 175*n*18
The Moon Pool (Merritt) 73, 144–45
Moore, C.L. 2, 25, 29–30, 31, 54, 86–87, 104, 108–9, 126, 142, 148–49, 164, 177*n*69, 180*n*120, 180*n*130, 180–81*n*131
Moore, Ward 175*n*13
More Issues at Hand (Blish) 19
Moskowitz, Sam 19, 170*n*5
Mullen, Richard 19
mutants/mutation 3, 54–55, 66, 75, 121–33
My Best Science Fiction Story (Marguiles & Friend) 38

"N Day" (Latham) 110
Neptune 86
"Nerves" (Del Rey) 97
Neuromancer (Gibson) 176*n*57
Neville, Kris 156
"The New Accelerator" (Wells) 25, 124
New Maps of Hell (Amis) 19, 174*n*49
"A New Sort of Magazine" (Gernsback) 11–12, 172–73*n*33
New Worlds for Old (Ketterer) 21
Nicholls, Peter 21, 176*n*53
Nicolson, Marjorie Hope 6, 10, 171*n*14
Nietzsche, Friedrich 53, 122
"Nightfall" (Asimov) 25, 29, 117, 178*n*85
"The Nightmare" (Davis) 30, 100, 177*n*61
1984 (Orwell) 181*n*132
No Enemy But Time (Bishop) 174*n*7
"No Woman Born" (Moore) 2, 29, 30, 148–49, 164, 180*n*130, 180–81*n*131
"Nobody Saw the Ship" (Leinster) 28, 81
North, Claire 176*n*45

O'Brien, Fitz-James 25, 43, 172*n*24
Odd John (Stapledon) 54, 124, 178*n*97
"Of Jovian Build" (Friend) 77–78
Of Worlds Beyond (Eschbach) 13, 18
Orwell, George 181*n*132
The Other Side of the Moon (Derleth) 26
The Other Worlds (Stong) 26, 46
Other Worlds (magazine) 38, 175*n*31

"P-Plus" (Phillips) 98–99
Paden, Bill 5, 6, 7, 17
Padgett, Lewis *see* Kuttner, Henry; Moore, C.L.
Panshin, Alexei 23, 173*n*40, 178*n*108
Panshin, Cory 23, 173*n*40, 178*n*108
Paradise and Iron (Breuer) 181*n*132
"Paradox" (Gunn) 17, 81, 171*n*12, 175*n*35
The Pattern of Expectation (Clarke) 21, 171*n*10
Patterns of Culture (Benedict) 99
Pebble in the Sky (Asimov) 18, 29
Pellucidar series (Burroughs) 72
The Penultimate Truth (Dick) 180*n*127
"The Person from Porlock" (Jones) 161

Phase IV 179*n*106
Phillips, Peter 3, 50, 98–99
Philmus, Robert 20
"The Philosophy of Science Fiction" (Gunn) 1, 7, 14–16
A Pictorial History of Science Fiction (Kyle) 22
Pierce, John J. 23, 178*n*92
Pilgrim Award 11, 170*n*4
"Pilgrims of the Fall" (Wolfe) 13, 19
Pilgrims Through Space and Time (Bailey) 3, 6, 10–11, 13–14, 35
"A Pinch of Culture" (Kahn) 99
Piper, H. Beam 86, 176*n*45
"The Piper's Son" (Kuttner & Moore) 30, 54, 126
"The Place of Science Fiction" (Campbell) 18
The Planet of Peril (Kline) 10
Planet of the Apes (Boulle) 179*n*107
Planet Stories 67
Plato 51, 172*n*16
The Players of Null-A (van Vogt) 28, 125
"The Plot-Forms of Science Fiction" (Gunn) 1, 7, 14–17, 24
Pluto 121
The Pocket Book of Science-Fiction (Wollheim) 26–27
Poe, Edgar Allan 10, 42–43, 67, 171*n*13, 172*n*22
Pohl, Frederik 2, 6, 7, 14, 18, 20, 24, 25, 174*n*49, 176*n*56, 178*n*82, 179*n*109, 179*n*112, 181*n*137, 181*n*141
Pratt, Fletcher 18, 34, 179*n*111
"The Prince of Liars" (Hansen) 10
"Private Enterprise" (Gunn) 28
Pronzini, Bill 175*n*16

"Quixote and the Windmill" (Anderson) 153
"Q.U.R." (Boucher) 148, 180*n*130

Rabkin, Eric S. 20
Rationalizing Genius (Huntington) 22
"Reason" (Asimov) 29
Rebirth (McClary) 76, 175*n*26
"The Red Brain" (Wandrei) 11
"The Remarkable Case of Davidson's Eyes" (Wells) 111
Replay (Grimwood) 176*n*45
"Rescue Party" (Clarke) 2, 14, 83–84, 176*n*39
"Resurrection" (van Vogt) 28, 83
Reynolds, Mack 50
Rhine, Joseph 181*n*134
Rieder, John 23
"Ripples in the Dirac Sea" (Landis) 176*n*44
The Road to Science Fiction (Gunn) 25–26, 29, 170*n*7, 171*n*11, 171*n*13, 172*n*22, 172*n*24, 175*n*14, 175*n*18, 176*n*48, 176*n*56, 178*n*93, 180*n*121
"The Roads Must Roll" (Heinlein) 27, 120, 178*n*88
"Robbie" (Asimov) 180*n*125

Index 203

robots 55, 79–80, 83, 140, 146–53, 180–81n125–34
"Robot's Return" (Williams) 83, 176n39
Rocketship X-M 38
Rocklynne, Ross 81
Rose, Mark 22, 174, 181n132
Ruddick, Nicolas 174n7, 178n79
R.U.R. (Capek) 146
Russ, Joanna 20
Russell, Eric Frank 78, 81, 88, 130, 132–33

Sagan, Carl 177n67
"The Sands of Time" (Miller) 69
satire 31, 41, 74–75, 77, 79, 81–82, 83, 85–86, 131, 174n49
Saturday Evening Post 37, 120
Saturn 77
Saving the World Through Science Fiction (Page) 17, 28, 32
Scarborough, Dorothy 15
The Scarlet Plague (London) 62
Schachner, Nat 3, 11, 159–60
Scholes, Robert 21
Science and Invention 45
Science Fiction: An Introduction (Allen) 20
"Science Fiction and Literature—or, the Conscience of the King" (Delany) 21
"Science Fiction and Sanity in an Age of Crisis" (Wylie) 18
"Science Fiction and the Mainstream" (Gunn) 176n39
Science Fiction and the Mass Cultural Genre System (Rieder) 23
Science Fiction as Existentialism (Wilson) 173n39
The Science Fiction Encyclopedia (Nicholls & Clute) 21
The Science Fiction Hall of Fame Volume One (Silverberg) 22
Science Fiction: History, Science, Vision (Scholes & Rabkin) 21
Science Fiction League 12
The Science Fiction Novel: Imagination and Social Criticism 19
Science Fiction Poetry Association 178n89
"Science Fiction: Preparation for the Age of Space" (Clarke) 18
Science Fiction Quarterly 14, 15–16, 169n4
Science Fiction Reader's Guide (Allen) 22
Science Fiction Research Association 11, 24, 170n4
Science Fiction Studies 9, 20
"Science Fiction: The New Mythology" 20
Science Fiction: What It's All About (Lundwall) 22, 169n16
scientific method 47–48, 58
Scientific Romance in Britain (Stableford) 22
"Scientifiction, Searchlight of Science" (Williamson) 12
"Seeds of the Dusk" (Gallun) 107

Seekers of Tomorrow (Moskowitz) 19
Seetee Shock (Williamson) 90–91, 176n52
Service, Robert W. 120
Serviss, Garrett P. 44
The Seven Beauties of Science Fiction (Csciery-Ronay, Jr.) 23
SF: The Other Side of Realism (Clareson) 20, 21
SFWA 2
"The Shadow and the Flash" (London) 124
"The Shadow Out of Time" (Lovecraft) 11
Shakespeare, William 39, 71, 73, 162, 175n16
"Shakespeare MCMLXXXV" (Malzberg & Pronzini) 175n16
"Shambleau" (Moore) 180n120
Shapley, Harlow 169n17
Sharp, D.D. 160
Shaver, Richard 43, 102
Shaver Mystery 43, 102, 172n20
Sheckley, Robert 27, 174n49
Shelley, Mary 10, 16, 22, 25, 43, 136, 141, 171n10, 172n18
The Ship of Ishtar (Merritt) 72–73
Shiras, Wilmar H. 54, 126, 173n46
A Shot in the Dark (Merril) 27
"Sidewise in Time" (Leinster) 175n13
"The Silly Season" (Kornbluth) 106
Silverberg, Robert 15, 20, 174n58
Simak, Clifford D. 11, 17, 71, 93, 132, 140–41, 179n25
Sinister Barrier (Russell) 130
"The Siren Songs of Academe" (Del Rey) 20
"The Sky Was Full of Ships" (Sturgeon) 28, 106
The Skylark of Space (E.E. Smith) 11, 46, 172n29
Slan (van Vogt) 28, 54, 125, 173n44
Smith, E.E. "Doc" 11, 13, 17, 46, 99, 173n40
Smith, George O. 11, 52
Smith, Lloyd 18, 29
The Snake Mother (Merritt) 73
"Social Science Fiction" (Asimov) 18, 172n16
"Solution Unsatisfactory" (Heinlein) 27, 30, 50–51, 96, 100, 173n35
"A Sound of Thunder" (Bradbury) 174n8
Space Science Fiction 5
spaceships 49–52, 59, 72, 77–82, 84, 88, 91, 105, 117–20, 128, 132–33, 142, 150, 154, 158, 160, 179n103
Stableford, Brian 22, 180n130
"Standing Room Only" (Fowler) 176n42
Stapledon, Olaf 10, 54, 85–86, 124, 173n44, 178n96
Star-Begotten (Wells) 31, 54, 124–25, 178n95
Star-Begotten: A Life Lived in Science Fiction (Gunn) 28, 178n95
Star Bridge (Gunn & Williamson) 31, 171n4
Star Wars Defense Initiative 171n1
Startling Stories 17, 66, 140, 171n12, 175n35
Station in Space (Gunn) 174n51, 182n142

Stephens, James 148
Stevenson, Lionel 17
Stilson, Charles B. 44
Stockton, Frank 44
Stong, Phil 26, 46, 60
"The Storm That Had to Be Stopped" (Leinster) 11
"A Story of the Stone Age" (Wells) 178*n*79
Strange Ports of Call (Derleth) 6, 26, 41, 61
Stuart, Don A. *see* Campbell, John W., Jr.
A Study of Imagination and Evolution (Pierce) 23, 178*n*92
Sturgeon, Theodore 2, 11, 25–26, 28, 30, 66, 100–2, 106, 179*n*113
"The Sun Came Up Last Night" (Gunn) 178*n*97
Super Science Stories 179*n*107, 180*n*125
The Supernatural in Modern English Fiction (Scarborough) 15
Suvin, Darko 20, 21
Swift, Jonathan 41
"Symbiosis" (Leinster) 28, 100–1
"Symbiotica" (Russell) 88

Taine, John 11, 13, 57, 158–59
"A Tale of the Ragged Mountains" (Poe) 43
Tarzan series 39, 67, 72, 114, 171*n*9, 174*n*6
Tarzan at the Earth's Core (Burroughs) 10, 72
Teaching Tomorrow (Calkins & McGhan) 20
telepathy/ESP 55, 125–26, 143, 148, 152, 156, 181*n*134
"Television Hill" (McLociard) 11
Tenn, William 20–21, 25, 71, 107, 174*n*49, 177*n*71
Terminal Visions (Wagar) 22
"That Only a Mother" (Merril) 25, 30, 54, 129, 179*n*104
Them! 179*n*106
"These Things Are Sirius" (Gunn) 162, 182*n*145
The Thing (1951 film) 38
"The Thing from Outside" (England) 104
"The 32nd of May" (Ernst) 73
"Though Dreamers Die" (Del Rey) 176*n*38
thought-variant 11
The Thousand Plus 38
Three Laws of Robotics 29, 147, 180*n*126
Thrilling Wonder Stories 17, 44, 45, 66, 85, 171*n*12, 175*n*35
Through the Looking Glass (Carroll) 109
"Thunder and Roses" (Sturgeon) 25, 28, 30, 101, 177*n*64
"Time and Time Again" (Piper) 86, 176*n*45
The Time Machine (Wells) 51, 74
Time Quarry [*Time and Again*] (Simak) 71–72, 140–41, 180*n*119
time travel 68–72, 74–75, 85–87, 101, 107, 111, 132, 141, 156, 175*n*17, 176*n*42
"The Tissue-Culture King" (Huxley) 25, 143, 180*n*121

"Tomorrow's Children (Anderson & Waldrop) 30, 54, 128–29, 177*n*61
Transcendental (Gunn) 173*n*41, 176*n*47
Transgalactic (Gunn) 178*n*91
A Treasury of Science Fiction (Conklin) 26, 63
"Tree of Wrath" (Christopher) 145–46
Tremaine, F. Orlin 11
"Trial by Fire" (Gunn) 24
"The Trial of Adam Link" (Binder) 180*n*128
"Trojan Horse Laugh" (MacDonald) 98
"A True Story" (Lucian) 11, 25, 40, 171
Turning Points (Knight) 22
Twain, Mark 44
"Twilight" (Campbell) 26
The Twilight Zone 175*n*34
"The Twonky" (Kuttner & Moore) 2, 30, 108–9, 177*n*69

"The Ultimate Catalyst" (Taine) 158–59
"The Ultimate Egoist" (Sturgeon) 179*n*113
"The Ultimate Metal" (Schachner) 159–60
Under the Dome (King) 182*n*143
Understanding American Science Fiction (Clareson) 23
"Universe" (Heinlein) 27, 51, 91, 128, 171*n*5, 173*n*36, 179*n*103
The Universe Makers (Wollheim) 22
University of Kansas (KU) 2, 5, 10, 17, 18, 20, 23–25, 27, 32, 171*n*7, 171*n*9, 174*n*4
Unknown Worlds 107, 179*n*113
utopia/utopian 34, 40–41, 51, 72, 74, 114, 129, 175*n*21

"The Valley of Spiders" (Wells) 131
van Vogt, A.E. 11, 13, 18, 25, 28, 54, 69, 83, 88, 116, 125, 135, 174*n*48, 176*n*48, 178–79*n*100
Végsö, Roland 174*n*1, 176*n*55
Velikovsky, Immanuel 177*n*72
Venus 72, 142, 148
Verne, Jules 2, 34, 43, 45, 50, 62, 97
Verrill, A. Hyatt 11
"Vintage Season" (Kuttner & Moore) 2, 30, 86–87
Voices Prophesying War (Clarke) 20
Voltaire 25, 41, 77, 105, 175*n*32
The Voyage of the Space Beagle (van Vogt) 18
Voyages to the Moon (Nicolson) 6, 10, 171*n*14
Voyages to the Moon and the Sun (Cyrano) 25, 41, 171*n*13

Wagar, W. Warren 22
"The Waging of the Peace" (Pohl) 181*n*141
Walsh, Chad 19
Wandrei, Donald 11, 104
The War of the Worlds (radio broadcast) 43, 80
War Stars (Franklin) 171*n*1, 177*n*64
Ward, Don 30
Warner, Harry, Jr. 169*n*5
Warrick, Patricia 22, 179*n*115, 180*n*126, 181*n*132

The Weapon Makers (van Vogt) 28
The Weapon Shops of Isher (van Vogt) 135
"The Weapons Shop" (van Vogt) 28, 116
Weinbaum, Stanley G. 26
Weird Tales 26
Welles, Orson 43, 80
Wells, H.G. 2, 10, 22, 25, 30, 34, 43, 44, 45, 51, 54, 74, 80, 111, 122, 124, 131, 144, 170n5, 173n7, 175n22, 178n79, 178n95, 181n138
West, Wallace 121
western genre 34, 38, 163, 170n1
Westfahl, Gary 23, 169n1
When the Sleeper Wakes (Wells) 175n22
When Worlds Collide (Wylie & Balmer) 10, 177n72
"Wherever You May Be" ["The Reluctant Witch"] (Gunn) 177n75
"Who Goes There?" (Campbell) 2, 28, 38, 48–49, 103
Wilkins, Bishop John 41, 171n14
Williams, Robert Moore 83, 175–76n38
Williamson, Jack 2, 11, 12, 13, 24, 25, 31, 50, 90–91, 147, 150–52, 164, 169n14, 181n132–34
"The Willows" (Blackwood) 176n66
Wilson, Colin 173n39, 179n100
"Wings Across the Cosmos" (Fearn) 107
Wise, Robert 175n29

"Witch Hunt" (Gunn) 24
"Witches Must Burn" (Gunn) 24
"With Folded Hands" (Williamson) 2, 24, 25, 31, 147, 150–52, 164, 181n132–34
Wolfe, Gary K. 13, 14, 19, 21, 27, 32, 170n8, 174n4, 178n81, 179n103, 181n132
Wollheim, Donald A. 22, 26–27, 80
The Wonder (Beresford) 178n96
Wonder Stories 12, 45
Wonder's Child (Williamson) 181n134
The World Beyond the Hill (Panshins) 23, 173n40
The World of Null-A (van Vogt) 28, 125, 178–79n100
The World of Science Fiction (Del Rey) 22
World Science Fiction Convention 1, 6, 9, 18, 24
Worlds in Collison (Velikovsky) 177n72
"The Worldview of Science Fiction" (Gunn) 25, 178n92
Wylie, Philip 10, 18, 94, 124, 176n55, 177n72

X Minus One 171n6

Yesterday's Tomorrows (Armytage) 20

Zagat, Arthur Leo 3, 160

www.ingramcontent.com/pod-product-compliance
Lightning Source LLC
Chambersburg PA
CBHW032058300426
44116CB00007B/791